T0323410

Susceptibility in Development

Critical Frontiers of Theory, Research, and Policy in International Development Studies

Series Editors: Andrew Fischer, Uma Kothari, and Giles Mohan

Critical Frontiers of Theory, Research, and Policy in International Development Studies is the official book series of the Development Studies Association of the UK and Ireland (DSA).

The series profiles research monographs that will shape the theory, practice, and teaching of international development for a new generation of scholars, students, and practitioners. The objective is to set high quality standards within the field of development studies to nurture and advance the field, as is the central mandate of the DSA. Critical scholarship is especially encouraged, within the spirit of development studies as an interdisciplinary and applied field, dealing centrally with local, national, and global processes of structural transformation, and associated political, social, and cultural change, as well as critical reflections on achieving social justice. In particular, the series seeks to highlight analyses of historical development experiences as an important methodological and epistemological strength of the field of development studies.

Also in this series

The Aid Lab
Understanding Bangladesh's Unexpected Success
Naomi Hossain

Susceptibility in Development

Micropolitics of Local Development in India and Indonesia

TANYA JAKIMOW

OXFORD
UNIVERSITY PRESS

Great Clarendon Street, Oxford, OX2 6DP,
United Kingdom

Oxford University Press is a department of the University of Oxford.
It furthers the University's objective of excellence in research, scholarship,
and education by publishing worldwide. Oxford is a registered trade mark of
Oxford University Press in the UK and in certain other countries

First Edition published in 2020

Impression: 1

Published in the United States of America by Oxford University Press
198 Madison Avenue, New York, NY 10016, United States of America

British Library Cataloguing in Publication Data

Data available

Library of Congress Control Number: 2020934958

ISBN 978-0-19-885473-9

Printed and bound in Great Britain by
Clays Ltd, Elcograf S.p.A.

Acknowledgements

This book would not have been possible without the help, support, and generosity of many. I am particularly indebted to the local development agents who shared with me their experiences and allowed me to join them in their work. Thank you for your time, friendship, and for entrusting me with your stories. I hope that I have done them justice.

In addition to the time given by volunteers, I spoke with many others in Medan: the recipients of benefits, *kaders*, officials in the Kantor Lurah, and facilitators in the PNPM office. I am especially grateful to officials in PNPM Medan who introduced me to BKMs, allowed me access to PNPM events, and were genuinely interested in my findings. Special thanks to Pak Tondi and Pak Freddy; I have rarely met such committed and energetic officials. In Dehradun, women Municipal Councillors invited me into their worlds of social and political activity, with their colleagues in political parties extending that welcome. Thank you also to various officials in the Dehradun Nagar Nigam for your time in patiently answering my questions, and for your support of the capacity building programme.

I have had the pleasure of working with amazing research assistants and collaborators. I am deeply indebted to Yumasdaleni and Aida Harahap—my constant companions in Medan—who brought so much to the project: insights, deeper understandings, relationship building, laughter, friendship, and more. We could not have made our appointments across the city without Pak Oji, who completed our team. Dr Fikarwin Zuska, Head of Anthropology at Universitas Sumatera Utara (USU), graciously helped me throughout the project. I met Dr Asima Yanty Siahaan in the Department of Public Administration (USU) when she assisted me in obtaining a research permit. She has become a great source of knowledge and inspiration, and I am grateful for her ongoing counsel and research partnership. To Dr Kurniawati Hastuti Dewi at Lembaga Ilmu Pengetahuan Indonesia (LIPI) I extend the same gratitude.

In Dehradun, I have had the fortune of collaborating with Panchayati Rule Awareness and Gender Training Institute: sister organization of Rural Litigation and Entitlement Kendra. Thank you to the chairperson Mr Avdhash Kaushal for being enthusiastic about the partnership, and to Namrata, Rekha,

Pushpa, Josphin, and Damani for making it successful. Not only have they assisted each stage of the research, through PRAGATI we were able to translate the findings into activities that had a discernible difference for women political actors in Dehradun. Thanks also to the Direct Aid Program, Australian High Commission in New Delhi, for financially supporting these activities. I am very grateful to all at the office and hostel for the thousands of ways they have made RLEK my home in Dehradun. Special thanks to Dharmendra. Two interns at RLEK provided critical support and insights during various stages of this project: Divya Joshi and Prashant Anand. Anil, Rina, Shubhang, and Sukrit Jaggi are my family in Dehradun, and I thank you for your friendship and hospitality.

This project was funded by an Australia Research Council Discovery Early Career Research Award (DE130100468). My thanks to all involved, from the Research Support Office and Grants Management Office at UNSW, to colleagues who provided feedback on drafts, to the assessors and College of Experts who give their time to the ARC process. Additional research for the Dehradun elections in 2018 was funded by the School of Social Sciences, UNSW.

The research in Medan and Dehradun were parallel projects until I had the mental space to bring them into conversation. A Sabbatical Research Fellowship at the Asian Research Institute at the National University of Singapore in 2017 offered the perfect opportunity. My deepest gratitude to Professor Jonathan Rigg for inviting me to ARI and being a wonderful sounding board, and to all the researchers there who critically engaged with my work. Likewise, my visiting position at the School of Global Studies, University of Sussex proved highly productive, not least in part due to the interactions with Dr Anke Schwittay, Dr Anne-Meike Fechter, and Dr Robert Nurick. Early ideas were also developed during a visiting position at the India Initiative, Watson Institute, Brown University in 2016. My thanks to Professor Ashutosh Varshney for facilitating that position, and for being such a generous distinguished visitor at our workshop at UNSW in 2017.

Ideas and theoretical propositions have been rehearsed in seminars. My thanks to participants at seminars at the University of Sussex, Yale University, KITLV Netherlands, University of Sydney, and workshops 'Women's Eyes' at Yale University (2016) and 'Encounters in South Asia' at UNSW Sydney (2017) for their sharp and astute commentary. Thank you also to anonymous reviewers of articles whose critical feedback helped me to sharpen my thinking in relation to key ideas that are further developed in this book. These include reviewers of *Anthropological Forum*, *Critique of Anthropology*,

Development and Change, World Development, Journal of Contemporary Asia, Journal of Royal Anthropological Institute, and *International Journal of Urban and Regional Research.*

The book manuscript has been strengthened by constructive feedback on earlier drafts. My thanks to the DSA Series editors and two anonymous reviewers for their comments on the initial proposal and chapters. I am especially grateful to Professor Giles Mohan who offered constructive comments on the near final manuscript. Dr Annabel Dulhanty and Dr Kristy Ward provided timely and very useful suggestions on draft chapters, graciously giving their time and insights. At OUP, Katie Bishop, Adam Swallow and Samantha Downes have enabled this project to get off the ground, and in print in a timely fashion. Kim Allen caught many errors and poor phrasing in the final edit. All errors, omissions, and faulty reasonings are of course my own.

I have been exceptionally fortunate to have had mentors and peers who have supported my work. Professor Duncan McDuie-Ra and Professor Ursula Rao both provided critical feedback on the funding application that made the research possible, and more so, have been constant sources of guidance and encouragement. I have also benefited greatly from the words of wisdom from Professor Michele Ford. Colleagues at UNSW have helped me sustain the energy required for a book project. Special mention goes to Nick Apoifis, Monika Barthwal-Datta, Melissa Crouch, Caroline Lenette, Jane Mowll, Philip Wadds, Melanie White, for their collective ability to keep me in good humour. Many more at UNSW have offered friendship and mentoring. My research has also benefited from my engagement in various associations, with thanks to colleagues in the Asian Studies Association of Australia, the South Asian Studies Association of Australia, and the Development Studies Association of Australia.

And to my husband R. Harindranath, who makes all things possible, thank you for everything.

Contents

1

The Politics of Susceptibility

My heart began to sink as I continued listening. I was crouched on a stool in the two room shack of Pak Alex:[1] a so-called 'beneficiary' of a community development programme in Medan, Indonesia and a key interlocutor in my research. It was becoming clear that this was the final time I would meet Pak Alex as he expressed his deep disappointment in my research:

> Research is of benefit when the results can be used as an example, to teach others. If we only give information, we do not get anything. It is only generating information, just useless talking. There is nothing that is given to the objects of your research. If I do not get anything then it is not a win–win situation....Only for you, you win. I only spend my time. You have come back after one year, and then we are still the same, and the next time you come back in another year, then we are the same again (May 2015).

Pak Alex's words stung. An *object* of research, useless talking, you win: seemingly long held but supressed interpretations of what our relationship actually was that contrasted sharply with what I thought it had been. The pain was not only on account of the loss of affection, but what his words indicated about me as a researcher and a person. My ability to develop mutually beneficial and non-exploitative relationships with research participants is critical to my identity as an anthropologist and my sense of self as a politically aware and ethical person. Pak Alex's words had the capacity to threaten this self-imaginary. The impact of his words, their capacity to affect, was magnified by the lack of conviction that I am the person that I present to the world, and the persistent and often unflattering self-evaluation of my actions. I am highly susceptible to challenges to my self-narrative.

If I had cried, it would not have been the first time that Pak Alex brought me to tears. I remember our initial meeting when volunteers in the community programme introduced us. Yumasdaleni (my research assistant) and I were

---

[1] The names of research participants are pseudonyms, most of them selected by the participants themselves.

Susceptibility in Development: Micropolitics of Local Development in India and Indonesia. Tanya Jakimow, Oxford University Press (2020). © Tanya Jakimow.
DOI: 10.1093/oso/9780198854739.001.0001

moved by the difficult conditions of his life and his unflinching optimism in the face of what seemed insurmountable odds. In that first encounter Pak Alex showed us misshapen baskets he hoped to export to places such as Australia, as the rain hammered down on his tin roof, flooding the mud path outside his home. Both Yumasdaleni and I were quiet on the way home, meeting the next morning with the tell-tale signs of red eyes and swollen faces betraying that we had both spent the night crying *for* Pak Alex. He would have hated our useless sympathy that was counter to the ways he was actually feeling (he later described the scene as one of pride). My first meeting with Pak Alex was, however, critical in highlighting the importance of affect and emotions in research on subjectivities, and to develop strategies to work in a team to try to understand these dimensions of our research encounters (Jakimow and Yumasdaleni 2016). The grief-like sensations that overwhelmed me that night resonated in subsequent meetings with Pak Alex. When I drew up my list of people who I wanted as key research participants,[2] his was the first name.

But I did not cry during or after my *final* meeting with Pak Alex. His words stung, but they did not derail (or perhaps only momentarily) my self-imaginary. I let them circulate in the air between us, but I did not allow them to penetrate too deeply. Instead, I kept my mind busy during the encounter, thinking of counter arguments that would allow me to protect my self-narrative. My field notes after our conversation betray an embarrassing lack of self-reflexivity and failure of empathy:

[Research assistants] said that [Pak Alex's] wife and daughter looked very embarrassed when he said these things. I was not surprised at his comments, and while I feel quite sad, I do not feel as if what we did was wrong. We were at pains to describe the research benefits from the beginning, and we also paid him for his time, precisely because the benefits were otherwise indir-ect.[3] So I feel I have been fair, and maybe he is forgetful. But it is otherwise

---

[2] I go into detail in Chapter Two about my research methods including the co-constructed profiles I developed with key research participants. The term 'co-constructed' is used to suggest that this was a team effort or shared endeavour with the participant. The scene with Pak Alex makes me question the use of this term.

[3] Paying participants is particularly controversial in anthropology and development studies. I decided to do so in Indonesia due to the cultural expectations of people involved in research, in recog-nition of their contribution to the co-construction of profiles for which I, and my research assistants, were paid well, and due to the opportunity cost for people with lower incomes in constructing these profiles. Payment was in the form of a donation to the BKM (community organization) for volunteers. Pak Alex, as a 'beneficiary' received a personal cash payment. Municipal councillors in Dehradun received a gift.

very interesting and speaks to his frustration of being stuck in the same place, people come and go and yet nothing really improves, nothing makes a big difference. The tone and his complaints are very different to our meetings with other respondents who have greeted us as friends.

I was happy to believe the interpretations provided by my research assistants I had also implicated them in this research. Their reading of Pak Alex's wife and daughter as being very embarrassed rather than an alternative interpretation that they too shared his indignation, protected them as well as me from a sense that what we had done was wrong. Rather than confront Pak Alex's accusations, I dismiss them through reference to the formal ethics process[4] and the time we spent going over the Participant Information Sheet that laid out in black and white what he could expect from the research. I further invalidate his feelings, or see them as unjustifiable, by comparing his response to other encounters with participants. Rather than Pak Alex's words provoking an ethical dilemma that I reconciled internally, I closed off the scene, dampened its affective power through self-assurances.

This book is about the capacity of people such as Pak Alex who are the targets or recipients of development (broadly conceived) to affect 'development agents', the people involved in the design and implementation of its numerous manifestations (myself included). I argue that this capacity to affect (Anderson 2014) is an under-recognized form of power that has the potential to disrupt development's seemingly inherent hierarchies. Pak Alex refused to abide by the expectations of the research established through the formal Participant Information Sheet. He argued for different expectations and research outcomes—arguments made forceful through the feelings engendered in our final encounter. This book is also about the capacity (Anderson 2014) and susceptibility of development agents to be affected. In it, I examine the affective investments development agents make in self-fashioning projects through development programmes and initiatives, and the way such investments come under threat when development fails. Threats need not translate into actual harm. Similar to my response to Pak Alex's words, development agents distract themselves from engendered emotions, avoid reflective practice that would expose their inner inconsistencies, hide behind formal

---

[4] Formal ethics processes are often designed to in part reduce the vulnerability of the institution to legal challenge. The ways they thereby frustrate vulnerability as an ethical practice is an important question.

processes and stereotypes of who is deserving or not to receive empathy. This book is about the politics of affects and emotions within development.

To examine this politics involves attention to the 'differentiated "capacities to affect and [susceptibilities to] be affected"' (Anderson 2014: 10). I argue that these capacities and susceptibilities are unevenly distributed within international and national aid chains, with local development agents bearing a disproportionate burden of development's failures. As an international researcher, I have stronger relational ties in Australia than Indonesia (or India), while the nature of my engagement with development is based on curiosity as to whether community development works, lacking affective investment in its success. These characteristics lessen my susceptibility to be affected by my research participants, and protect me from any serious threats to my self-imaginary. The volunteers who introduced me to Pak Alex do not have this luxury. As local development agents they are socially embedded and entangled in complex relations in the societies in which they work. I argue that these characteristics make them highly susceptible to threats to their self-imaginaries and self-narratives, which have themselves been propelled by the development enterprise.

The capacity/susceptibility to affect/be affected augments, or helps us to think anew existing understandings of power configurations in Development Studies in three ways. First, the framework reveals mechanisms through which development ideologies and discourses gain their productive power. It helps move beyond examining the way discourse shapes practice, to understanding its efficacy in recruiting and constituting development subjects. Second, it helps identify and explain scenarios that seemingly confound power regimes and patterns of distribution that are counter to unequal power relations (as conventionally understood). That is, the framework is attentive to forces of destabilization and creativity (Legg 2011). Finally, studies examining development as a technology of power have been *mirrored* by accounts of resistance to all-encompassing regimes, but there has been little work that deals with the murky ground between them. As Legg (2011) notes, the two are not in hostile opposition, rather 'each state contains the traces, remnants, seeds and potential for the alternate state' (2011: 129). The proposed framework aims to overcome this binary in both post- and anti-development thought, by presenting the relationship between resistance and acquiescence as much more complex and ambivalent (see also Ortner 2006; Li 2007; High 2014). The capacity/susceptibility to affect/be affected holds these two aspects of power—regimes of power *or* creative potentialities—in productive tension.

The protangonists in this book are two types of local development agents: women municipal councillors in Dehradun India, and volunteers in a state-led community development programme in Medan, Indonesia. I use the term 'development agent' loosely to include anyone involved in an aspect of the practice of development. Municipal councillors and volunteers may seem an unlikely pairing, but it was through comparing their diverse yet similar experiences that their shared susceptibility became apparent. Indeed, I argue that it is the relative lack of in-depth studies of local development agents compared to expat volunteers, development practitioners, and our own reflections as academics that has prevented a thorough investigation of the affective intensities generated in sites of development. This disproportionate focus on actors of the Global North (including elites in so-called 'developing countries') is understandable. Trying to understand the inner workings of another person is wrought with danger at the best of times (Beatty 2014), and is a task made all the more difficult when one's own experiences are very different.

Perhaps for this reason I have started writing this book with an account that I am more sure of, one in which I interrogate my own emotions and affective responses. However, to maintain a focus on myself, or people like me, would be to continue to ignore the importance of local development agents for how development operates in practice. So despite the difficulties, I believe that the venture is worth attempting. Opening the book with an account of myself also attempts to achieve some degree of parity with my interlocutors. As I share moments of development agents' vulnerabilities, insecurities, failures, and successes, it is only 'fair' that I share some of my own, even at the risk of professional embarrassment: 'her respondent said *that* to her!' Of course I protect the identities of my interlocutors with pseudonyms that they have chosen themselves. I believe they will feel pride rather than embarrassment when they recognize themselves in these pages. I am deeply impressed by their work, and readers seeking a critique of local development agents will be disappointed. What I offer instead is an account of their day to day experiences and the ways the larger development sector fails them by not appreciating or sharing the burden of susceptibility.

Susceptibility

Ibu Hanum is one such local development agent: a volunteer with the community based organization that introduced us to Pak Alex. I take us back to the first time we met Pak Alex in June 2013, which was also the first time we met Ibu Hanum. We had been accompanying government officials as they visited and evaluated volunteer organizations of a community development programme (explained in Chapter Two). Each organization selected 'benefi-ciaries' to give an account of their experiences with the programme. Pak Alex was a 'good news' story; the misshapen baskets he aimed to export were the result of a training programme sponsored by the organization. As the govern-ment officials asked Pak Alex questions, the eight volunteers peered through the door and window of the small home. My photos show Ibu Hanum in her uniform, grinning from ear to ear. She subsequently told us several times of the pride and satisfaction she feels during such moments that reconfirm for her that she is doing something positive for her neighbourhood.

As we came to know Ibu Hanum better, we realized that her volunteer activities were tied to both a sense of who she was (whose 'nature' was to be socially active) and who she desired to be (a pious Muslim who engaged in acts of charity with her energy). In other words, being and becoming a development agent were part of her 'self-formative activity—what some would call "self-fashioning"' (Butler 2015: 6): terms that capture the agentive nature of becom-ing, while recognizing that the discursive, affective, and symbolic 'set the stage for the subject's self-crafting' (Butler 2005: 18, see also Moore 2007). For local development agents such as Ibu Hanum, joining as a volunteer enabled her to become a person she had long desired to be: a self-fashioning project with much at stake (Ortner 1996). Her everyday activities as a volunteer are also critical for her more durable idea of who she is, a provisional 'sense of self' that has a narra-tive coherence, even as it is comprised of multiple positionings. The opening argument of this book is that these ideas of becoming, the essentially unfinished process of the formation of the self made within and in relation to multiple social fields and materialities (Biehl and Locke 2017) are of great significance for development as both intentional practice and immanent change (Jakimow 2015).

In this book, I focus on one aspect of the becoming of local development agents: their susceptibility. By this I refer to the way our 'sense of self' and 'self-fashioning projects' can be derailed, modified, or threatened in our rela-tions with others. Susceptibility arises from our fundamental dependence on our relations and encounters with the world, its human and non-human actors; 'without the "you," my own story becomes impossible' (Butler 2005: 32). Our accounts of ourselves are always expressed in discourses, moral and ethical frameworks that exist beyond and through us. Butler's paradox of subject formation captures the ways we are at one level self-forming, but fundamentally dependent on the world. This paradox leads to susceptibility;

'I am affected not just by this one other or a set of others, but by a world in which humans, institutions, and organic and inorganic processes all impress themselves upon this me who is, at the outset, susceptible in ways that are *radically involuntary*' (Butler 2015: 6–7, emphasis added). We engage in agentive self-formation, but we are not the sole, or even primary actors in the provisional 'self'; 'I am never simply formed, nor am I ever fully self forming' (Butler 2015: 6), rather I am susceptible to being formed in ways counter to prior ideas and imaginaries of self.

While Ibu Hanum has a narrative of who she is and desires to become, it is dependent upon others for its legibility, credibility, and even viability. Acts of relationality put the self at risk through the formation of new relations and new selves. I explore empirical examples of this throughout the book, but here I take literary licence to present a fictional account of what could have transpired in our first encounter with Pak Alex for illustrative purposes. This time, instead of warmly greeting the volunteers Pak Alex turns to the government officials and says: 'It is good you have come. These people [waving an arm at the volunteers] have not taken responsibility for their project'. Pointing to the misshapen baskets that fill one of his two rooms, Pak Alex says:

> Two days I lost to learning how to make these baskets, and I took a loan for the material as well. These people promised to help with marketing but they have done whatever they had to do to get the money, and nothing else. Now I am left with the cost. Who will buy these baskets?[5]

Ibu Hanum deflates and slowly leaves the shack with her friend and fellow volunteer, leaving the coordinator to explain. They walk down the street towards another 'beneficiary' with a small store. They chat distractedly about nothing in particular.

Against the expectation that Ibu Hanum would experience the pride and satisfaction of showing her 'good work', an alternative account threatens her evaluation of her actions and even her intent. The encounter reveals her susceptibility, that is, the precariousness of her ambitions to become a better person and her idea that she has a 'social nature' that motivates her to do good. This moment could be interpreted as a 'moral breakdown', a moment when her 'already cultivated way of being in the world' is brought to attention and ceases to be something taken for granted, disturbing one's sense of dwelling or being in the world (Zigon 2009: 81). For Zigon, this is also a

---

[5] Pak Alex made this complaint to us in a later interview, several months after our first meeting.

moment of self-creativity as the moral breakdown demands reflection, resulting in 'new moral ways of being' (2009: 85). What interests me in this scene is not, however, the potential for self-(re)fashioning or modulations in one's sense of self. Rather I focus on the conscious and unconscious responses to diminish the threat, to retain or recover the self and one's self-fashioning project. Ibu Hanum does not confront the accusation or reflect on her practices. Instead she diverts her attention, seeks out an encounter with another beneficiary that can reaffirm her self-narrative. In this book I aim to lay bare the unreflective responses required to sustain one's sense of self in a world of moral ambiguity and incertitude of the impacts of one's actions, and the consequences of these responses for development.

Vulnerability

Susceptibility is an *analytical* rather than *normative* framework through which I examine heretofore ignored aspects of power configurations in development. That is, I am interested in what an analysis of susceptibility reveals about how development works in practice, rather than an argument as to how development should be. I do not bypass the normative altogether, however, and explore the potential of susceptibility to advance more responsive relations between the doers and targets of development. '[S]usceptibility to others that is unwilled, unchosen' is, as Butler notes a 'condition of our responsiveness to others, even a condition of our responsibility *for* them' (2005: 87–8). Our *affective responses* to others, manifest as confusion, anxiety, desire for example, are prompts to recall our relationality with others, and our mutual responsibility (Butler 2005). In a related move, Butler et al. (2016) place vulnerability at the heart of a radical politics, in which vulnerability is not a condition to be 'overcome', but the starting point for resistance. Calling attention to vulnerability as a condition that is 'pervasive, fundamental, shared and something we cannot ever entirely avoid', Gilson (2014: 2) underlines our mutual inter-dependence, demanding a new relationality. She describes it as a 'matter of practice...vulnerability is the basis for learning and for empathy, connection and community...extend[ing] oneself beyond oneself' (Gilson 2014: 2).

I want to posit a difference between susceptibility and vulnerability in order make them useful analytically and normatively to development studies. I consider susceptibility as a fundamental condition in which we have the *potential* to be affected in ways that inform our sense of who we are, or are becoming. Following Gilson (2014), vulnerability is an ethical resource that invites openness to being affected, experiencing pain and joy that is not necessarily our own, inviting new imaginations as to what it is to live as the other. I use vulnerability to denote the opening of oneself to being affected in such a way that it challenges one's sense of who one is or is becoming. While susceptibility is a part of our human condition, I use vulnerability as an intentional practice. Used in this way, vulnerability is compatible with and perhaps essential to an 'ethic of care': a feminist project that seeks new forms of relationality. Within that project, emotions, or the susceptibility to be impressed upon, are valued for the way they evoke attentiveness, responsiveness, and ultimately responsibility (Tronto 1995; Lawson 2007). I suggest that vulnerability as part of an ethic of care can help to break down rigid hierarchies between the doers and the recipients/targets of development, making development practice responsive to the people affected by it.

Experiments in practices that could be broadly conceived as based on, or at least requiring vulnerability, have started to take place in international development. Pedwell (2012) examines one such experiment, in the form of an immersion programme in which development practitioners (from the Global North) spend time with beneficiaries of their programme. The ability to get to know one another and put oneself in another's shoes—the 'unsettling experience of empathy' (Pedwell 2012: 170)—has the potential to transform the thinking of development practitioners. As Pedwell (2012) demonstrates, however, these programmes often fail to produce intersubjective ways of knowing, and instead augment the claims to knowledge of development practitioners whose affective capacities are seen to provide them privileged access to 'truth'. I agree with her conclusions that vulnerability practised this way may result in a speaking on behalf of the other, rather than true responsiveness. The point I make when considering the potential of such experiments is, however, a different one. I argue that more attention needs to be placed on the journey from impression/affect to self-transformation that, until now, is taken for granted, thereby under-estimating people's *resilience* to vulnerability. In other words, while development agents are all, on account of being human actors, susceptible, their vulnerability, that is the extent to which an impression leaves a trace (Ahmed 2004), is highly contextual.

The conditions of an encounter and the pre-existing relation between actors influence the extent of vulnerability: a development agent may be more vulnerable to the impressions engendered in one scene than another. I outline an analytical frame to examine these conditions below, but here I want to unpack the difference between susceptibility and vulnerability in terms of the movement between them. The difference is not strictly one of intent, although vulnerability can form the basis of ethical practice (Gilson 2014) as seen above. Rather the difference lies in the process between impression, the way the body is modified in the encounter, and its qualification as emotion. The difference between affect and emotion can help to clarify this point. Affect is the 'passage...of forces or intensities' other than consciousness and beyond emotion (Seigworth and Gregg 2010: 1). Emotions in contrast are pre-eminently cultural; we make sense of the way we feel through a particular socio-cultural context (Lutz 1986; Wetherell 2012), even as emotions are personally experienced (Beatty 2014). We are moved, affected, and this experience is then expressed in feelings and qualified or articulated through emotions (Anderson 2014). 'Feelings mark the embodied modulations' from one state to another (Hickey-Moody 2013: 81), while emotions capture how one processes the experience, drawing upon cultural-linguistic repertoires embedded within power relations.

This 'gap between how bodies feel and subjects make sense of how they feel' is enormously productive intellectually and politically (White 2017: 177). Using the opening scene between myself and Pak Alex, we can see how the difference between susceptibility and vulnerability raises all kinds of ethical questions. I am affected in the scene, as my pre-existing ideas about my intentions, my relationship with Pak Alex, and who I am as a researcher, are severely challenged. In my day to day living this kind of susceptibility is part of my formative processes, it is unavoidable. The scene does not, however, shift in any *discernible* way my relationship to myself, my sense of self, or self-fashioning project. I was not open to Pak Alex, I did not *experience* his frustration, I did not learn from his accusations, at least not at the time. Instead the impressions were qualified and processed as denial, disregard. I was not vulnerable, and it was this invulnerability (which I emphasize has a negative connotation here) that diffused his capacity to affect me. If I had been more open to being affected in ways that challenge my idea of self, I would invite the possibility for a different kind of relationship between researcher and research subject.

Susceptibility and vulnerability are not in opposition (from Chapter Two onwards, I talk of degrees of susceptibility, returning to vulnerability only in the conclusion). The difference is the degree to which the impression leaves its mark, the extent to which the 'affect' affects, its intensity and forcefulness. The critical point is that we are more vulnerable in some encounters than others; that which affects us deeply and that which we 'blow off' is at least partially shaped by unequal relations. A different encounter to the one between Pak Alex and me, let's say with a professor, may be more forceful.

The academic challenges the legitimacy of a well-funded academic from Australia to do research on community development in Indonesia. Rather than deflect the accusation, I reflect on the words, I process them using the repertoires of my culture and my academic discipline. The impression left on me is qualified as shame, embarrassment, doubt. The different encounter points not only to how differential vulnerability is often aligned with and thereby reproductive of certain power configurations, but also the way vulnerability may not always be positive. What are the implications that a professor can challenge my sense of self more than Pak Alex: a man lacking in cultural and economic capital?

While this book is in part an argument for greater vulnerability by development elites, it is more so an argument for critical analysis as to how and when people are more or less susceptible in development. This analytical project is inextricable from the normative one, as it is only in understanding different degrees and consequences of susceptibility that we can propose a course of action that seeks to turn this fundamental condition into more positive relations. Both projects raise several questions that are critical to development practice: Who has the capacity to affect? Under what circumstances are development agents more or less susceptible? And what happens in the moments between affect and emotion that prevents a fundamental susceptibility transforming into vulnerability? As we will see in this book, answering these questions sheds light on different forms of power operating within development.

Rethinking Power in Development

The analytical concept of susceptibility can, I argue, shed new light on power configurations in development. The large volume of writing on emotions and affect that has helped rethink power across the humanities and social sciences has barely penetrated the field of development studies (see Wright 2012; Hoffman 2013; Schwittay 2014; Malkki 2015, for exceptions). Post-structuralist accounts of power remain dominant. Development is seen as a mechanism of governmentality (Foucault 1979, 1991), that is the 'attempt to shape human conduct by calculated means ... by educating desires and configuring habits, aspirations and beliefs' (Li 2007: 5). Discursive practices institutionalize and naturalize certain 'truths', setting the limits of thought and action in ways that are taken for granted. As Ferguson's (1990) seminal work in Lesotho demonstrated, this structure of knowledge powerfully shapes the thoughts and actions of development practitioners. Much 'Aidnography' adds nuance to these accounts of discursive power, revealing development as a 'site of struggle', in which development discourses are multiple, contested, and reinscribed with local meaning (Hilhorst 2003; Li 2007; Pandian 2009; Bulloch 2017). While these are important interventions, this anthropological literature often remains bound to understanding social life solely through its discursive dimensions. That is, they neither dislodge discourses as the central organizing element in social life, nor explain the productive force of development discourse.

In a much needed intervention, Kapoor (2017) argues that treating development as purely discursive fails to capture the unconscious underpinnings of power, and the way power is mediated at the level of the subject. He characterizes Foucault's theorization of power as 'realtight', with 'no gap between the discursive space and its positive content or effect' (Kapoor 2017: 2667). Reliance on Foucault, he argues, has thus prevented an understanding of how development persists or how real alternatives might arise. While Kapoor (2017, see also High 2014) draws upon Lacan's concepts of the Real and 'desire' to unsettle notions of development as discourse, affect theory also has much to offer. Here I draw upon Legg (2011) who notes that while Foucault concentrates in his writing on apparatuses that orient, determine, and govern action, his letters and activism explored the possibilities to disrupt the sedimentation and stratification of social life. That is, Foucault's understanding of power is not 'realtight', as there is always life that escapes discourse; here, Legg (2011) is referring to the affective dimensions of life.

Affect arose as a conceptual apparatus in response to post-structuralist accounts that failed to capture the *texture* of life (Pedwell and Whitehead 2012). A focus on the discursive as the means through which we and the world are made and remade ignores that which lies beyond representation, the forces and intensities that move us and which make up 'our qualitative experience of the social world' (Hemmings 2005: 549). The body is not an automaton, or cog within systems of signification, but rather the body prepares for action, 'in such a way that intentions or decisions are made before the conscious self is even aware of them' (Thrift 2008: 7). Affect thereby introduces indetermination and contingency into power's reproduction, underlining the potential for new forms of being and breaks to existing social orders. But affect can augment, as much as break the apparatuses that organize life and living. Some scholars argue that affect gets its force precisely from the way it is embedded in meaning. Wetherell (2012: 19) insists that affect is not some prior potential that is tamed by discourse, rather 'it is the discursive that very frequently makes affect powerful, makes it radical and provides the means for affect to travel'.

That is not to say that affect is *captured by* or *reducible to* discursive power configurations, but rather to see affect as a means through which power is augmented. Affect is 'embodied meaning making', and hence the way politics is felt and experienced at its most intimate levels, which can, but does not necessarily reproduce social orders (Wetherell 2012; see also Pedwell and Whitehead 2012). As a material intensity it has a force that circulates power in ways that are not only tied to discursive regulation, but also that which escapes it, that has the potential to 'become otherwise' (Pedwell and Whitehead 2012). It is this tension between affect as augmenting and amplifying the force of discursive regimes, while not being fully captured/being in excess to them, that helps interrogate the *space between* discourse as an all-encompassing governing apparatus, and the potential for dis-order, de-territorializations, disruption.

In outlining an alternative approach to understanding power I am attentive to this productive tension between affect as part of apparatuses without being fully reducible to them, and locating within that irreducibility the potential for creativity and disorder. This section aims to outline what affect theory can bring to our understanding of power in development studies. I examine three levels of power, starting from the most intimate (the self), through to the micro-level (encounters in the development arena), to the broader conditions/environment. Each of these levels corresponds to a line of enquiry in my book, respectively: (i) the capacity/susceptibility *to be affected* (examined in Part I); (ii) the capacity/susceptibility *to affect* (Part III), and; (iii) the *conditions* engendering capacities/susceptibilities (Part II). I provide a brief explanation of each below, with a fuller theoretical elaboration found in each chapter.

The Capacity/Susceptibility to be Affected

The tension between affect as related to but in excess of discursive regimes makes the capacity to be affected (and processes of selfhood) a key means to rethink power in development. The discursive constitution of persons as self-governing and disciplined subjects has become central to the way we conceive of power in and through development (Li 2007; Agrawal 2005). Governing behaviour can be reinforced through the employment of affect, the intensifying of emotions, so that citizens will become attuned to their own stirrings of the heart, compelling them to act in ways aligned with government ambitions (Rose 2000). In this way, 'power works through affect to shape individual and social bodies' (Pedwell and Whitehead 2012: 120, see also Muehlebach 2012; Hoffman 2013; Rudnyckyj 2014). While affects may mobilize sentiments in ways that produce governable subjects, they can also open up 'possibilities for future actions, desires or feelings' (Fox 2015: 307). As affect captures the ways feelings slip, overflow, evade capture by signification (White 2017), our 'embodied experience[s]...[have] the capacity to transform as well as exceed social subjection' (Hemmings 2005: 549). Affect is therefore not only a potential mechanism in the governing of subjects, it also lies at the heart of self-creativity, or reproduction. Understanding how and why subjects evade governmentality or engage in creative self-fashioning is a critical line of enquiry to understand the workings and consequences of development, as explored in Part I.

Following this line of enquiry, attention to the *capacity to be affected* refers to the condition of being responsive to the world (fundamental to social existence), as well as the affective and emotional resources that people draw upon in their processes of selfhood. I argue that these resources are critical to agentive processes of self-formation: processes that occur in relation to, but are not fully captured by, discursive regimes. One of the striking findings of local development agents in Medan and Dehradun (Part I), is the importance of their development activity for projects of self-fashioning made possible through the emotional and affective resources in the development terrain. I describe these increased possibilities as a form of empowerment, that was particularly striking for individuals for whom these opportunities for self-hood were previously foreclosed due to class, gender, or caste (Chapter Four). As affective and emotional resources are unevenly accessible, the *differential capacity to be affected* points to inequalities in possibilities for self.

At the same time, development agents are also *susceptible to be affected* in ways that challenge ideas of an autonomous self, and individual self-fashioning projects. Critical here is the tension between the voluntary and involuntary way that we are moved or affected. Sentiments may be engendered that produce certain ways of being commensurate with the aims of government, but not everyone becomes a model development subject (Li 2007). Attention to differential susceptibility to be affected can nuance understandings of governmentality, by providing explanations as to why some people, but not others, imbibe the discourses of development in their ideas of self, and the consequences of this susceptibility for the force of programme rationalities (Chapter Three). Differential susceptibility also refers to unevenness in how certain scenes involuntarily impress upon the self, and therefore the limits of self-authorship (Chapters Six and Seven). As some individuals are more susceptible than others to having their idea of self threatened by external impressions, differential susceptibility alludes to forms of privilege and disadvantage.

The Capacity/Susceptibility to Affect

The second level at which I explore power is the encounters between bodies in the development 'arena' (Long 2001). Arenas are important as sites of everyday politics, where differential access to resources and opportunities is determined, and hierarchies between different actors consolidated or challenged (Hilhorst 2018). Attention to the capacity/susceptibility to affect/be affected sheds new light on everyday politics by (a) drawing attention to the role of affect and emotion in the distribution of resources (Sultana 2011, and as seen in Chapter Eight), and (b) inviting reconsideration of unequal power relations in development arenas (Chapter Seven).

By 'capacity to affect' I am referring specifically to the body's force or charge that engenders affects, understood as bodily modifications or engendered emotions. The capacity to affect emerges within encounters. It is not a quality of the body; it is only available in relation (Ahmed 2004; Anderson 2014). To use Fox's (2015) example, the 'capacity' of an apple is realized in its relationship to a hungry child, not as an inherent object. Or in terms more relevant for this book, the capacity of a poor child to engender sympathy is in relation to a person with the capacity to be moved. This latter example underlines that the capacity to affect, in particular to engender feelings, is an overlooked resource that people may (un)consciously draw upon in their negotiations with others in development arenas. For example Chapter Eight examines how both poor and middle-class 'voters' consciously or unconsciously affect municipal councillors in ways that shape access to resources. Importantly, 'voters' have differential capacity to affect, shaped in part by their social identities: gender, caste, class, and so on.

Although the encounter has an immediacy to it (Anderson 2014), engendered affects are not pre-discursive. Returning to the above example, the poor child engenders sympathy due to the social meanings of poverty inscribed on their body, discourses of charity, and societal values of helping others. The capacity to affect is not, therefore 'pre-discursive, in the sense of existing outside of signifying forces' (Anderson 2014: 85). At the same time, the capacity to affect is not pre-determined, or fully contained within discursive regimes. The child may elicit scorn or disgust, or unarticulated ambivalent feelings. There is, therefore, a contingency in the actual affects engendered in the contact between two bodies and hence the capacity to affect. Attention to the capacity to affect in development therefore refers to understanding the differential forces that each body has within particular encounters, and their relation to, without presuming a determination by, broader symbolic and representational regimes.

Examining the capacity and susceptibility to affect sheds light on heretofore overlooked factors shaping development encounters and the relationship between the doers and targets of development. Wright (2012) makes a strong case for a 'sensible' approach to examining development, which is sensitive to the ways emotions compel actors to action and are central to understanding suffering. Her account of a land reform programme in the Philippines is a particularly poignant example. The scene entails a group of activists wearing shabby clothes accompanied by children descending on a Land Bank. The visibility of their wretched condition, alongside the immediacy of the encounter, 'shamed' the officials into providing the necessary documents for their land claims. Wright (2012) demonstrates the capacity of poor and marginalized people to affect officials as a conscious or unconscious strategy to get access to resources (see also Sultana 2011). This capacity is a form of power: the power to engender feelings that animate and mobilise. The capacity to affect thereby has the potential to disrupt hierarchies that determine the flow of resources.

'Development agents' also have the capacity to affect. At times, this capacity is involuntary, and development agents may engender affects in others in ways that are detrimental to their work. I therefore also refer to the *susceptibility to affect*, to move away from the positive connotations of 'capacity' found in Anderson (2014). Sara Ahmed's work on cultural politics is useful to examine these negative consequences. Ahmed (2004) argues that emotions sometimes 'stick' to particular bodies, that is, bodies engender certain responses in others. Ahmed is particularly interested in what it is like to live in a body made sticky by emotions of disgust, fear, hate, such as those engendered involuntarily by the 'black body' within racist systems of signification (Fanon 1967). In Chapters Five and Six, I examine the way that development agents' bodies are made sticky with the emotions of suspicion and cynicism, reversing the assumed hierarchy between them as 'development agents' and the targets of aid, and ultimately frustrating their work. The *susceptibility to affect* draws attention to how development actors—both agents and recipients of aid—engender affects that are detrimental to their ability to perform their work, acquire resources, or develop bonds of sociality.

I argue that the capacity/susceptibility to affect are under-recognized forms of power in development studies. Attention only to material claims, or the transformation of social norms, fails to capture what is the greatest potential of otherwise powerless or power-deficient individuals (the capacity to affect) as well as the weakest links in elite domination (the susceptibility to be affected in ways that animate individuals to act against their own interests). I am not suggesting, however, that the capacity to affect is only, or even primarily a resource for the poor, or that development agents are always more susceptible in their encounters with others. Extant research, while still relatively thin, indicates that like other capacities and susceptibilities, they are distributed in ways that reinforce rather than challenge existing social hierarchies (Pedwell 2012). Further, as the capacity to affect is relational, it is not a resource that can be acquired or given. Rather to enhance or diminish one's capacity to affect demands a change in the forms of relationality shaping an encounter. Collective affect is an important constituent shaping these forms of relationality.

The Conditions Engendering Capacities/Susceptibilities

Differential capacities and susceptibilities are partially shaped by the collective conditions in which they occur, including collective forms of affect. Anderson's (2014: 106) observation that 'Affects become the environment in which people dwell' draws attention to the ways collective affects are part of the conditions for the formation of self, and of relations with others. As noted above, people draw upon resources within the socio-cultural context (or topography of self, see Chapter Four) in their self-fashioning projects: resources that include emotional and affective experiences. Collective affect is therefore one factor in the differential capacity to be affected, while intense forms of affect may recruit individuals into self-regulating governance. In relation to the micro-level, the bodies charge of affect may be realized in an encounter, but the encounter itself is framed by conditions in which collective affects are a critical part. Collective affect in part determines the differential capacity to affect in an encounter, as well as one's susceptibility to be affected. In other words, attention to the conditions engendering capacities and susceptibilities to affect/be affected is critical to understanding power configurations.

Anti- and alternative-development schools of thought have argued that people need to delink from global capitalist development and discard the ideology of 'development' in favour of indigenous, non-growth, and non-capitalist models of social organization (Acosta 2017). What remains under-theorized in these accounts is why and how certain ideologies take hold and become sites of personal investment, and the conditions under which their hold is weakened. Collective affect can shed light on these questions. In this book, I am particularly interested in how collective affect shapes differential capacities/susceptibilities to affect/be affected at the micro-level. Chapter Five examines how discourses of anti-corruption and good governance create an atmosphere that envelops encounters between volunteers and members of the general public, creating the conditions in which the former are highly suscep-tible to the charges of the latter. Chapter Six reveals the ways that the hype surrounding 'democracy' and the lived experiences of democratic processes (voting, campaigning) establish new affective practices (Wetherell 2012; 2013) that challenge established social hierarchies. In both cases, collective forms of affect are critical to understanding the capacity of one person to affect another, and hence the configuring of power relations within the development arena.

The three aspects of power outlined above provide an analytical framework to augment existing understandings of power in development, while poten-tially helping us to move beyond them. Affect prompts us to recognize the unconscious underpinning of power and the ways discourses work through human subjects, providing a means to understand how development persists, as well as offering a pathway to alternative politics (see also Kapoor 2017). Affect and emotions nuance understandings of the processes of subjectifica-tion, drawing attention to the affective and emotional resources that individ-uals draw upon in their self-fashioning projects, while also highlighting how one may be affected in ways that disrupt or threaten these projects. Attention to differential capacity to affect points to an under-recognized power that the 'targets' of development can draw on in their negotiations with development agents, while differential susceptibility (and resilience in the face of suscepti-bility) provides an alternative way to examine power relations across inter-national aid chains. Finally, collective forms of affect or social feeling that shape the development arena offers a productive means to examine how hier-archies between development practitioners, the recipients of welfare, and the general public at large, are sustained, or challenged.

Chapter Outline

These three aspects of power map loosely (with some overlaps) onto the three Parts that organize the arrangement of empirical material in the book. Part I explores the processes of selfhood for development agents: the capacity/susceptibility to be affected; Part II examines the collective conditions that shape differential capacity and susceptibility: the development arena; while Part III examines the texture and consequences of encounters between doers and targets of development, paying particular attention to the capacity/susceptibility to affect. Each Part brings together empirical material from Medan and Dehradun to underline the common experience of susceptibility across two different types of local development agents. Reading across the book, Chapters Three, Five, and Seven present a narrative of volunteers in Medan, Indonesia, the importance of their social activities for their self-fashioning projects (Chapter Three), the difficulty of maintaining an idea of who one is and is becoming in an atmosphere of cynicism (Chapter Five), and the consequences for reflexive practice of a community development programme (Chapter Seven). Chapters Four, Six, and Eight trace a similar narrative for women municipal councillors in Dehradun, India, from the acquiring of new self-imaginaries during the election (Chapter Four), to being positioned as servants in relation to assertive voters (Chapter Six), to the ways differential susceptibility shapes citizen entitlements (Chapter Eight). In this way the book hopes to cater for scholars interested in power configurations in development writ large, and for those with a particular interest in how these are realized in relation to the two case studies.

In Part I, I examine how affect operates in processes of self-formation, analysing both the disciplining potential of affect, as well as the way that affect can open up creative and new possibilities for being. In Chapter Three, I examine how individuals are affectively mobilized to become volunteers in a community development programme in Medan, Indonesia. Rather than examining their 'becoming' through a Foucauldian lens, I use volunteers own theories of personhood that reframe this mobilization in agentive terms. Understood in this way, their activities provide the affective resources that they perceive as critical to their self-making projects: projects that distinguish them from others, but which nonetheless are bound by the discursive and affective/emotional possibilities of their work. Chapter Four examines the creative possibilities of becoming for women municipal councillors in Dehradun, India. I pay particular attention to how the affective experience of campaigning, and winning an election lead to radical re-imaginings of self. This hopeful chapter points to the possibilities for women's empowerment through opportunities for self-imagining and self-actualization. At the same time, the differential opportunity and capacity to be affected has gendered dimensions that limit self-realization.

As Part I examines the individual self, and the way that they are formed in relation to a broader socio-historical context, Part II examines this context, with an emphasis on collective forms of affect (Anderson 2014). In Chapter Five I examine how a 'moral atmosphere' engenders feelings of cynicism, suspicion, and disillusion in community development. These collective affects shape the ways that encounters are interpreted and felt, so that acts of care between volunteers and beneficiaries are viewed cynically; rituals of 'success' engender scorn and jealousy. At the same time, volunteers engage in affective practices that produce collective conditions supportive of their projects of self-making, which dilute the force of other forms of collective affect. Chapter Six reveals a collective sense of entitlement that has emerged from the discourses and emotions associated with democratic practice in Dehradun. I demonstrate how the expectations of 'voters' on their elected representatives have increased, at the same time that the power of municipal councillors has diminished. The demands from 'voters' that female municipal councillors do menial and time-consuming work positions the latter as servants: a positioning that conflicts with a prior sense of self as a respected person in the community.

Part III examines the capacity of the recipients/targets of development and welfare to affect local development agents, the ways that local development agents respond, and the consequences for development practice. Chapter Seven shows how community volunteers exhibit resilience in moments of susceptibility. Encounters between volunteers and others have the potential to inflict what I describe as an affective injury: moments when the 'other' impresses upon the individual in ways that are counter to, rather than aligned with their emergent or durable ideas of self. Rather than prompting self-reflexive practices, volunteers deploy strategies to repress feelings and seek self-assurance, sustaining the self at the cost of reflection on development practice. Chapter Eight investigates the affective configurations that mediate and are (re)produced in the encounters between municipal councillors and 'voters' (constituents/citizens). I argue that voters' differential capacity to engender emotions in councillors' encounters with voters, are overlooked determinants of citizen entitlements: their access to services and resources from the state.

These chapters serve to counter any argument that resilience to susceptibility is necessarily always negative, while vulnerability is positive. The intensified force of affective injuries for 'development agents' who come from, and live in the 'community' that is the target of community-based interventions, raises additional questions about the duty of care towards local development agents, and the way that susceptibility is differentially distributed within international aid chains. The empirical chapters are therefore not an argument for weaker or stronger forms of susceptibility, but rather an analysis of its unevenness, and its consequences. In the conclusion I change tack, aiming to recover an idea of vulnerability as a means through which power relations cannot only be understood, but acted upon in ways that lead to more equitable, responsive, and responsible development. Analysis that examines differential susceptibility leads us to rethink power configurations in the broader development enterprise; a normative project to make the powerful more vulnerable would be a step towards more ethical development practice.

First, however, I examine the characteristics of local development agents that make them particularly susceptible to being affected. In Chapter Two, I map out an agenda to study local development agents in their own right, as important actors shaping development outcomes. The next chapter also introduces in more detail the particular actors I focus on in this book—volunteers and municipal councillors—and the conditions of urban development in Medan and Dehradun.

2

Local Development Agents

The aspects of power outlined in Chapter One revealed themselves through a comparison of two types of local development agents: volunteers in a community-driven development programme in Indonesia, and women municipal councillors in India. Volunteers and political actors may seem like two groups with little in common, but they share similarities in being responsible for the implementation and success of development and welfare programmes. Both the type of development actor, as well as examining them in comparative perspective, were critical to revealing the importance of the differential susceptibility/capacity to affect and be affected. I argue that susceptibility is heightened for development agents who live alongside and with the people who are the targets of development, and hence is more conspicuous as an observable phenomenon through ethnographic research with such actors. I would have missed the significance of this susceptibility that I first saw among volunteers in Medan had I not also observed it among municipal councillors in Dehradun, pointing to the fecundity of comparative research. In this chapter I argue for the distinctiveness of local development agents as an object of study in development studies, not only for their importance to local development practice, but also for their ability to reveal heretofore overlooked aspects of development writ large.

My use of the term 'development' needs some qualification. While I am referring to *intentional* development, inasmuch as these are activities with the expressed intention of improving the lives of others (Bebbington 2004), they are not limited to aid-funded programmes and projects. I also include everyday social practices of decision-making, resource distribution and other forms of assistance that are critical to people's well-being. Local development agents are those individuals who have some power or authority over resource distribution and/or decision making at the local level, and/or who assist others beyond their familial relations. Therefore, while they may be involved in 'multiply scaled projects of intervention in the "Third World"', what Hart (2010: 119) describes as 'big D' Development, they also act on little 'd' development or immanent development, the 'processes of structural, political, economic change' (Bebbington 2004: 726). Local development agents thereby

Susceptibility in Development: Micropolitics of Local Development in India and Indonesia. Tanya Jakimow,
Oxford University Press (2020). © Tanya Jakimow.
DOI: 10.1093/oso/9780198854739.001.0001

exemplify what Lewis (2019) argued recently about the difficulty of disentangling big D and little d development in practice; he suggests they should be considered different *dimensions to* rather than *types of* development. While Lewis (2019) expertly traces the interactions and interrelations between these different dimensions in relation to Bangladesh's garment sector, the local scale reveals different entanglements. Practices of intentional development (big 'D' development) are extensions of, while also profoundly shaping local political economies and social processes (little 'd' development) (Bornstein 2012).

My understanding of local development agents is similar to Mosse and Lewis' (2006: 12) conceptualization of 'brokers' and 'translators': 'a specific group of social actors who specialize in the acquisition, control, and redistribution of development "revenue". Indeed the collection of actors examined in their edited book are examples of local development agents. I too share an ambition to theorize about development through close attention to practices, subjectivities, and meaning making at the local level. I differ, however, in that I see my account not as an 'ethnography of the social spaces that exist between aid funders and recipients' (Mosse and Lewis 2006: 12), but a study of locales that are thick with the discourses, practices, and institutions of 'development', which need not be traced back to international aid. I argue that while highly significant, Mosse and Lewis's (2006) focus on the ways development projects come into being through the work of translation still centres a development imaginary in which the global North is primary. Instead, I position this book in studies of 'Global Development', which aim to move Development Studies beyond North–South binaries (Horner 2019) and the focus on international aid flows: a relatively minor element of people's everyday struggles to get by (Chandhoke 2009; Harrison 2013). I argue that such a move must necessarily include a greater acknowledgement of, and attention to, the role and importance of local development agents in their own right, and for whom their embeddedness within local social worlds and relations are much more significant for development practice than their exposure to the world of international aid.

When development is about more than discreet programmes and instead reflects wider processes of resource distribution and decision-making, we must include as development agents all people who intervene in these processes. There are advantages to studying traditional actors alongside nonconventional ones. Development professionals working in small local NGOs (Arvidson 2008; Jakimow 2012), volunteers in community development projects (Lewis 2015), brokers (Mosse and Lewis 2006; Berenschot 2010), 'techies' (Ong and Combinido 2018), loan officers (Kar 2013), donors to local charities (Bornstein 2012), information agents (Huang 2017), municipal councillors (Van Djik 2011), and so on share characteristics that I map out in this chapter. Crucially here, they all have power over the distribution of development resources, and or mediate to help disadvantaged groups to gain access to those resources. Many of these resources can be traced to state development and welfare budgets, or international aid and charity, and hence I argue they are part of larger development assemblages. In doing so, my argument is not to reduce their experiences as significant only in relation to international aid flows. Rather my aim is to theorize from actors who occupy a marginal position within these wider assemblages to reveal aspects of power operating at multiple scales that have heretofore been overlooked. These aspects of power affect not only projects of intervention, but also broader processes of change, further collapsing the distinction between intentional and immanent development.

I argue that attention to the narratives and experiences of local development agents can reveal much about these different dimensions of development. In this way, my study belongs to the genre of 'Aidnography', contributing to understandings of the personal dimensions of development. Chambers (1997) first argued for the 'primacy of the personal', as practitioners values, perceptions, motivations, and behaviour have far-reaching consequences for development. Several collaborative projects have taken up Chambers' call for such studies, leading to insights of the ethical practices and personal relationships of development agents, the role of development professionals in producing 'expertise', and its consequences for knowledge practices in international development, and the world of expat living (Fechter 2012a; Mosse 2011, see also Feldman 2007; Roth 2015). Understanding the agents of development is seen as a critical step towards what Chambers (1997) described as a pedagogy of the non-oppressed: a self-critical awareness by elites who can bring about change, encouraging new ways of thinking and acting that challenge abuses of power.

Ethnographies of development agents have, however, been critiqued for their triviality in relation to more pressing issues related to economic and social change (Gardner and Lewis 2015). Harrison (2013) argues that studies of 'Aidland' (Apthorpe 2011) rests on a dated view of development, that does not take into account the rise of South–South cooperation, the importance of sectors beyond international aid such as the state and market, and the securitization of aid. While I am somewhat sympathetic to these views, such criticisms are a symptom of the overemphasis in the genre on practitioners and volunteers from the global North, rather than a problem with studies of the personal per se. Attention to local development agents' personal experiences and subjectivities can help to reveal the interactions and interrelations between *both* intentional and immanent development (Lewis 2019), rather than seeing ethnographies as being about *one or the other*. The social worlds in which local development agents dwell are much more buffeted by, and con nected to broader processes of socio-economic transformation (Bornstein 2012) compared to the expats in the bubble of Aidland. Further, reading local development practices as 'infused with cultural codes' can make visible larger social processes (Bornstein 2012: 14).

The definition of 'local' matters here. There have been calls to dismantle North–South imaginaries in the study of development actors and to recognize the significance of 'South–South' volunteering in particular (Ballie-Smith et al 2018; Laurie and Ballie-Smith 2018). While such calls are laudable, they only take us so far in reconceiving who is a legitimate development actor. In this re-imagining, the 'global South' seemingly stands in for other terms long discarded such as 'developing countries' and the 'third-world'.[1] Laurie and Ballie-Smith (2018) demonstrate the ongoing salience of such categorizations, where the shared experience of colonial histories and of being a recipient of aid establish a sense of solidarity and mutual understanding between development agents and host communities. At the same time, the volunteers in their study are still part of the global elite, and I would argue, likewise live in a bubble of 'Aidland', disconnected from local relations, histories, and futures (Watanabe 2017). Furthermore, national elites that often 'stand in' for 'local' development practitioners are similarly disconnected, and while interesting in their own right (for example Beck 2017), are not equivalent to the actors that are the focus of this study. I now map out exactly what I mean by local development agents, and why they are an important, and distinctive, object of study.

The Significance of the Local

By *local* development agents I am referring to people engaged in delivering 'development' who share a close socio-economic and geographical location

---

[1] For me, the purpose of terms such as 'global South' is to overcome a division of the world based on geography, to one based on structural positioning, recognizing that privilege and marginality do not map on to national borders, without downplaying the still significant differences across countries (Fischer 2019).

with the recipients of welfare and development. Local development agents are not 'provincial' in comparison to the 'universal' or 'cosmopolitan' national or expat development actor, rather the socio-cultural context of 'home' fundamentally shapes the constitution of all 'aid workers', influencing the way they are affected in the field (Malkki 2015). Local development agents are distinct, however, in sharing a social milieu with the targets or recipients of assistance (see Pigg 1992; Crewe and Harrison 1998; Hilhorst 2001; Heaton-Shestra 2006; Kar 2013), with significant consequences as I demonstrate throughout this book. As such, local development agents are 'materially light and socially heavy' in contrast to expat workers who are 'materially heavy and socially light' (Redfield 2012: 360). That is, local development agents lack high incomes and are often only marginally better off economically than the 'beneficiaries' of their programmes and activities (Ong and Combinido 2018). At the same time, they carry the gravity of local attachment; they are embedded within social relations that extend beyond development transactions, and that last beyond short-term interventions.

These actors share several characteristics that influence their role in local development and their positioning within broader development assemblages. The first are diverse yet distinct motivations compared to development actors from the global North. Sharing a similar socio-economic position to the beneficiaries of aid, they are often motivated by lived experiences of poverty or disaster (Ong and Combinido 2018), or are targets themselves of development projects, in which becoming a development agent is a part of self-reinventions as entrepreneurial subjects (Hoffman 2013). With low social and economic capital, local development agents also seek opportunities to enhance their employment prospects (Brown and Prince 2015), to extend and strengthen social ties (Smith 2003), and accumulate symbolic and material resources (Crewe and Harrison 1998). Development agents from the global North may similarly be pursuing social mobility and 'CV-building' (Laurie and Ballie Smith 2018), but rarely are these strategies a matter of survival or entail substantial shifts in social status. While important factors, material and status conferring motivations are arguably over-emphasized in the literature; altruism remains central (Brown and Prince 2015). Further, like other development volunteers and professionals (Allahyari 1996; Malkki 2015), many people become local development agents as part of projects of self-cultivation and transformation (Arvidson 2008; Bornstein 2012; Scherz 2014). Rather than pursuing cosmopolitan identities (Malkki 2015), local development agents are more likely to tie their ambitions of self-making to nation-building and citizenship (Hoffman 2013; Brown and Prince 2015). These themes are taken up in Part I of this book.

The second characteristic is that these motivations alongside low socio-economic status, can make local development agents easily exploitable as a cheap workforce. The cost effectiveness of community development is considered a positive in much of the development studies literature (Mansuri and Rao 2004), yet volunteers often complain that this comes at the cost of the exploitation of their labour (Russell and Vidler 2000; Boesten et al. 2011; Jakimow 2018d). For example volunteers in Kenya described volunteerism as 'working for less than what you are worth' (Lewis 2015: 73). Women in particular are often taken advantage of due to their socially prescribed 'altruistic behaviour' (Brickell and Chant 2010). Huang (2017) notes the fine line between empowerment by becoming an information agent in a market-driven development project, and the exploitation of agents' labour in underpaid time-intensive work. The link between empowerment and exploitation is explored in Chapter Four among women political party workers, encouraged to affectively and financially invest in self-imaginaries barely realizable within the constraints of party structures.

The third characteristic common to all local development agents is being culturally and ethically embedded within the societies in which they work. Ideologies, social norms, and symbolic power shape the relationships they have with others, and their possibilities for self. The symbolic terrain carries a greater intensity for local development agents (Bulloch 2017) compared to expats living in the 'bubble of Aidland' (Apthorpe 2011), with gender, caste, and other ideologies having a weightier affective force and socializing power (Heaton-Shrestha 2006; Roy 2017). While expat volunteers and workers face ethical dilemmas associated with their greater material wealth and outsider status (Fechter 2012b; Shutt 2012), local development agents face difficulties due to their belonging to the same moral universe as the targets of development. Often the beliefs that motivate or drive development and welfare activities are in tension with social norms, creating irreconcilable ethical dilemmas for local development agents (Kar 2013; Scherz 2014). These agents must also contend with evaluative frames (Bornstein 2012) and 'moral atmospheres' that frustrate their work and create anxieties and tension as explored in Chapter Five.

As members of the community in which they work, local development agents are also positioned within multiple social relations of unequal power (Crewe and Harrison 1998; Smith 2003; Ong and Combinido 2018). Their multitude of relationships include not only those with the recipients of assistance, but also government officials, party leaders, NGO partners, donor agencies, and the general public. They must carefully navigate the hierarchies and social relations in their working environment (Huang 2017; Ong and

Combinido 2018), and their own status as simultaneously insider and outsider (Crewe and Harrison 1998; Heaton-Shrestha 2006). Critically, most of these relations predate discrete development projects and endure far beyond the project cycle, and are important to future livelihoods or even social survival. If relationships break down, local development agents cannot retreat to 'home' and an altogether different set of self-sustaining relations as expats or national elites do. Further, local development agents experience different ethical relationships with 'beneficiaries', characterized by inter-dependence, care, empathy, personalization, and desire for respect (Bornstein 2012; Kar 2013; Scherz 2014). While expat workers are 'proximate' to locals in the development terrain, their identity as operating without borders and *in situ* only temporarily, gives their work a lightness in comparison to the 'social heaviness' of local development agents (Redfield 2012).

The fifth characteristic particular to local development agents is that becoming one can be status conferring, but it can also risk present and future selves. Becoming a doer of development rather than a recipient can be a means of social differentiation and mobility (Pigg 1992), as development agents have access to material and symbolic resources that enhance their socio-economic status. The ideology and discourse of development is pro-ductive in structuring their relations with others, with ideas of 'backwardness', 'remoteness', or *'orang belum mampu'* (people not yet capable) central in the formation of beneficiary *and benefactor* identities (Heaton-Shrestha 2006). Often, however, the distinction between categories of 'people who receive development... and those who bring development' is ambiguous (Hilhorst et al. 2012: 410; Huang 2017). Statuses are fluid, and people slip between them (Hilhorst 2003). Indeed the overlapping of identities so that one is an agent of development, as well as a local who benefits from this development, is a defin-ing feature of *local* development agents. Further, as I explore throughout this book, it is too simplistic to state that becoming an agent of development always results in tipping power relations in their favour. Local development agents are 'marked' in ways that do not necessarily bring them prestige and social status, or in other terms, they are susceptible to engendering affects in others that are at variance with their own self-understandings or ambitions (see Chapters Six and Seven; Bornstein 2012; Hilhorst 2003). The ways local development produces anew social relations can be revelatory of transform-ations and reproductions in the broader political economy.

This book explores under-recognized instances in which becoming a local development agent puts at risk the self one is, or is becoming—their susceptibility to being affected in ways that are involuntary, and potentially harmful. Other development agents—expats or national elites—are lighter, less embedded within local social worlds and therefore less susceptible to being affected in ways that challenge their fundamental sense of self. Greater susceptibility relative to other development agents is the final feature common to local development agents, and the one most relevant to this book. It is a product of the other characteristics mentioned above, namely: affective investments in projects of self-making (their motivations for joining); their embeddedness within cultural and moral universes that gives social norms and expectations greater affective force; the importance of enduring relationships with other actors in the development terrain, and; the dangers and possibilities that come from their changed social status by becoming a doer of development. As I argue throughout this book, this differential susceptibility to be affected has significant implications for development. At the local level, it shapes resource flows (who gets what within local political economies) and produces anew unequal social relations. At the meso- and macro-level, I argue that differential susceptibility is an unrecognized constituent of power within broader development assemblages, reinforcing 'top-down' hierarchies while also providing the possibility for these to be disrupted (see Chapter One).

Bringing together the literature on local development agents reveals distinct characteristics that are consequential for development, and hence I argue that treating them as a distinct object of study is overdue. I contribute to this task through a comparison of two very different development agents: volunteers in Medan and municipal councillors in Dehradun. The above mentioned similarities in what are otherwise substantially different actors underlines the utility of bringing them together in a study of local development agents. Having outlined what makes them a single category of understanding, I now provide details of the very different contexts in which they work.

Community Development in Medan, Indonesia

Medan is a city of 2.1 million inhabitants in the province of North Sumatra, and is the largest city in Indonesia outside Java and the fourth largest overall. Medan is an important economic and commercial hub, connected to one of the busiest shipping lanes in the world, and is a centre of crop trading for commodities in the region (Tarigan et al. 2017). Its economic growth rate of 6.4 per cent is higher than the national average. Medan nonetheless faces considerable urban challenges, including energy shortages leading to frequent power cuts, overreliance on private transportation resulting in traffic congestion, inability of the city government to provide clean water to more than 30 per cent of the population, and creaking solid waste management processes (Tarigan et al. 2017). Poverty rates have fluctuated greatly over the past twenty years according to available statistics, reaching the highest point in 1998 at 19.27 per cent, and the lowest in 2002 at 4.8 per cent. The latest figure is 9.3 per cent, calculated by the number of people with monthly expenditure below 330,663 rupiah (around US$24).[2] According to residents, the official poverty line is far too low, and does not take into consideration the high cost of living in Medan relative to other cities such as Yogyakarta or Bandung. Urban poverty remains a considerable, and perhaps understated problem in Medan.

As an economic hub with a long history of migration, it is arguably the most ethnically diverse urban centre in Indonesia. The 'indigenous' Malay today make up only 6.6 per cent of the population. The Batak people (34 per cent) comprise a family of different ethnic groups—the main ones in Medan being Toba, Karo, Mandailing—while the next largest ethnic group are Javanese (32 per cent). Two minority populations are particularly significant in Medan (Aspinall et al. 2011). The Chinese population comprise 11.2 per cent of the population, who retain a distinctive culture and continue to speak a Chinese dialect (Hokkien) unlike in other parts of Indonesia. The visibility of economic success for some ethnic Chinese has led to resentment, and assumptions that all Chinese people are comfortably off: stereotypes that betray a wide variety of economic circumstances. We heard multiple stories of local level officials treating Chinese people like 'milk cows', or ATMs, to be milked for money and Chinese people were often left off lists for government assistance. The Tamil population is a much smaller minority group (only 0.8 per cent), yet nonetheless a visible part of Medan cultural diversity. Large Tamil temples are in central parts of the city, and the Tamil language can still be heard on the street in parts of Medan. They do not, however, seem to play a large role in the delivery of state aid programmes or become local development actors.[3] Despite significant religious diversity, Medan remains a Muslim majority city with close to 68 per cent of the population.

---

[2] https://sumut.bps.go.id/dynamictable/2016/10/10/17/persentase-penduduk-miskin-kabupaten-kota-1993-2016.html; http://www.thejakartapost.com/news/2015/01/09/north-sumatra-poverty-level-increasing-says-bps.html.

[3] The head of one lingkungan (neighbourhood) in which we worked was Tamil, in an area with a large Tamil population.

Associational life is vibrant in Medan, with various ethnic and ethno-religious associations reflecting the ethnic diversity of the city (Aspinall et al. 2011). Many of these are involved in community work aimed at addressing the problems of urban poverty mentioned above. The church, masjid, and temple are significant sites of social and community activities. Associational life in Medan also includes a darker side. While their presence has been reduced since the early 2000s, *preman* groups are a significant feature of the urban landscape, so much so that preman, meaning gangster/thug, has become synonymous with Medan (Sitompul 2016).[4] Preman groups are often associated with the Pemuda Pancasila—the paramilitary youth group for the five principles of the Indonesian state. Oppenheimer's (2012) film *The Act of Killing* captured the strength and notoriety of these groups in Medan, and the way members harass and extort money from residents (Wandita 2014). Nonetheless, for some Medan residents, the Pemuda Pancasila used to have higher ideals, even as these have faded in recent years.

Across Indonesia, a large infrastructure exists at the local level to aid the implementation of state development and welfare programmes. Medan sits within North Sumatera province, and has its own city government (*pemerintah kota*). The governor and mayor are the popularly elected heads of the province and city respectively. Beneath the *kota* are the *kecamatan*, or sub-districts, below which are the *kelurahan* (which I translate as urban locality). Medan has 21 districts, and 151 *kelurahan*, with populations in the latter ranging between 10,000 to 20,000 residents. The Camat (head of the *kecamatan*) and the Lurah (Head of the *kelurahan*), are appointed by the government rather than popularly elected (the equivalent level of governance in villages are elected). The community based organizations that feature in this book are also based at the level of the *kelurahan*, who must then interact with the Lurah to get works accomplished. Below the *kelurahan* is the level of *lingkungan* (approximately 9–12 per *kelurahan*), which I translate into neighbourhood. The Kepling (*kepala lingkungan*, or head of the *lingkungan*) is also appointed, but is (variously) seen as being closer to the local people than the Lurah. There are no *Rukun Warga* (RW) or *Rukun Tetangga* (RT) in Medan as there are in other parts of Indonesia.

At the level of *lingkungan*, the *posyandu* (*pos pelayanan terpadu*: integrated service post) deliver health services to mothers, babies, and infants. An important figure in this infrastructure is the *kader* (cadre), primarily women

[4] Sitompul, Martin (2016) 'Preman Medan dari Zaman ke Zaman', *Historia*, https://historia.id/kota/articles/preman-medan-dari-zaman-ke-zaman-P1Bm4 accessed 9 February 2020.

from each *lingkungan* who provide assistance to the state (Chung 2015). Their duties include assisting at the *posyandu*, collecting household level data, conducting mosquito eradication drives, and so on. In the past, there was an element of coercion to this volunteer labour. During the New Order, women were compelled to participate in the PKK (Pembinann Kesejahteraan Keluarga—Family Welfare Guidance), Dharma Wanita, and Dharma Pertiwi (Suryakusuma 2011). Positions within the organizational structure mirrored a woman's husband's position; her active involvement obligatory for his promotion prospects (Robinson 2008). Gerke (1992) argues that Dharma Wanita was 'the final expression of *ikut suami* (follow the husband) mentality' (Gerke 1992: 47), and further confirmation that in public life, women were seen solely as facilitating their husbands: '*pendamping suami*' or 'the companion at the husband's side' (Robinson 2008: 71). Today, women take on roles as kader willingly, and often benefit materially, economically, and socially. As brokers, kaders are often crucial nodes in mediating citizen entitlements, part of the personal networks through which citizenship becomes socialized (Berenschot and van Klinken 2018).

The dominant development discourse in Indonesia has shifted from guidance (*pembinaan*) to empowerment (*pemberdayaan*) (Robinson 2008), although the language of empowerment has faded in recent times (Robinson 2014). The Program Nasional Pemberdayaan Masyarakat (the National Program for Community Development, hereafter PNPM) exemplifies this change, and the opportunities such a shift in paradigm provided for men and women to become local development actors. The Yudhoyono Government launched the PNPM as its flagship poverty alleviation programme in 2007. At the time it reached all villages and urban wards, making it the largest community driven development programme in the world. The aims of the PNPM were 'fostering community participation, improving local governance, and delivering basic needs at the community level' (World Bank 2013: vi).[5] At the urban level, the PNPM-Perkotaan was a continuation of the Program Penanggulangan Kemiskinan di Perkotaan (Urban Poverty Alleviation Program), or P2KP. Both programmes were based on the premise that the people know best how to solve their problems, at the same time that communities were undergoing a period of moral crisis (Li 2006; Effendy 2015). Backed by financial and

---

[5] The Jokowi government has ceased funding the PNPM-Perkotaan in order to focus on rural development. As my research mostly predates this change in government policy, it has not affected the empirical material.

strategic assistance from the World Bank, and later the Islamic Development Bank, central funding for the PNPM finished in 2016.[6]

An important feature of the PNPM-Urban is the establishment of a Badan Keswadayaan Masyarakat (Board for Community Self-reliance) of volunteers in each Kelurahan. BKMs are responsible for developing a Community Development Plan and implementing projects in three areas: infrastructure (building of roads and drains, etc.), economic (rotating funds and small enterprise development), and social (small gifts of welfare and training). BKM members liaise with the *masyarakat* (people/community) to decide on appropriate projects, oversee small group lending, and select recipients of social programmes. They also work with the Kelompok Swadaya Masyarakat (community self-help groups) who develop proposals for their *lingkungan* to be funded by the PNPM. Trained facilitators recruit individuals to become BKM members, approaching potential candidates individually or in community meetings and religious forums. Elections are held for residents to select the most appropriate individuals as BKM members and coordinators. BKM members describe themselves as volunteers, as they receive no honorarium or salary for their work.

BKMs reflect the ethnic diversity of Medan, with Bataknese (Karo and Mandailing), Javanese, Malay, Banjar, Sundanese, among others claiming membership. The exception is the low level of participation by the Chinese and Tamil minorities, and to my knowledge, no BKM member in Medan identified as such, although a couple of our respondents had mixed parentage. As a large city with a high cost of living, residents are busy with livelihood activities, frustrating 'community mobilization' (see also Marcus and Asmorowati 2006). BKM members are therefore exceptional in their desire and/or willingness to volunteer their time. The political and economic status of BKM members in Medan is diverse, but the majority are from modest socio-economic backgrounds. One was a former Lurah, and several BKM members were, or had been, a *kepling*. Other BKM members were little known in their locales prior to becoming involved in the programme. Livelihood activities included security guards, *becak* drivers (similar to a rickshaw), running a home-based laundry or small *warung* (street-side restaurant), and housewife. Many BKM members had spent periods of their

---

[6] Rural CDD (PNPM-perdesaan) continued with the Undang-Undang Desa 'Village Laws' that guarantee a budget direct to villages, with a set of institutional frameworks to ensure community involvement in development.

life below the poverty line and had been, or were currently eligible for government assistance.

Urban Development in Dehradun, India

Dehradun is the provisional capital of Uttarakhand: a Himalayan region carved out of Uttar Pradesh in India in 2000. This geology presents distinct development challenges in the largely rural hills and mountains (*pahar*), distinct to those of the (more urban) plains (*maidan*). As a consequence of what was considered the neglect of mountain areas, and the loss of control over land, forest, and livelihoods, the Uttarakhand *andolan* (meaning movement) emerged as a mass protest movement in the 1990s demanding their own statehood. Drawing from a longer history of political movements, of which Chipko is most famous (Guha 1989), momentum built for a new state. The Bharatiya Janata Party (BJP) government established the state of 'Uttaranchal', in November 2000, which later became Uttarakhand in 2006.[7] Dehradun was made the provisional capital until facilities could be developed in Gairsain: a small town that is in the hills and thus a symbolic move of political power from the plains to the mountains. The failure to move the capital is one example of the unmet demands of the Uttarakhand *andolan*. Further, massive migration to urban localities is seen as symptomatic of the failure of statehood to result in the development of the hills (Koskimaki 2017).

As a state capital, Dehradun has been granted Municipal Corporation status. Its population of just over ten lakh (one million people) is expanding rapidly due to migration from the hills and other parts of North India. During the summer months, the main roads are clogged with traffic as holiday makers escape the heat on the plains, passing through Dehradun to the hills of Uttarakhand. High population growth places a heavy burden on city infrastructure, resulting in growing *bastis* (informal housing colonies), and increasing stress on roads, electricity, water, and urban transport (Mittal 2014). Dehradun's recent low ranking of 61 out of 73 among India's cleanest cities epitomizes a transformation from a city of orchards and grey hair, referring to the lychee trees that were common to the city and its attractiveness to retirees,

---

[7] Uttaranchal was one of three states formed by the BJP government in 2000, led by Vajpayee, and also included Jharkhand and Chhattisgarh. Uttaranchal is a name with strong Hindu connotations, and was a contentious choice against the more inclusive and widely demanded 'Uttarakhand'. The name was eventually changed to the latter in 2006 under the Union government.

to one of traffic jams and rubbish (*Times of India*, 4 May 2017). At the time fieldwork started in 2015, its governing body, the Dehradun Nagar Nigam, comprised 60 wards, each with between 5,000 and 12,000 voters (adults registered to vote in the locality). In 2018, a process of delimitation increased the municipal limits to include areas formerly under the *panchayat* (village governance), and reduced the size of large wards to between 5–6,000 voters.[8] Each ward elects a representative, locally known as *Parshad*, but also called ward member, and the equivalent in the literature of Municipal Councillor.

Dehradun Nagar Nigam (DNN) is significantly smaller and less resourced compared to other municipal corporations in India. There has been little by way of devolution of state funds through the 12th Schedule—a list of items that are in the functional domain of urban local bodies—and DNN must rely on House Tax. The starving of municipal corporations is a feature of urban governance across India, as state governments have prioritized rural constituencies and guarded their power over cities through the establishment of agencies that bypass municipal institutions (Weinstein et al. 2014; Ahluwalia 2019). Dehradun seems particularly hard hit. Parshads received only 5 *lakh* (US$8,000) of discretionary development funding in 2015. In contrast, MCs in Ahmedabad received 9 *lakh* rupees in 2006 (Berenschot 2010), in Delhi, MCs received 30 *lakh* in 2017 (Chettri 2017), while Bhopal MCs protested in 2016 to lift their development fund from 20 to 30 *lakh* (*Hindustan Times*, 4 April 2016). To undertake substantial development works, Parshads in Dehradun must convince MLAs to spend their discretionary budget in their wards (an argument made significantly easier when the MLA is from the same party), or submit proposals through agencies such as the Mussoorie Dehradun Development Association. Unlike MCs in other states and the Pradhans (elected village heads) in Uttarakhand, Parshads do not receive a honorarium or 'sitting fee'.

The official duties of Parshads reflect their limited power. They are responsible for waste removal and liaising with government departments to ensure electricity, water supply, and street lighting. They undertake small development works and cooperate with other agencies (such as the state Public Works Department) to facilitate larger scale infrastructure projects. Parshads are also signatories to a range of documentation required by the Indian state: such as domicile certificates, income certificates, pension forms, electricity applications,

---

[8] Challenges in court against the process of delimitation resulted in (or was the reason given for) the delay in the 2018 urban local body elections due April 2018, which were eventually held in November 2018.

and so on. Municipal councillors play an 'intermediary' role (Berenschot 2010), helping citizens with 'social handicaps'—such as illiteracy, poverty, caste status (de Wit 2017)—to access the state through its often recalcitrant and indifferent bureaucrats (van Dijk 2011; Ciotti 2012; Shekhar Swain 2012).

According to the 74th Constitutional Amendment, women must hold no less than a third of seats in local urban bodies including municipal corporations. Scheduled castes (SCs, the government designation for *Dalit*), scheduled tribes (STs), and other backward classes (OBCs) also have seats reserved in accordance with their proportion in the population. Uttarakhand has increased the reservation for women in rural areas to 50 per cent, however it remains one-third in urban areas. For the 2013–18 term, seven women were elected into general seats, making the total number of elected women ward members 29 out of 60. There is a tendency among the general public, and academics, to diminish the importance of women MCs by focusing on so-called proxies, that is women who contest elections on behalf of men. The phenomena of *Parshad Pati* (or the husband of the Parshad as the real source of power) is less than is often assumed, however, and research on such women outlines a more complicated picture (see de Wit 2017: 165–6; and Ghosh and Lama-Rewel 2005; John 2007 for more nuanced accounts). Often women are elected on behalf of men, but then come to have a significant role and political ambitions of their own. For the 2013–18 term, only three women Parshads had no public presence and took part in no activities (see also Chapter Four).

The conditions for women's involvement in Dehradun politics are more conducive than other parts of North India. Bimla, a woman Parshad who moved to Dehradun from Haryana after marriage, claimed she had drawn strength from the local saying: 'We are not flowers but fire, we are the power and we are the women of Uttarakhand.' In the hills of Uttarakhand, women have a history of involvement in political movements such as the Anti-Alcohol Movement (1956–65), Chipko movements, and *jan andolan* (Kumar 2011). In particular, many men and women first cut their political teeth during the Uttarakhand *andolan* in the 1990s, and still call upon the fictive kin ties established during that time. Being able to claim that one is an *andolan kari* (a fighter in the movement for Uttarakhand) brings material benefits and is an important political claim. Women political actors in particular draw upon a narrative of sacrifice during the andolan. Many were present during the Rampur Tiraha incident in Muzaffarnagar Uttar Pradesh on 1–2 October 1994, when police fired on activists. There were also allegations that security forces raped women activists, and women often shed tears relaying the events of that night. Collective memory thereby legitimates women's place in politics.

A Research Approach of Affection

Comparative ethnography of these two distinct types of local development agents revealed shared experiences—including the susceptibility to be affected—not possible through other research methods. The ethnographic approach, with its attention to seemingly trivial and localized everyday practices, reveals the invisible side of social life and power (Herzfeld 2015). At the same time, this demand for in-depth specificity can lead to an endless particularism that frustrates anthropology's contributions to broader debates and questions (van der Veer 2016). Comparative ethnographies overcome this problem, rendering visible operations of power that transcend cultural specificities (Herzfeld 2015), and helping researchers identify that which is of analytical import, but taken for granted when focusing on a single context (Manor 2016). Van der Veer (2016: 9) argues that ethnography is well-suited to comparison due to its 'necessarily fragmentary approach to social life, in which the intensive study of a fragment is used to gain a perspective on a larger whole'. The study of 'fragments', allows anthropologists to ask questions and reveal insights about the larger questions—such as personhood, nationalism, power, and so on—without falling into the trap of generalizing across large diverse populations. I consider 'susceptibility' as one fragment, shared across two settings but with diverse manifestations and consequences. By examining susceptibility through a comparative ethnography, I aim to gain insight into how it influences power relations at the local level, while pointing to broader implications within the development enterprise as a whole.

The comparative ethnography of these different development actors entailed participant observation and the co-construction of in-depth profiles. Between April 2013 and April 2015 I, along with two research assistants (Yumasdaleni and Aida Harahap), conducted ten months of ethnographic research in Medan, Indonesia, following the activities of three BKMs, conducting interviews with relevant individuals (government officials, beneficiaries, etc.) and co-constructing seventeen in-depth profiles (nine volunteers and eight recipients of benefits). In Dehradun, India, I worked with PRAGATI (Panchayati Rule and Gender Awareness Training Institute), a local NGO, to undertake five months of ethnographic research between May 2015 and June 2016, returning for the urban local body elections in April 2018 when they were scheduled, and again in November 2018 when they were held. We interviewed half of Dehradun's sixty municipal councillors (elected for the term 2013–18), in addition to government officials and MLAs. We co-constructed in-depth profiles with ten women municipal councillors, entailing at least five formal interviews as well as informal discussions and observing them in their role. There are thus several elements to my research methods: capturing experience as it is lived (participant observation), as it is later recalled (interviews and conversations), and presentations of self.

Emotions and affects that are personally experienced are particularly difficult to capture methodologically, as affective pedagogies and culturally learnt emotional responses shape our interpretations. We therefore took a methodological approach that involved purposeful reflection on our pathways from affect, to emotion, to thought, in order to understand how we reached certain interpretations, while also deepening them (see Jakimow and Yumasdaleni 2016). After each interview or observation, my co-researchers and I shared our impressions of the scene, and unravelled the meanings behind respondents use of words such as 'fear', 'anxiety', 'satisfaction'. The cross-cultural research teams were important, as the conversation between Australian and Indian/Indonesian researchers helped to reveal the cultural basis of our interpretations. Biographical details also matter for the way people are affected or moved (Beatty 2010). The intimate understanding developed through the co-constructed profiles enabled us to interpret the resonance, intensity, and practical significance of emotions and affect that we observed and felt in the field (Beatty 2014). An intimate understanding of people's lives alongside direct observation, interrogated through reflexive research practice, thereby informs my interpretations. At the same time, I recognize the difficulty of researching emotions and affects necessarily means there is a degree of speculation.

I deploy what I describe as a research orientation of affection. On a simple note, what I mean by affection is a willing fondness for my research partici- pants, I empathized with them and tried to see the world through their eyes. I took their self-representations seriously, not as truth, but as their genuine attempts to describe their reality. As such, I am often accused by reviewers of naiveté for taking narratives at face value, without critically (or cynically) enquiring into their *real* motivations. The presumption of ulterior motives seems particularly strong when describing local development agents, who are often reduced to caricatures seeking only material or political gain. The vast majority of the literature likewise misses the essential humanness of politi- cians, who are feeling thinking beings, rather than purely rational calculative machines (Mahler 2006). In contrast, few dare question the sincerity of the accounts of people considered 'poor' or 'marginal'. In this book I have sus- pended disbelief around local development agents' claims to be motivated to do good, while being cautious of the complaints and rumours made against them. I am not suggesting that this holds a greater claim to truth, but rather that accounts generated through affection for research participants are equally worthy of consideration as more cynical ones, and that in doing so, we open up new pathways to understanding.

Affection also means, following Throop and Duranti (2014), the allure or the pull that the world has upon us. As a research orientation, I see affection as a willing openness to be imposed upon and affected by the world I am encountering, being attentive and responsive to the affects, moods, and sensibilities of my surroundings (Throop 2018). Describing the *capacity to be affected* as a resource is to underline the importance of our responsiveness to our social worlds for personhood. I too am a social being, and as outlined in the introduction, also susceptible to be impressed upon. Methodologically I opened myself up to these impressions, tried to heighten them, pick at them, allow them to lead me to new pathways of thinking. Already as an outsider, I was in a process of attunement to be able to dwell comfortably in a world that was not yet natural or taken-for-granted. The ability to dwell in and reflect on the unfamiliar or the not-so-natural background of life, is, according to Throop (2018), one of the possibilities for anthropological thinking. I have found that working comparatively assists in the ability to practically suspend ones unquestionable adherence to the world, potentially leading to insights about the particular context as well as the human condition more generally.

A degree of modesty is required, however, in what I have been able to achieve. The horizons that come in and out of prominence, the ebbs and flows of life, were different for me on account of the temporariness of my dwelling in that space. Further, as I touched on in the introduction, I did not always succeed in being responsive to a world that was putting at risk my sense of self, or who I am. These experiences, and failures, also help me to understand susceptibility as a human condition that not only leads to reflexive change, but also resilience to the world imposed upon us. The tension between openness and resilience is a core theme of this book, and critical to understanding power in development.

PART I

SELFHOOD

3

Touched by the Heart

> Finally I became a part of the PNPM, and I felt that my life had more meaning, for myself. I am only a graduate of SMA [Year 12], just stupid, [but] with principles that the meaning of life is to do things for the family and for other people, the people who need our help. Because help does not have to be material. We can also help with our energy, with our thoughts. After I joined the PNPM, I am more at ease living this life. Even though I have not yet had a child, I have found activities to keep me busy that are useful. After joining the PNPM, I thought maybe this is the place for me to become my self [*menjadi diri sendiri*], what I have, and what I have been desiring ardently [*idam-idamkan*] all this time, and finally I can find happiness
>
> (Pak Anto, BKM Coordinator, 2013)

At the time of this interview in 2013, Pak Anto was coordinator of one of the most successful BKMs in Medan: the community-based organization established to implement the PNPM at the local level. He became aware of the programme two years earlier through a socialization initiative in a community meeting at the Kantor Lurah: the government office of the urban ward. '*Sosialisasi*' (socialization) is a common feature of state-led development in Indonesia (Gibbings 2017), entailing in this case information about a new development programme (the PNPM) in order to gain people's support, encourage them to volunteer, and persuade them to adopt the programme's values (Carroll 2009). Pak Anto responded enthusiastically to the invitation, incorporating the values of the programme into his own personal project to live a meaningful life. Indeed, he credits his involvement in the PNPM as having a transformative effect on his being, allowing him to become the person he long desired to be.

Accounts of local development agents often express cynicism that local volunteers are motivated by anything more than material or political gain. Research in other parts of Indonesia have shown that BKM members use their roles to benefit politically, economically, or both (Prahara 2016). BKM members in Medan have diverse reasons for volunteering, including building

Susceptibility in Development: Micropolitics of Local Development in India and Indonesia. Tanya Jakimow, Oxford University Press (2020). © Tanya Jakimow.
DOI: 10.1093/oso/9780198854739.001.0001

social connections, securing access to government entitlements, and becoming known in the locality. Yet as this chapter demonstrates, many volunteers (the majority in my small sample) are motivated by the opportunity to engage in activities that give their life meaning and to realize self-making projects. These personal dimensions of development are not inconsequential, as 'beliefs and attitudes are implicated and impact on the outcomes of aid', and hence aid workers 'can become points of intervention' (Fechter 2012a: 1386; Chambers 1997). Arguably, local volunteers are already considered points of intervention, in that their recruitment and participation in community development is part of a programme's design. I suggest, however, that insufficient attention has been paid to who is recruited, the processes of recruitment and retention, and how these processes shape local development practices.

The body of literature that explores these processes tends to be cynical not only of volunteers' claims that they seek to do good, but of their autonomy within self-making projects. The recruitment of Pak Anto to become a volunteer in service of state objectives can be interpreted as an example of governmentality (Hoffman 2013). The PNPM, with its explicit focus on 'educating desires, and configuring habits, aspirations and beliefs' (Li 2006: 3, see also Effendy 2015; Marcus and Asmorowati 2006) is almost exemplary of 'government' in the Foucauldian sense (Carroll 2009). The *sosialisasi* that is an important component of community development in Indonesia (Guggenheim 2004) awakens feelings in potential recruits, encourages citizens to expend their energies strengthening civil society and building social capital in the forms directed by development experts (Li 2006). This mobilization of sentiments extends regimes of governance, using what Rose (2000) describes as 'Ethopower': the self-regulation of individuals as social beings by appealing to and intensifying emotions and affective forces, enlisting individuals' sense of obligation, shame, guilt, and so on. In this way, 'values, beliefs, and sentiments . . . underpin the techniques of responsible self-government and the management of one's obligations to others' (Rose 2000, 1399). Read simplistically, the PNPM dupes Pak Anto into engaging in a project of self-cultivation that ultimately extends disciplinary power through state-led development.

Such an interpretation of Pak Anto's recruitment into the BKM would not, I argue, do justice to both the disciplining *and creative* possibilities for self available through state-led development. Many people attended community meetings that included socialization for the PNPM, but very few people put their hands up to become volunteers. Fewer still remained and were active volunteers throughout the life of the programme. Answering why some individuals are particularly susceptible to being affected through the socialization programme, while others are left cold, is necessary if we are to move beyond a simplistic understanding of community development as merely a form of self-regulation. Further, the expansiveness in Pak Anto's sense of self is missed when the focus is on the prescribed nature of this becoming. In this chapter, I use volunteers' own theories of personhood to understand why they were drawn to the PNPM and to unravel how they 'became' within the programme. In particular, I examine the tension inherent in processes of self-formation that are both agentive, but also responsive to and dependent on the external world. I argue that close attention to the dialectic between susceptibility to affective animations and the capacity for emotional experiences that provide opportunities for self-realization provides insight to the workings of power through the self.

These 'personal dimensions' of development have important implications for how development is practised in urban Medan. I demonstrate how the heightened susceptibility to take up the invitation to 'become' through the PNPM is a factor in the force of its rationalities. Volunteers affectively invest in this sense of self and the processes of its realization through the programme. The emotional returns from their involvement, which are craved and required for this realization, make them vehement adherents of the objectives of the programme. That is, the conditions that make people like Pak Anto more likely to volunteer—ethical ambitions in personal circumstances of limited opportunities to fulfil those ambitions—gives these self-making projects immense personal significance, as well as increase the precariousness of these projects and their susceptibility to challenges.

Differential *susceptibility* to be affected thus sheds light on unconscious underpinnings of power and the force of discourses as mediated through the development subject (Kapoor 2017). At the same time, differential *capacity* to be affected sheds light on how the reaffirmation of volunteers' self-one-wants-to-be through BKM activities is an overlooked and positive consequence of the programme. The opportunity to become a development agent is uneven; the consequence of this unevenness is not only (or even) differential access to material and political resources, but also differential possibilities for self. This chapter draws attention to the dialectical nature of the capacity/susceptibility to be affected, in which the conditions that make one susceptible to being recruited into the programme and invest in its rationalities are the same as the conditions that enable self-realization through the capacity to be affected. Doing so reveals the huge stakes involved in community development for volunteers, which are no less than a sense of who one is, or is becoming. As seen throughout this book, these stakes shape urban local development and social relations in significant ways.

Becoming

Before examining how volunteers' own theories of personhood shed light on their processes of self-formation, I map out my starting framework of 'becoming'. The use of the word 'becoming' rather than 'being' is deliberate, pointing to the unfinished nature of the self, its plasticity in relation to human and non-human relations (Biehl and Locke 2017). Not only are we always 'unfinished', our sense of who we are is always in relation to a self we are becoming; a future orientation is woven into past biographies (Moore 2011). There is no singular interiority representative of an 'authentic self' (Bauman and Raud 2015). Individuals are a multiplicity of selves, belonging to and mutually constituted by the cultural and material particularities of the spaces they inhabit. Biehl and Locke (2017) describe such becoming as cartographic, rather than archaeological. That is, the self is not (only) an accumulation of past experiences with traces of the present self found in the past; we also inhabit and 'become' in our engagements with *multiple* worlds. We move through or are blocked from these worlds, resulting in differential possibilities of becoming. These possibilities change according to ascribed characteristics (such as gender and race), the biographical history of the individual, and transformations in the worlds themselves. In the next chapter I describe the entirety of these multiple worlds as they are differentially available to an individual as the 'topography for self': the socio-historical resources for self that are drawn upon in self-fashioning projects and impose upon the self in their ongoing becoming.

I take the anthropology of becoming as an invitation to hold 'agentive' and 'constitutive' aspects of self-formation in productive tension. That is, I examine the 'becoming' of volunteers as, on the one hand, an intentional striving to achieve a (culturally defined) self-making project (Ortner 2006), and, on the other, as responsive and attuned to the worlds they inhabit and traverse. There is no inconsistency here, as the worlds we inhabit provide the resources for these self-making projects (a theme I return to in Chapter Four). Rather I am speaking of two 'senses' of self. The first is the 'grand narrative', the 'life-long accumulation of self-fashioning' (Berlant 2011: 99) that self-making projects serve. My starting point to understanding these projects is Foucault's concept of ethical self-cultivation, the 'exercise of the self by which one attempts to develop and transform oneself, and to attain to a certain mode of being' (Foucault 1994: 282). The agentive language implied in these projects captures the *freedom* that individuals have in cultivating themselves through 'active processes of reflective self-formation' (Laidlaw 2014: 101). Freedom is not liberation in the sense of returning to a 'true self' however. Rather the self is stylized drawing on socio-historical ethical models of the right way to be, or in Foucault's (1986) terms, the operations of truth (see also Moore 2011).

The second sense of self refers to the 'ongoingness' of being in the world as 'an activity exercised within spaces of ordinariness' (Berlant 2011: 99). This sense captures the everyday responsiveness to the world, the daily micro and imperceptible fluctuations in self as one attunes to the world. We are attuned to world(s) (Throop 2018), impressed upon by the worlds we inhabit (Butler 2015), modifying ourselves in ways that are not an object of reflection. Our sentiments are developed inter-subjectively with others (Throop 2012), or in other words we are 'mutually arising' relational beings (Jackson 1998), with our responsiveness to multiple 'Others' a core aspect of the human condition. Zigon (2009: 81) describes this sense of self as our morality, our 'already cultivated everyday way of being in the world'. He contrasts morality with 'ethics' as referred to above, which he describes as the 'conscious reflec-tion on, or the turning of one's attention toward . . . morality' (Zigon 2009: 82). While this distinction has rightly been critiqued for its (mis)reading of Foucault (Laidlaw 2014), it is useful to capture the difference between a sense of self that is formed through reflective practice, framed by ambitions and hopes related to an unfolding future (Moore 2011), and a sense of self as an ongoing attunement, undulating and responsive to the worlds it is traversing.

I visualize the relationship between these two senses of self as a swimmer in open waters. While there is a destination in mind, one is rocked by the waves, demanding responsiveness to and working with the underlying cur-rents rather than fighting against them. The water is critical to reaching the destination. In relation to the first sense of self, as a self-fashioning project, socio-historical conditions (water in my analogy) contain the resources through which we make ourselves. These resources include not only ethical frameworks for living the good life as outlined by Foucault, but also the affect-ive experiences that reaffirm such a self is right for you. As we will see in this chapter, the *capacity* to be affected—to be able to feel a particular way—is critical to self-making projects. At the same time, we are also *susceptible* to being affected, imposed upon or moved in ways that demand a responsiveness to the conditions. These are the currents or waves that we work with, or attempt to diminish their force so that we can continue along the desired pathway. Sometimes, however, the swimmer may be driven off course, thrown in an uncharted direction, requiring a reorientation and new sense of destin-ation. One of the underlying themes of this book is what happens when the turbulent waters in which the ongoing sense of self dwells and attunes, makes unrealizable self-fashioning projects or the sense of who we are becoming (see in particular Chapters Six and Seven).

In this chapter, I am interested in how the capacity to be affected through the PNPM programme is critical to the self-fashioning projects of volunteers in Medan. Seizing on these opportunities is followed by processes of attunement to the rationalities of the programme. Their susceptibility to be affected, I suggest, makes them especially responsive to these rationalities. As they strive to reach the destination of respected, useful, and ethically upright 'self', they undulate, are rocked and carried, as they traverse the 'world' of community development, shaping where they eventually end up.

Recruitment

Pak Anto's antenna were up for opportunities to help people and contribute to the nation. He had previously been a member of the Pemuda Pancasila: part of the gangster fabric of Medan, in which strong-arm tactics and intimidation are used to gain control of localities and to reap financial reward. Pak Anto was in charge of a local carpark and was the security guard of his *lingkungan* (locality). According to Pak Anto, he was unusual in that he never demanded money from the people; a disposition that was so out of alignment with the Pemuda Pancasila that people were confused. His refusal to take advantage of people also caused him trouble with the Lurah, and eventually led to him leaving the organization. 'Why did I leave? Because the Pemuda Pancasila started to take a form that was counter to its previous goals. . . . We used to be the guardians of the community, help weak people to get justice. But now the paradigm is reversed. Now it has become a scourge for the people'. Further, he did not fit with the leadership '*tidak ada kecocokan dengan pimpinan-pimpinan*'. In lieu of these activities, he established himself within another community related to his workplace, but it was distant from his home.

Pak Anto's narrative of his pre-PNPM days provides an account of his 'grand narrative' of self, his more durable understanding of who he is and the type of person he wants to become. This grand narrative helps to explain why he eagerly volunteered to become a BKM member while other people were left cold by the invitation. His eagerness was a result of the limited opportunities he had to engage in activities that gave his life meaning, due to his meagre economic and cultural capital. The message of the PNPM communicated through socialization events resonated with Pak Anto, and he repeated them in his account of why he joined: 'help does not only have to be in material form. We can help through our *tenaga* [energy, labour, or person-power] and with our *pikiran* [thoughts, ideas]'. Such an idea appeals to someone like Pak Anto who lacks money and whose self-narrative is based around being useful to people. He is susceptible to the invitation to imagine himself as serving the community, at the same time such an invitation is empowering as it allowed Pak Anto to realize a 'self' that had been latent, but not possible given his circumstances. The PNPM also comes with the status and recognition of a government programme; people associated with the PNPM become well known and respected in the locality. Such 'benefits' are particularly significant for people who previously lacked such status or recognition. Hence the pro-gramme appeals to people from low socio-economic groups, a fact that is reflected in the general characteristics of BKM members across Medan.[1]

Another BKM coordinator, Pak Alrasyad, shares a similar socio-economic status to Pak Anto. After coming to Medan following his marriage, he knew few people in the area. He had a relatively poorly paid job in a nightclub: a profession which does not confer status and reflects his relative lack of education. He (therefore) made a conscious effort to become involved in the mosque and other community activities. I put 'therefore' in brackets, as it is a little speculative to suggest that part of the reason he sought status in the locality was due to his otherwise poor socio-economic status. Although Pak Alrasyad did not describe it in these terms, other BKM members who were of a similar economic background referred to their poor occupation (I am *only* a *becak* driver, or *only* a housewife) as part of their motivation to join the programme and to describe the significance of the recognition that they now enjoyed. Pak Alrasyad differs from many of these other volunteers, however, in that his wife's sister was *kepling*. He therefore knew about and had an invitation to attend community meetings, including the first meeting at which he was introduced to the PNPM.

The process of socialization piqued Pak Alrasyad's curiosity: 'I became involved after the socialization made me *penasaran* about the program, actually, what is this? What will happen to this program in the end'? *Penasaran* translates uneasily into curiosity, or even to be anxiously curious, or in suspense. It is a term that is sometimes used to denote a curiosity to *know* more, and the feeling of being uneasy or unsatisfied with limited knowledge (Boellstorff 2005b). Pak Alrasyad was curious because there was no salary

---

[1] These characteristics are not generalizable across Indonesia. Village BKM members (who receive an honorarium) are generally better off, or politically connected individuals, while Asmorawati and Marcus (2006) found in Bandung that they were 'elites', however they do not seem to account for the social mobility that occurs after joining the programme.

attached to the work of the BKM, which for his friends seemed ludicrous. A proposition of volunteer labour for the state is not unusual in Indonesia (Guinness 2009; Jakimow 2018a), where *keplings* and *kaders* are routinely paid a small honorarium or nothing at all for their labour in support of government programmes. The PNPM had a different feel to it, however, as it was presented as a professional programme in which BKM members had leadership responsibilities. Pak Alrasyad told us on several occasions that his friends and even his wife thought he was being fooled by becoming involved in a programme where he was not paid. He told his wife that he joined to help out the facilitator who was having trouble recruiting people, but he reiterated to us that 'I was only encouraged by a feeling of *penasaran*'. As he attended more and more meetings about the PNPM, his knowledge increased (or his *penasaran* was increasingly satisfied) and 'the desire to do more, do more for the benefit of the people, from the start it grew by itself' (Pak Alrasyad).

Sosialisasi is not merely a sharing of information about a programme, it is also an engendering of emotions that encourage some people to volunteer. These emotions are in no way uniform, rather they speak to the sense of potential self: who they are, or would like to be. For Pak Anto, the programme spoke to a durable self-narrative of community involvement; to Pak Alrasyad, it engendered curiosity about a potential opportunity that he could not pass up. For the majority of people, *sosialisasi* left them cold, or perhaps cynical, or in the least, uninterested. While we could read the recruitment of BKM members as Ethopower, the stirring of the heart strings to produce a passionate citizenry (Muehlebach 2012; Hoffman 2014; Rudnyckyj 2014), this would fail to capture this diversity. The differential susceptibility to the affective mobilization of the programme, and the diverse emotions engendered in such scenes complicates a simple picture of governance versus autonomy.

The Capacity to be Affected

BKM members had their own explanation as to why they, and not others, were susceptible to being recruited into the programme, in the process revealing their own theories of personhood (Geertz 1984; Moore 2007). Ibu Rosa is the coordinator of a BKM located in a poor neighbourhood known for its history as a centre for drugs and prostitution. She is not well to do in economic terms, and she starts her narrative with her humble beginnings before describing the changes that have occurred to her since joining the BKM.

I only used to sell *nasi goreng* [fried rice]. Indeed I was just a housewife and a member of the *masyarakat*. If I put it like this, I received a *panggilan jiwa* [call of the soul]...[that] I should use my hands to serve the *masyarakat* [people]. Maybe [pause], indeed it is because I have a *sifat* [characteristic] of compassion in my *hati* [heart]...after coming to know this program, I could not sleep, I looked around the locality. Apparently there were people who did not eat, could not buy medicines. I got a headache and I could not sleep.

(November 2014)

Ibu Rosa says she was deeply affected by the conditions of her neighbourhood only after hearing about an avenue of action, animating her to act.

Ibu Rosa describes the moment of recruitment as responding to *panggilan jiwa*: the call of the soul. Being called by the *jiwa* was a common phrasing among BKM members to explain why they joined the programme, and their ongoing motivations. *Jiwa* directly translates into English as soul or spirit. As used by Ibu Rosa and others however, it has the connotation of one's nature. So for example Pak Adnan states: 'I do not have any expectations from the BKM, I do not want reward. Why? Indeed my *jiwa* is like this...my *jiwa*, I like to help people' (Pak Adnan).[2] The *jiwa* explains why individuals become volunteers, and why they expect no material benefits for the work that they do. Pak Wibawa described the difficulties of finding people who were willing to work without a salary; 'it is volunteer work. If s/he is not called by his/her *jiwa*, if s/he does not care for the *masyarakat*, then they will be less able to do this work'. He said that he cannot explain why he works so hard as a BKM member without any reward, but notes that the work is light because he is *berjiwa sosial*. Having a social soul (*berjiwa sosial*) is essential to be able to invest time and energy without feeling burdened. The *jiwa* is often used as a response to the question of why they, but not others, find satisfaction from this work.

Jiwa as a symbolic form helps volunteers to make sense of their being; it is a vehicle through which people negotiate life and is therefore critical to agency (Geertz 1984). In other words, *jiwa* is part of a cultural theory of the will, its origin and interaction with society.[3] In this rendering, the *jiwa* is not an object of reflection and improvement, but rather is understood as a force external to the self, to which the conscious self aligns. The ambitions for self-making

---

[2] The missing section is due to an inaudible section of the recording.
[3] See Boellstorff (2005a) for an account of *jiwa*, and Jakimow (2017a) for my response to his interpretation.

arise from locating and realizing this nature. The *jiwa* is personal, a characteristic of the individual, but the self that one becomes is not unique. Rather, one must realize one's *jiwa* within the grammar of Indonesian society (Boellstorff 2005a) and the socially recognized ways of being. I return to the word fit [*cocok*, or *pas sama*] in relation to the people's account of *jiwa*. Ibu Rosa appeals to her husband that her soul fits (is suited to) the PNPM. Pak Anto said he longer fitted with the Pemuda Pancasila. The *jiwa* does not enable an individuality, or pre-cultural self, as much as it identifies which social positions or activities are aligned with one's real nature. The PNPM provides one positioning and a range of activities through which the self gains expression. In this way, the PNPM expands the possibilities for self of people predisposed to social activities, yet who previously had no means of realization.

The capacity to be affected is critical to this realization of self. Ibu Rosa notes that she has a 'characteristic of compassion in my *hati* [heart]...after coming to know this program, I could not sleep'. Whereas the *jiwa* represents one's calling, the *hati* aligns the individual to this calling by ensuring that they are affected in appropriate ways. *Hati* is the seat of emotion in Indonesia: a word that literally means liver (Boellstorff and Lindquist 2004). I translate *hati* as heart (see also Simon 2009; Rudnyckyj 2011; Munsoor 2015) as it more accurately captures the figurative meaning in English, the organ that is moved or moves us. My heart beats faster, my heart sinks—these are somatic responses that I feel in my chest. In Ibu Rosa's account, it was the *hati* who *moved* her, that impressed upon her that she should engage in social work. She was not moved by the problems in her locality before she had the ability to take action. The programme thereby provided the capacity to be affected, in ways that mobilized her, and prompted her to realize her self.

According to Ibu Muslimah, a BKM coordinator, the *hati* does more than respond to experiences, it also demands actions that will satisfy it.

> My friend asked, 'why do you want to go to the BKM every day, every Monday you have a meeting until night, why go'? It is not [pause], it is my *hati*, my *hati* which makes me happy....I am also amazed, why I want to do it, but I have to. It seems like an action [interrupted]
>
> Ibu Utari (BKM member): The *hati* is feeling happy, right!

Ibu Muslimah is amazed why she wants to work hard, but she *has* to. This could be interpreted as an inner compulsion, but is better described as an animation, as the *hati* can also be a source of energy. Later in the interview Ibu Muslimah explained that she was able to undertake the BKM training during Ramadan from morning to evening without tiring because her *hati* made her happy. The *hati* affects those *berjiwa sosial* in particular ways so that they are satisfied by, and energized to engage in social work.

Attention to the words BKM members use to represent themselves provides some explanations as to why some people are more susceptible to being recruited as BKM members than others.[4] Their *hati* attunes them to opportunities to realize their *jiwa* by engendering affective responses that draw them to some activities and subject positions and not others. In this way, the attunement that lies at the heart of becoming is also an attunement to the self, or a reading of one's desires within available possibilities (ways of being that are culturally legible as well as practically achievable). The PNPM provided the biographic moment when this self-recognition was possible, or the conditions in which a latent self was able to enter the imagination and become an animating force. This reading of the processes of becoming has important implications. First, responsiveness, attunement, and dependence on others as basic conditions for human life is not only a theoretical proposition (Duranti 2010; Throop 2018), but it is woven into the fabric of volunteers' existential understanding (Jackson 1998). They need to experience feeling the right way for their realization of self. Second, that volunteers perceive their 'calling' to be tied to their very core of being increases the stakes of the project of self-making, making urgent the need for affective experiences that reaffirm their understanding of self. I argue that these stakes and the gravity of feeling makes BKM members particularly susceptible to reproduce the rationalities of the programme.

An Election

The election, an important part of the recruitment process of BKM members, is an ideal site to examine the dialectic between susceptibility to affective recruitment and the capacity for emotional experiences that provide opportunities for self-realization. An election is held in each *kelurahan* in Medan to select BKM members. The election is not a demand from the *masyarakat*: 'it is *wajib*

---

[4] Interestingly, anger at the injustice of poverty was not cited as a motivation by any of the volunteers; nor did it appear as an animating force (with thanks to the series editor for highlighting this). I speculate that this is due to the discourses of self-responsibilization in Indonesian development that sees poverty as an outcome of personal characteristics, rather than structural conditions. See Jakimow et al. (2019) for a discussion of the difference between how volunteers and recipients of benefits talk about poverty.

[compulsory] that we hold an election for the BKM. The concept comes from the government' (Pak Maritim). The election has a particular tone and campaigning or having candidates is strictly prohibited. As Pak Adnan explains: 'The election is important because people express their aspirations in this meeting, and it is like a democratic process. But it is not really like an election, in that we are not candidates who campaign for people to vote for us' (June 2013). These rules are in order to give 'the villagers a freedom to select the best... [most] virtuous persons among themselves' (Effendy 2015: 14), with the most important moral virtue being *ikhlas* [sincerity]. Campaigning is seen as counter to the idea that volunteers work sincerely and selflessly, resulting in '[e]lite domination accompanied by their vested interests... [rather than] collective leadership whose membership signifies moral virtues' (Effendy 2015: 14).

This idea of representation without campaigning appeals to volunteers who understand themselves as people interested in working for the people, unlike politicians who work only for their own self-interest. Several BKM members were explicit about this difference. Pak Adnan described how he was predisposed to a more 'civil' mode of being involved in the *masyarakat*, rather than 'politics' which creates bad relations: 'I do not like to sit in coffee shops, talking nonsense, stories about nothing'. He refuses to join politics, explaining 'Why? If I am invited by some people, it is better to avoid, better to succumb than be confrontational. In politics, politics is *keras* [hard, but also crass, uncivilized]'. The 'civil' nature of the PNPM elections is more aligned with his nature, his *jiwa*. The idea of politics is unappealing for him, he does not enjoy confrontation and the feelings it engenders. Indeed, unlike in villages throughout Indonesia, we heard of only one BKM member who became involved in electoral politics. Her candidature in the 2014 legislative election was a cause of much amusement among her fellow BKM members. Compared to messy politics, a non-campaign-based election provides reinforcement from the people, with the right emotional tone.

PNPM elections are not ringing endorsements of BKMs. Attendance is poor, and the vast majority of residents that we spoke to, including the recipients of PNPM loans and benefits, were unaware that they even took place. They are nonetheless significant for individuals, who see it as an essential part of the process of legitimately holding the position of BKM member. Ibu Rosa relayed the scene:

At the [local] level we were truly democratic. I was surprised; there were no candidates, no campaign like that. Frankly we were confused as to what this

means, how should we conduct this election.... Actually we were volunteers...
I cannot be a candidate.... So in this room in my mother's garage we used a
noodle packet. The paper was torn to pieces... and they invited residents to
select the person according to who is good. Without any campaigning, many
names appeared, who knows who these people are.... But by the time of the
election, it was indeed apparently democracy without campaigning. My
name was drawn, and we formed the group.   (November 2013)

The excitement and animation of the narrative gets lost through it being
recounted and translated on the page: an excitement that was evident in many
BKM members. Respondents noted the joy and thrill of having their name
selected; the election was public recognition that the people considered them a
person of good conduct, reaffirming that they had the right qualities for the job.

This recognition further animated volunteers to work for the people.
Despite heavy government involvement in what was at the time a centrally
controlled development programme, BKM members were adamant that they
were part of the community rather than associated with the state. Being
elected by the people was critical to this sentiment as it showed that the people
trusted them, and hence there was an obligation to return that trust. Although
this may seem mundane, being involved in government programmes in
Indonesia is more often a way to get closer to people in the government, to
differentiate oneself from others and use this position for political or material
gain (Berenschot et al. 2018). The election was one way through which BKM
members distanced themselves from other programmes, and in particular
from local unelected government officials (see Jakimow 2018a).

Consequently, BKM members worked hard for the *masyarakat*, thereby
fulfilling the aims of community-driven development. These affective properties
of the election contribute to the mobilizing of subjects that are commensurable
with the norms and values of the programme. The election can therefore be
considered a technology and affective transaction that stirs individual sentiments in ways that animate them to act in the interests of the state (Rose 2000),
and in which 'affect is mobilized to produce subjects' for community-driven
development (Richard and Rudnyckyj 2009: 57). At the same time, this
animation did not occur on a blank slate, a subject waiting to be formed.
Rather people were drawn to these kinds of programmes due to their pre-
existing ideas of self, as well as their ambitions for becoming particular kinds
of people. They were thus susceptible to being moved in particular ways
through the election, while the election also provided the capacity to be
affected in ways that reaffirmed this sense of self. The dialectic between

capacity and susceptibility to affect complicates simplistic readings of the PNPM as a technology of government. At the same time, examining BKM members' emotional and affective responses to the discursive practices of the programme reveal the limits of self-authorship.

Being Useful

To be successful, the PNPM not only had to recruit BKM members, they had to motivate them to continue working for the programme. There was a steep attrition rate of BKM members in the first couple of months as members realized there was no financial benefit from their involvement. Within Medan only a small percentage of the 149 BKMs were active, or even functional. According to Pak Alrasyad, their *semangat* [enthusiasm, spirit, zest] had weakened, and needed to be reinvigorated. Even within successful BKMs, it was sometimes difficult to maintain active involvement or retain membership. During the time we knew Pak Anto there were several years of high levels of activity in the BKM, after which the majority of volunteers left. Rather than examine why people left, the more pertinent question is why people remained committed to a programme from which they received scant reward and that had significant costs (see Chapter Five). I argue that the positive emotions engendered through their work—which reaffirmed their sense of who they were becoming—were critical factors.

Many BKM members explained that the experience of helping others encouraged them to want to do more. Pak Anto described how after becoming a BKM coordinator he started to look at the neighbourhood in a different way, he was drawn to the problems of the people and had a desire to help them. Such activities brought him joy: 'I am extremely happy to be a BKM member, that in the context of my life, I can be very useful for the people'. *Berguna*, being useful, *bermanfaat*, being of benefit, or *manfaatkan* benefiting others, were the most common terms male volunteers used to explain the satisfaction they received from their work. 'Actually I used to feel that I was not of much benefit (*kurang bermanfaat*). But after becoming involved in the BKM, it is evident that I am beneficial to the community' (Pak Alrasyad). The desire to be useful or of benefit to the people is tied to citizenship discourses in Indonesia, in which responsibilities or duties (*kewajiban*) are inextricable from rights (*hak*) (Gibbings 2017). For many, being able to contribute to Indonesian development is important to citizenship claims. For example the people with a disability in Tsaputra's (2019) study in Indonesia consider the inability to contribute to national development due to prejudices or inaccessibility an important element of their marginalization, with the right to contribute a key demand. People lacking in economic, social, or cultural capital may also lack the capacity to contribute, which must be considered part of the lived experiences of disadvantage. The flip side is the consequent force of affective experiences in which one is of of benefit or useful to people. The discourse of citizenship in Indonesia intensifies the feelings associated with such work.

Gendered ideologies and hegemonic masculinities may also play a role in enhancing the satisfaction that Pak Anto and Pak Alrasyad feel from being useful. While much has been written on women's limited role in Indonesian citizenship, in which they are considered wives and mothers first and foremost (Robinson 2008; Suryakusuma 2011), there has been less discussion about the effects of such gendered discourses for men, who are expected to play a public role in national development. To do so requires social networks, potentially financial capital, and requisite skills and education.[5] Men lacking these characteristics, and therefore excluded from contributing to society, fail to live up to the masculine ideal. Again, the flip side is the positive affective experience of achieving these masculine ideals.

The evaluation of an action as good and hence engendering positive feelings is attuned to the rationalities of the programme. For men, these include material achievements and the undertaking of work in accordance with the rules of the programme. For example, male BKM coordinators emphasize achieving the performance indicators of the PNPM, such as repayment rates of the *dana bergulir* [rotating funds] component of the programme. Across Medan repayment rates were abysmal, and achieving a high rate of repaid loans became a source of pride for successful coordinators. Also significant was successful implementation of infrastructure projects and the management of BKM accounts according to the strict conditions of the programme. These requirements emphasized transparency and accountability, requiring substantial paperwork. Many coordinators had limited, if any experience in such work, and were helped by government appointed facilitators. When they achieved some degree of independence they were immensely proud. On the other hand, failure to achieve high repayment rates, problems with project implementation or the budget, could be emotionally difficult. When the rotating funds in Pak Anto's BKM became *macet* [stuck, that is, not repaid], he was anxious and deeply embarrassed. I suggest his self-imaginary as a capable

---

[5] See Nilan (2009) for a discussion of hegemonic masculinities in Indonesia.

contributor and leader in the community alongside insecurities as to whether he is the person he thinks himself to be, added to the affective force of these 'failures', even when the causes of these were largely out of his hands (see also Chapter Five).

It appears, therefore, that the biographical and personal characteristics that make people such as Pak Anto and Pak Alrasyad susceptible to affective mobilization into the programme are similar to the characteristics that increase the affective intensity of perceived successes and failures. Due to their marginal position within the broader development infrastructure, I suggest that, for local development actors in particular, success and failure is largely measured *as per the parameters* of the programme. The ways volunteers experience 'being' a BKM member are tied to nascent ideas of self or more durable yet still tenuous self-narratives. As such, failures can threaten who one thinks one is, or desires to become. I argue that this susceptibility makes BKM members invest in the rationalities of community development. Men seem particularly loyal to the values of good governance and empowerment through the entrepreneurship that is promoted through the programme.

Ikhlas

The way that this susceptibility to be affected is shaped by discourses and gendered ideologies beyond development is evident in the different ways women explain their recruitment and ongoing motivations. Unlike men who mostly came to know about the PNPM through secular community meetings, the majority of women found out about the programme at the *wirid pengajian*. These weekly meetings are times of prayer and the reading of the Qur'an, but are also opportunities for *sosialisasi*. For example, as a condition of their job, university lecturers must devote some time to community activity, and women lecturers in particular will provide information sessions during the *pengajian* on topics such as health, enterprise, or crafts. Ibu Hanum started to attend the *pengajian* soon after moving to the area as she did not know anyone in the locality. The PNPM facilitator came to her *masjid* to promote the programme as a social activity for 'people with a generous heart'. Ibu Hanum recognized herself in this description and was touched. She explained that she had also experienced poverty and was only marginally above the poverty line herself. She saw people in greater need and this moved her to want to join the programme.

Ibu Hanum's husband initially protested her involvement as it detracted from her duties in the home but did not bring in additional income.[6] She convinced him by stating 'If I want to give alms [*sedekah*], just like them [potential beneficiaries] I do not have money or wealth. I can only give alms [*sedekahkan*] with my energy [*tenaga*] and thoughts [*pikiran*]'. *Sedekah* has significance for Muslim Indonesians as being the giving of alms or the helping of others voluntarily [*sukarela*] and with sincerity [*ikhlas*]. Being involved as a BKM member thereby enables Ibu Hanum to engage in Islamic acts of charity despite lacking financial means. Note she uses the same language as Pak Anto and many other BKM members stating that one does not need to have money as one can help with energy and thoughts. Such messages are powerful for people like Ibu Hanum who otherwise lack the opportunity to engage in charitable acts.

The PNPM also provides women a legitimate way to 'publically perform piety' (Deeb 2006: 5). Boellstorff (2005a) notes that in Indonesia, civic life intersects with Islamic principles and Islam is lived publicly. Women have fewer opportunities than men to engage in civic life as domestic responsibilities are considered their most important role (Suryakusuma 2011; Robinson 2008). Women's exclusion from other roles in national development beyond those tied to domesticity and reproduction restricts their ability to engage in public expressions of their morality through contributions to the community.

It is perhaps for this reason that more women than men used Islamic terms to describe their work. Ibu Asmara describes her work as BKM coordinator as 'a form of *ibadah*.... This is *ikhlas* there is nothing to lose. We just hope that we will receive *pahala* [reward] from God'. *Ibadah* has three connotations. It means a form of obedience, a type of devotion or worship, and is also associated with being humble and submissive to Allah. For devotion and obedience to be properly directed, it needs to be done with *ikhlas*: a term that has a religious significance of undertaking action not for selfish purposes, but for God's blessing. *Ikhlas* describes not only a motivation based on reflection of what it means to live a good life, but also a feeling. One does not feel that the work is heavy or a burden as one receives satisfaction from the deed itself.

The moment of recruitment in the *wirid* therefore touches upon the sentiments of women's religious devotion, as well as potentially sparking an

---

[6] Earning additional income outside the home has long been a socially appropriate role for women in Indonesia (Robinson 2008), however there can be resistance to wives devoting time to non-economic social activities.

imaginary in women who see the programme as an opportunity to take part in social activity. It sparks, or responds to a desire to feel the satisfaction of social work without any expectation of reward. The different sentiments engendered in this site of recruitment compared to the secular community meeting is mirrored in the ongoing motivations of many BKM members. As noted in Chapter Two, the BKM's activities are divided into environmental (infrastructure), economic (largely rotating funds), and social activities. This latter set of activities—which primarily consisted of small gifts that provide immediate assistance to people in need—was often the sole prerogative of women BKM members. Environmental activity was dominated by men, and the responsibility for economic activities was shared, although there are exceptions across Medan. The act of giving with *ikhlas* brings great satisfaction that lifts the spirits, which women BKM members describe as a benefit of their work.

Ikhlas is also part of the discourse of community development in Indonesia, arguably supporting the rationalities of good governance. Being able to conduct good work with *ikhlas* is not only identified by respondents as a benefit of their work, it is also one of the universal values that the PNPM promotes as being essential to BKM members, along with *kejujuran* (honesty), *keadilan* (fairness), and *peduli* (care). At the moment of recruitment, the promotion of the values of the programme are an invitation to locate these within the self, to be animated by them. Associating oneself with these values helps achievement of the rationalities of the programme. As will be seen in Chapter Five, the prevailing distributional logic of development in Medan is characterized by corruption and favouritism. Honesty, fairness, sincerity, and being caring is aligned with the discourses of good governance that aim to combat this logic. BKM members are invited to identify themselves with these values, and in doing so, augment the affective force of actions that are either in accordance with, or opposed to them.

Although men were more likely to express their desire to join the programme in order to be *useful* for the people, and for women to use religious terms in their explanations of their motivations, the distinction between male and female BKM members is not as stark as I have presented. Women coordinators in particular often mentioned being useful and doing something tangible for the people, whereas a number of men spoke of the importance of *ikhlas*. Nor do I want to suggest that these were motivations particular to Muslims. The majority of the BKM members we interacted with were Muslim, but we also spoke at length with two Christian Batak respondents, one of whom spoke of the importance of her religious motivations. These qualifications do not, however, detract from the overall impression that men expressed their ambitions for self in ways that subscribe to hegemonic forms of masculinity in Medan—being useful, with a focus on infrastructure and enterprise development—while women subscribed to emphasized forms of femininity—being a social worker, selfless, with a focus on the social activities within the BKM.

Conclusion

The PNPM offers a place where volunteers are able to pursue self-making projects that critically depend upon their capacity to be affected through their activities. Volunteers' self-representations reflected, or established, a deeply held set of beliefs about the self they were, or were becoming, through the PNPM. The emphasis on the disciplining and governing effects of processes of subjectification have often over-emphasized the negative, while failing to see development as a site of self-realization and expansion. Malkki (2015) is an exception in this regard, examining humanitarian action as a particularly important site for the processes of self. She observes how Swedish humanitarian workers have a *need* to help, not as a disciplined global citizen, 'but as specific social persons with homegrown needs, vulnerabilities, desires, and multiple professional responsibilities [that prompts people to seek...] to be part of something greater than themselves, to help, to be actors in the lively world' (Malkki 2015: 4). The affective dimensions of their work are critical; to be able to *feel* that they are helping people, often in extreme situations, is central to the self-transformations that many of them desired. The same can be said of BKM members, for whom mobilization as a volunteer was most often an empowering moment, a way to be touched by the heart and to realize their true nature. The capacity to be affected is critical to these self-making projects.

At the same time, the precariousness of the projects increases the volunteers' susceptibility to be affected and produces an acute responsiveness to the sensorium of the programme. Kapoor (2017) critiques Ferguson's 'Anti-politics machine' for being cold-hearted, ignoring the human element in the discursive production of development. He argues that people desire development; they enjoy it even when it is doing them harm, and passionately invest in the power structures that produce it. While Kapoor (2017) examines this investment in development through Lacan's concept of desire, I have turned to the attunement to moral sentiments as an additional explanation for the production of development rationalities. As noted above, the self is responsive to the world and self–Other relations. We undertake 'an education of sentiments, to cultivate certain sentiments over others' (Throop 2012: 151) in our becoming a virtuous person. These moral sentiments are socio-historical, specific to time and place, and cartographic, in the sense that people move through multiple social fields and 'moral sentiments' (Biehl and Locke 2017). Development is one such social field.

Volunteers such as Pak Anto who are susceptible to the emotions engendered in processes of socialization become loyal recruits to the rationalities of the programme. Missing in accounts of governmentality are the inner and outer dialogues of people struggling to feel that they belong, that this is right, that they are who they think they are. Attention to affect points to how 'Ethopower' is a part of contemporary governance, urging the self-regulation of individuals through the animation of sentiments that 'stir the heart' (Rose 2000). At the same time, affect theory underlines the contingency of such processes as a means through which power's reiteration is disrupted or transformed. In this chapter, the contingency of 'feeling' the right way can make individuals invest more heavily in the discourses of the programme. Playing by the rules brings an affective buzz; failing to do the right thing can be emotionally devastating. The fear of not feeling the right way, the sinking feeling in the stomach that comes from doing something wrong or from failing, is particularly high for people who feel their occupation of a role is tenuous. People like Pak Anto, who describe themselves as uneducated and stupid, are therefore some of the most assiduous rule followers, carefully following the programme guidelines as closely as possible, basking in the affective rewards for doing their job 'right'. Pak Anto affectively invests in an emergent sense of self. He is highly responsive to the social world of the programme and craves the opportunity to feel the right way through his activities.

Examining the moments of recruitment and processes of becoming a local development agent is important to understanding how development works in practice, as I show in the remaining chapters. Here, I argue that doing so is also critical to our ethical obligations to volunteers in community development. Encouraging affective investments in a sense of self realized through involvement in development needs to come with a realization of what is at stake for these volunteers. The stakes became apparent several years after our first meeting with Pak Anto. The main source of funding had wound down, most of his fellow BKM members had become inactive, and the BKM office where we had usually met was being rented out. Pak Anto welcomed us to his home, saying: 'Finally you have come to my *gubuk*....I am so sorry that we have to meet here, in my *gubuk* [small shack]'. He had always struggled to hide his embarrassment at his low socio-economic status and his eyes were cast downwards and he laughed nervously. As we sat chatting, I noticed the photo I had given him next to the television showing Pak Anto receiving a certificate of appreciation for participating in my research project. This certificate was now hanging on the wall with apparent pride.[7] I was filled with discomfort and sadness seeing these items displayed in Pak Anto's home, reminders of what Pak Anto had become, as well as the loss of aspects of that version of self. His five years as coordinator have been incorporated into his durable self-narrative, yet the ongoing enactment has concluded. The invitation to realize an expanded sense of who we can become, is rarely accompanied by an acknowledgement of the risks entailed in these projects of becoming (Duranti 2010), or the sense of loss that accompanies the end of projects.

In the remaining chapters of this book, we consider some of the consequences of the high stakes involved in becoming a local development agent, and how their capacity and susceptibility to be affected shapes development practices. In Chapter Five, I consider the collective conditions that shape volunteers' susceptibility to both affect and be affected, while in Chapter Seven, I reveal how volunteers protect themselves from a loss of self, in the process hindering reflexive practice. In Chapter Four, however, I continue to examine the line between the susceptibility and capacity to be affected in the 'becoming' of women municipal councillors in India. I emphasize the empowering potential of the capacity to be affected, while also showing the limits of self-authorship arising from women's attunement to their social world.

---

[7] I have considered the possibility that Pak Anto had pulled the photo and certificate out of a box under the bed to display them solely for our visit. Such an action would make sense in the context of my family and social relations, but is not one that was entertained by my research assistants. Of course if he had, this would challenge my interpretation, although not my own emotional response to seeing the artefacts displayed.

4

Expansion

In her final days as Municipal Councillor, or Parshad, we asked Meera what was the most memorable moment of her five-year term. She quickly replied: 'The time when we won the election [in 2013]. Then, we had thousands of people coming with us and supporting us. This was the best time'. Her son quickly jumped out of his seat and showed us photos on his phone. The first one was from the day the results were announced. Meera was slumped in a chair looking exhausted and exhilarated. Her neck was laden with garlands, and her cheek and hair were marked by the coloured powder spread liberally on successful candidates. Other photos showed Meera at the time when she was nominated as the party candidate. I had known Meera for three years by this stage, yet she still looked somewhat unfamiliar in the photos surrounded by her supporters, walking confident, tall, content. As I flicked through the photos Meera was smiling widely, giggling as I responded with my own exclamations: 'Oh, look here! You look so happy!'

The election may have marked the moment Meera occupied the position of Parshad, yet her process of becoming was a gradual attunement (see Chapter Three). She had contested the elections on behalf of her husband, Kapil, as the seat was reserved for women, and she had no political ambitions of her own. The first time she held a microphone Meera's hands shook. The days after the election were disorientating as her status changed literally overnight. She felt embarrassed to be 'playacting' as a politician when she had no background in social work. She slowly adjusted to her relational self—the self she is in relation to others—becoming attuned to the expectations that other people had of her. She learnt to respond to constituents in a manner that endeared them to her: the subtle inflections of voice, the warmth of a hand on a shoulder, the assertiveness in a request. She describes her transition into someone 'ready' to be a politico as occurring only in the second year of her five-year term. By 2018, however, she was preparing to contest the elections again. In other words, occupying the role of Parshad gave her the experiences to develop her own political ambitions and dispositions.

That some women contest reserved seats on behalf of husbands in India is often used to diminish women's contribution to local politics. Yet many

Susceptibility in Development: Micropolitics of Local Development in India and Indonesia. Tanya Jakimow, Oxford University Press (2020). © Tanya Jakimow.
DOI: 10.1093/oso/9780198854739.001.0001

capable and fully independent women contest and win elections in their own right.[1] Many more, like Meera, stand on behalf of their husbands, yet grow into their new status, going on to develop a new sense of self from previously inconceivable self-imaginaries. As noted in Chapter Three, such processes of self-formation are critical to development practice, and a worthy object of study. The stakes are slightly different for local politicos compared to volunteers in Medan, as candidates are elected from a large pool of hopefuls rather than recruited from a largely uninterested populace. Alternatively, women like Meera are thrust into the position by circumstance rather than choice. Accounts of personhood in India have highlighted the greater need for women to be malleable, that is, willing to cultivate a self commensurate with people's expectations within the family and significant others (Lamb 2000). In the case of Meera and other women politicos in Dehradun, they become moulded as a 'social worker': a social positioning that is attuned to people's expectations, but that also provides women a status from which they can act (Bedi 2016). Although Meera's identity as Parshad was in a sense imposed, she became 'affectively attached' to this self-imaginary, that is, she invested emotionally in the idea that she is a Parshad, with the loss of this sense of self painful.

In this chapter I examine these processes of self-formation of women politicos. Continuing on from Chapter Three, I examine the agentive aspects of becoming, as well as the unconscious attunements and responsiveness that shape the self one becomes. I interrogate the co-potentialities of, on the one hand, the reproduction of women's political marginalization due to foreclosures of self and, on the other, empowerment through an expansion in the possibilities for self. I argue that the capacity and opportunity to be affected are critical to these potentialities. Feeling the 'right way' can reaffirm one's sense of self, while experience that breaks with one's expectations can engender responses that spark creative self-fashioning. In this way, the possibilities for self are a product, and productive of relations of power. As we will see, an affective attachment to a sense of self as 'social worker' makes women politicos exploitable, undertaking political labour that benefits party elites, without being rewarded for their efforts. At the same time, biographic moments in which the possibility for self-becoming arises within a particular juncture (Jackson 2014) are also triggered by the capacity and opportunity to be affected. Moments that engender feelings that transgress gendered emotional

---

[1] In the 2013 elections these were seemingly the majority. In 2018 women did not fare as well, with a larger number of tickets going to the wives of male party workers.

repertoires can spark creativity and alternative self-imaginaries, including unabashed political ambitions and a sense of entitlement to positions of power that challenge social hierarchies. Unravelling the affective dimensions of political power can thereby provide additional explanations for women's under-representation in politics and potential ways to increase it.

Topography for Self

In this chapter I outline an analytical framework to further examine personhood as interconnected processes of self-fashioning and an everyday 'ongoingness' sense of self (see Doucet and Mauthner 2008 and Chapter Three). These two senses of self aim to capture our innate responsiveness to the world, alongside our capacity to fashion a 'self' within these conditions. The actual selves we become is not solely a product of our environment, but is in part a result of our biographies and personal (autonomous) desires and proclivities (Jackson 2014). As Butler (2015: 6) notes, 'I am never simply formed, nor am I ever fully self-forming.... [That is,] we live in historical time... [that also] lives in us'. I take this to mean that multiple selves are possible within a socio-historical context, just as others are impossible. What I describe as the 'topography for self' aims to highlight how these possibilities are uneven; they are differentiated not only due to personality and biography, but due to ascribed characteristics such as gender, caste, class, and so on. The topography for self is the map of unevenly available resources within a socio-historical context that people draw upon in their self-making projects, and that impresses upon individuals in ways that shape, but do not determine them (Jakimow 2018b).

The topography for self provides a framework to understand the differentially available resources for this self-fashioning. These resources include discursive formations and practices that 'hail' individuals into certain subject positions or social identities (Hall 2000), providing the socially recognized identities from which a subject can act (Butler 1997). The topography for self also contains socio-historical ethical imaginaries (Moore 2011); that is the socially inscribed 'right ways of being' through which human subjects define themselves 'as a speaking, living, working individual' (Foucault 1994: 281). Pandian (2009) describes a topography of self as a terrain of moral cultivation, in which the self undergoes processes of transformation in relation to socio-historical virtues. These virtues are both resources and demands for self-fashioning that are available/impose unevenly on to gendered and racialized bodies.

Thus far, the topography for self is equivalent to Foucault's operations of truth, but like Moore (2011), I draw attention to the possibilities of affect and emotion. The topography for self includes the 'affective hinterland' (Wetherell 2012), the possibilities for being moved or impressed upon that arise in our contact with others. This affective dimension is particularly pregnant with potentialities, with its many 'possible semiotic connections and meaning trajectories' (Wetherell 2012: 129). That is, unlike discursive apparatuses and socio-historical terrains for moral cultivation, the affective hinterland 'always escapes entire articulation' (Wetherell 2012: 129), and hence is not fully captured by power.

The topography for self sheds light on the political economy of personhood by revealing how resources for self-fashioning are differentially available to individuals according to socially ascribed characteristics, resulting in some selves being possible within certain socio-historical junctures, while others are foreclosed, or impossible. Understanding this topography can shed light on moments in which possibilities for self can be expanded, or foreclosures transgressed. Elsewhere (Jakimow 2018b) I define empowerment as a process in which possibilities for self are expanded, through transformations in the topography for self or the differentially available resources for self-fashioning. I identify three possibilities for the empowerment of women in this sense. First is an increase in the number of socially recognized positions from which one can act, that is, what is seen as a socially appropriate way of being within the discursive and cultural context (Foucault 1994; Butler 1997; Hall 2000). So, for example, gender quotas provide a social position of woman Parshad, bolstered through legal frameworks and discursive practices that emphasize women's legitimacy in local level politics. The second is an expansion of self-imaginaries. So, for example, the request for Meera to contest the election to Parshad was also an invitation for her to see herself in a way that was formerly inconceivable (Moore 2011). And third are opportunities for self-enactment, that is, the action and experience of being (Jakimow and Harahap 2016). The possibility for self as a Parshad is reaffirmed through experiences such as speaking to a crowd, campaigning, meeting constituents. As seen in Chapter Three, being affected in ways that are attuned to our sense of who we are and who we are becoming is critical to our ongoing sense of self, as well as our ambitions for who we want to be.

In this chapter I am particularly interested with the third expansion of self—enhanced opportunities for self-enactment—within the affective hinterland of the topography for self. The ability to conceive of oneself in a particular way is distinct from the *opportunity* to engage in conduct that fits this understanding (Jakimow and Harahap 2016). Not all people have the material resources or social standing to engage in acts in the manner of their choosing, and therefore lack the opportunities for embodied experiences of being that they desire or imagine. The affective dimension is important, as it is through the way that one is moved, touched, or affected that reaffirms or casts doubt as to whether such action is 'right for me' (Butler 2015). Picking up on the themes of Chapter Three, the opportunity to experience feelings that can be qualified as emotions is critical to the accomplishment of self; that is, feeling the right way reaffirms for volunteers in Medan who they are or are becoming. Enactments of self facilitated the satisfaction of the heart that could be read as meaning such actions were aligned to one's *jiwa*, that is, that one's nature was compatible with social activities. *Opportunities* for affective experiences are, like other resources for self-making, unevenly available.

The *capacity* to be affected is one of our relational capacities that are a pre-condition of our social existence (Butler 2005). The way we are affected or recruited by affect is not neutral, however, nor solely (at best partially) a matter of inherent individual characteristics. Rather our social locations within representative regimes influence the way the world impresses upon us, how these affective experiences resonate through the body and are felt, cognized, and expressed as emotion (Pedwell and Whitehead 2012). Gender is one significant social location that shapes affective biographies and predisposes persons to feel a particular way. Ahmed (2010: 59) invites us to see gendered scripts of being as 'happiness scripts' providing a set of instructions for what women and men must do in order to be happy, whereby happiness is what follows being natural or good'. In Chapter Three I showed how volunteers found 'happiness' and 'satisfaction' in social work. There are many parallels with the women in this chapter, yet here I take a more critical approach in order to consider how such engendered feelings reinforce women's marginalization in politics. I argue in this chapter that the happiness women find in social work is both a starting point of agency and offers the possibilities of becoming within normative ways of being, as well as foreclosing possible selves, namely being a politically ambitious actor.

Affect not only augments power regimes, it also lies at the heart of self-creativity, and new self-imaginaries. Wetherell (2012: 139) locates affective routines, patterns, and emotional repertoires that reinforce social hierarchies, but sees these not as 'pre-packed with a raft of innate psychological processes, and with a large number of pre-organized routes' but rather with 'relational capacity, and tendencies'. These conditions create the 'textures, shapes, potentialities, repetitions, creativities' (Wetherell 2012: 139) of a possible self.

Unbidden but not asocial responses to the social world are 'not just about conformity to the normative or to power' (Moore 2011: 21), but about possibilities and new self-imaginaries. In the ethnographic material that follows, I examine these possibilities for self: the foreclosures within the topography for self, the ways they are expanded through different forms of political activities, and the moments of transgression that challenge or modify this topography.

Sevak Semajik

In April 2018 Dehradun's municipal elections seemed imminent. The term of the current Parshads was due to end on 3 May, and tension was mounting as people speculated about the expected announcement. It was also a time when party workers were jostling to get the party ticket for their ward, as each party can only nominate one person per seat/ward. It was in this atmosphere that PRAGATI, the NGO I collaborate with, held workshops to provide a supportive atmosphere in which women could decide whether to contest, to learn about the nomination process, and the rules of the election campaign. The workshops began with each participant introducing themselves. A microphone was handed from woman to woman, passing over the handful of husbands who had accompanied their wives. The invitation was to tell the assembled group about their work in the area, and why they wanted to become a Parshad. Some women could barely wait to get hold of the microphone, standing up and speaking at length until we gently pried it from their hands. Others were shy, speaking briefly while remaining seated.

Ananda's introduction was textbook. She spoke clearly rather than loudly. Her words were careful, unrushed but not laboured. She explained that she had been a BJP *karya karta* (party worker) for eighteen years, and that during that time she had built a great deal of support in her area. She ran off the usual list of activities: health camps, organizing ration cards, solving problems of electricity and water supply. Now was the right time for her to contest the election: 'I have everything. I run a small shop, have my own home, my son is now working and my daughter is married. When my children were small, I worked so much for the party, I feel that now I am free.' She explained her motivations further: 'Doing small things for people makes me feel happy.... They give me blessings and I feel very good. I enjoy this social work and I want to be able to do more. That is why I want to become a Parshad.' Ananda was an exception in her clear articulation, yet the content of her introduction was common. Most women were in their 40s and 50s with adult, and hence independent, children: traits common to women politicians in India (Ghosh and Lama-Rewel 2005; John 2007). Party workers had devoted years of their lives to party activities and expected that the party would reward them with the ticket to contest the elections in their ward.

Becoming a Parshad was usually, however, presented merely as a means to an end in which the final goal was to further social work, or *sevak samajik*. 'Social worker', is a common political 'style' for both men and women politicians in India (Price and Ruud 2010), but is particularly effective for women due to its compatibility with socially acceptable models of femininity (Ghosh and Lama-Rewel 2005; Ciotti 2012; Bedi 2016). In interviews, women hoping to contest the upcoming elections told us without exception that they desired a position of power to extend their social work, not vice versa. When asked why they personally had such desires, women described social work as a part of their habit, or nature: 'the feeling [to do social work] comes from within'; 'it is my habit to do social work since childhood'; 'the only benefit is satisfaction' were common responses. Ananda too said that she wanted to do more as she enjoyed the feeling associated with helping others. Much of the literature is cynical of such self-representations, viewing 'social worker' as solely a strategic political identity (Alm 2010; Berenschot 2014). I suggest that the overwhelming focus on male politicians overlooks how for women, in particular, *seva semajik* is central to their self-imaginary, the very core of who they believe themselves to be (see also Ciotti 2012).

The sentiments expressed by the women as to the emotional value of social work are gendered. Women receive positive affective cues when engaged in such work, as opposed to other forms of activity in the public domain. At the workshop for example, sharing a long list of one's social activities engendered admiration in others, perhaps even jealousy, reaffirming that such actions are admirable and that the woman undertaking them is a person to be admired. In reading these responses in others, the self as a social worker is reaffirmed, further encouraging affective investment in this idea of self. The identity of 'social worker' thereby brings an alignment with one's affective community (Ahmed 2010). At the same time, 'social worker' provides a socially recognized position from which women can act, including within the public sphere and in political worlds.

Padma, a two-term Parshad, is a loyal party worker. She explains, however, that 'it is not from the party, it is from working for society that I get personal satisfaction ... that I have this feeling.... And it is not only today that I feel this way...it is from childhood'. Having spent years watching Padma in her everyday work as Parshad, serving not only her own constituents but anyone who came to her home, nobody could doubt that her sense of who she is is tied to being a social worker, someone doing good for the people. In the act of helping she adopts a serious tone, a sense of a fight in the face of injustices. These are moments when she is most animated and energetic; her chest puffs, her pace quickens, her movements are assured. Being with her in these moments, the 'buzz', the good feelings that she experiences in her relations with others, is obvious. Being a social worker was not just a political style, it was core to her very sense of who she was. Given her record of work during her two terms as Parshad, it seemed inevitable that she would be given the party ticket. When speaking of the elections in April 2018, she said 'my motivation is not to win the election but to serve the people....I am very confident and hope that I will win. But if I do not, I will continue my *seva*'.

Rather than regard social worker as a style or identity that people adopt to fulfil political ambitions (Price and Ruud 2010; Berenschot 2014), I consider it a modality of being, attuned to the moral sentiments (Throop 2012) of a social world. Women are susceptible to the unspoken insistencies that arise in their relations with others, responsive to the moral demands to 'be' a particular way. This becoming is not only an attunement, but an invitation to affectively invest in this sense of self. To give up on the idea that 'I am foremost a social worker' is not only a social transgression, it is a betrayal to women's durable idea of self and 'ongoingness' in the world. Hence, when we asked women what they would do if the party did not give them the ticket for their ward, the response was usually restrained. While a small number said they would run as independents, the vast majority professed to not being too concerned. '*Theek hai*' [it's okay], they would say, in a neutral tone and with no visible emotion on their face. 'If I get the ticket, or not, I will continue my social work. Whoever the party selects, I will help in their campaign' paraphrases a response we heard numerous times. No amount of prodding could change their tune. The desire for the position was related to selfless social work and hence whether they got the ticket *should* not engender strong feelings.

Loyalty

I argue that the processes of becoming a politically oriented social worker makes some women particularly loyal to political parties that exploit their labour. To make this simple and admittedly simplified argument, I unravel the complex project of self-making of Bimla.[2] A controversial choice for the BJP party ticket for her ward in 2013, Bimla had shown promise by mobilizing supporters during the State Assembly elections the previous year. She professed to wanting to become a Parshad to improve people's conditions, yet at this stage she had only a slim record of social work. She still wore the veil that was common to women in her village but unusual in Dehradun, and extremely rare for women social workers. She too felt as if she had been plucked out of relative obscurity when she was given the ticket to contest the elections in a seat reserved for SC (scheduled caste, Dalit) women. When the party leaders came, their invitations to see herself as a Parshad were seductive and she quickly developed a new self-imaginary.

Bimla's circumstances changed rapidly, with new experiences reinforcing the emergent possibilities for self. Her small three-room house in a congested part of the city soon buzzed with activity. Her face appeared on banners throughout the ward. From being 'only a housewife', she rapidly became a public figure. The election results for Bimla's ward came late in the night. Bimla had been at the counting centre with her supporters since midday, nervous knots in her stomach. At three in the morning, their patience was rewarded. Bimla was dazed by her win. She barely comprehended as supporters smeared her with coloured powder, garlanded her, and she became the centre of a ring of dancing men. She noted how disorientating the next few days were: 'even my friends are teasing calling me Parshad-Ji. [The day after the election] there was an old man, maybe in his sixties. He called me Parshad-Ji in all seriousness. I was taken aback'. Ji is an honorific used across the Hindi belt in North India to denote respect, and both the title 'Parshad' with the addition of 'Ji' represented a remarkably different social positioning to that which she occupied prior to the election.

The election was a 'biographical moment', a time of heightened emotions sparking new self-imaginaries. The process of becoming a Parshad was far from over on election night, however. Shortly after the ceremony when she was officially sworn in as Parshad, she stopped wearing a veil and her husband bought her an Activa scooter to get around the ward. Suddenly, over a thousand people knew her and called her Parshad: 'People I did not recognize knew me. I used to greet people, now they greet me'. Such a status was

---

[2] Bimla is a composite profile made up of a woman I had known 2015–18, and a woman I met in the lead up to the November 2018 elections. This composite profile enables me to produce a narrative arc in which to explore the significance of the 2013 elections, without having directly experienced them with the respondents.

remarkable for a village Dalit woman. She told us of her family's happiness: 'My father-in-law has started loving me even more. People from [my village] are also very proud of me. People think that I have become different'. Beyond the change in her formal status was the readjustment of her attunement to others. Her relational self changed, so that each interaction had a different affective charge that was initially unfamiliar.

The first eighteen months were also exceptionally difficult, however. The Parshad has a long list of tasks, such as helping people get their pension, fixing lights, accompanying people to the police station. Each task requires a knowledge of the process and in many cases the ability to complete necessary paperwork. Having never dealt with her own paperwork, the forms looked alien and incomprehensible. Her husband lived out of town, so Bimla used to send him photos of the forms via WhatsApp so he could help her complete them. Being Parshad also made Bimla the target of insults and personal attacks. After one such incident, Bimla rang her husband in tears, saying that she would resign. Her husband told her: 'next time someone talks about you, understand that you are growing and doing the right thing'. Bimla explains with emotion in her voice: 'I was very scared in my first year and six times I decided to resign from my post. But now things have changed'.

In 2015, two years into her five-year term, Bimla was, by her own accounts, a completely different woman.

> Earlier I was unaware that a Parshad is powerful. Earlier I used to think that it was not a big deal that I won an election, but when I saw others, I learnt that—I am a woman! That is the biggest thing. I was not from this field [of social work] I had no experience. But when I saw other Parshads show so much ego, this [ego] also arose within me. Now I have no fear.

We saw confidence and fearlessness as she filled out people's paperwork with ease, rang officials to get works completed, or walked around her ward showing us the material improvements she had accomplished. Her everyday engagement with the world was full of micro-encounters of helping people, getting people to do things for her, affecting others—and in the process also experiencing satisfaction, pride, and confidence.

We continued to watch Bimla, in the words of her husband, 'grow' over the next three years. By the end of her term, she was fearless and precocious. It had been almost a year since I had seen Bimla when we met again at BJP headquarters (*Mahanagar*) in April 2018. The hall was packed with *karya karta* who had come to vote for their choice of candidate to contest the mayoral election. Her personality was larger than life. She noisily announced her arrival, sitting on the laps of her friends, taking photos and performing affection for her friend from the 'West'. Her style was always out of sync with the tone generated by the mostly high caste women party workers. Bimla, and other SC *karya karta*, were tolerated as the BJP needed them to generate support among Dalit voters and to contest reserved seats. Nonetheless the other women looked askance at her and were keen to gossip. None of this seemed to phase Bimla. She either did not pick up on the ways she was perceived by others, or was simply unmoved by their disapproving glances (or so it seemed). Her status as a Dalit woman perhaps provided her the assuredness to act in ways that were unconventional. She dwelled in the world of the party, yet her attunement to its sensibilities was imprecise. The nature and foundation of this imprecision—innate personal characteristics or a cross-over from the low-caste, low-class social world in which she otherwise dwelled—is an interesting, yet unanswerable puzzle.[3]

Bimla's location within the low-caste, low-class social world of her locality was very beneficial to the BJP. Dalit groups have only recently turned to the BJP: a party whose high-caste Hindutva message is arguably a threat to Dalit interests. Incremental shifts in Dalit support for the BJP in recent years (Sardesi and Attri 2019) have in part been attributed to the capacity of local level political actors (social workers and brokers) to be 'fixers', that is, connect Dalit voters to state entitlements and resources (Berenschot 2014). Much of the day-to-day activity of social workers entails such acts of mediation, including after they are elected into positions of power, such as Parshad. As we see in Chapter Six, such activities have financial and opportunity costs for women Parshads in particular, and Bimla was no different. Yet she mostly enjoyed such activities, got a thrill from helping others, being important and competent (for the effects of these on resource distribution see Chapter Eight). While voters are thought to engage instrumentally with such mediators (Berenschot 2010; van Dijk 2011) the BJP also benefits from the generation of positive sentiments towards a party that 'cares'. These activities are therefore a critical form of labour within what Bedi (2016) describes as 'affective grids', generating political support.

When it came time for the party to reward Bimla for this labour with the ticket to contest the 2018 elections, she was overlooked, with the BJP ticket

---

[3] Biehl and Locke (2017) talk about the importance of not being afraid to leave conclusions tentative and imprecise when talking about 'becoming'. When so much of my ethnographic material is located in inner worlds, inaccessible to direct readings, available only through interpretations, mine and theirs, I cannot help but have such an openness reflected in my writing.

going to an SC man. She barely sounded disappointed, and unlike other party workers, was not considering running as an independent: 'I was expecting to get the ticket, but...I am not angry with the party....I am who I am because of the party. *Mera wajood party kii wajah se hai* [my being is because of the party]'. *Wajood* is an Urdu word meaning existence, but also one's very being or self that comes from within. It is more weighty than identity and status, with a spiritual rather than material meaning. *Wajood* is not how other people recognize the subject but how one knows oneself. It is hard to imagine a more profound statement of empowerment if by which we mean an expansion in the possibilities for self. A new social positioning, new capabilities, but most critically, the affective experience of having achieved so much have been expansive. At the same time, as Bimla attributes the possibility of this becoming to the party, she is fiercely loyal to it. She worked tirelessly during the 2018 campaign canvassing for another candidate who benefited from the work she had done for others during her tenure as Parshad. Rather than being bitter about not being given the party ticket, it was okay, *'theek hai'*. Bimla was grateful to a party that made her who she is, and the opportunity to continue to be a social worker.

Anger, and its Limits

Bimla's gratitude towards the party was perhaps exceptional on account of the centrality of its role making her who she is. As mentioned above, other women social workers also made considerable sacrifices to a party without holding the post of Parshad. While many expressed hope if not expectation that their loyalty would be rewarded with the party ticket, when they missed out, the majority professed that 'it's okay' they could accept the decision. Although this *'theek hai'* attitude was consistent and unbreakable in interviews leading up to the elections, anger seeped out when hopeful women candidates came together. Emotions that were usually contained, unfelt, unqualified, or simply not expressed, bubbled to the surface, allowing a new sense of possibilities.

The aforementioned workshops in April 2018, when the announcement of tickets seemed imminent, provided an outlet for pent up frustration about the treatment of women in both major parties (Congress and BJP). Rather than take up the invitation to talk about their social work, some women took the opportunity to express fears that men would be given the tickets for all unreserved (general) seats, and that even the tickets for seats reserved for women would go to the wives of male party workers. In one memorable workshop the discussion was frequently interrupted by women lamenting this situation. An invitation to a group interview after the workshop turned into seventy minutes of women talking over the top of each other about the issue. Sadhika was one of the loudest. She explained that she had been a loyal party worker for over twenty years, devoting time and money. When the party needed busloads of supporters she always arranged at least one, paying out of her own pocket. She sacrificed time with her family to help people at any time of the day: social service in the name of the party. Now her children were independent, she felt it was her time to be rewarded with the ticket. Even before decisions could be made, however, she was tense, frustrated, and clearly very angry. The issue of party selection provoked an outpouring of emotion about the treatment of women in the party more generally: 'Men will never let women get ahead', Sadhika said.

The workshop was unusual in being a place for women across party lines to come and talk about their own political ambitions. It was, I suggest, a time when they received affective cues that reaffirmed or challenged their sense of being, their self-making projects. Within the topography for self, gender norms intersect with discourses of *seva samajik*, encouraging women to represent and make themselves in that manner. At the same time, there is a tension in the air. The anticipated emotional consequences of the distribution of party tickets infect the women and emotions are allowed to ferment. Anger, anxiety, and frustration arise. When affections are qualified as emotions, articulated and released, they push the limits of the women's sense of self as being first and foremost a 'social worker'. They let slip (the pretence), reveal (to themselves), and enable political ambitions and a self-imaginary of being a political leader running for election. The workshop was hence a moment in which latent selves were allowed expression.

When I returned in November 2018 after the delayed elections were finally called, it became apparent that the women's fears had played out. We spent a depressing afternoon ringing the approximately eighty participants of our workshops only to hear that less than a handful had received the party ticket. Most of the women were sanguine, saying that they would contest next time, but this time they would support their party candidates. Some were devastated. Marava could barely talk through thick sobs, apologising that since hearing the news she had fallen ill and was too sick to receive us. She spent the election at home, refusing to campaign for the party.

Needing some good news, we called on Padma, the two-term Parshad mentioned above, but even she had not been given the ticket. She was angry but more so dazed: 'I was always certain of the fact that I will get the ticket. The person who has got the ticket will win because of me and all the work I have done'. For three decades she had worked for the party, yet when it came to running as an independent (without a party ticket) she could not bring herself to do it. 'People know me and it is my moral duty to work for them. People still come to me to get their things done. It makes me happy when I help people. It is my *seva*. The rest is just a matter of a stamp [the seal of the Parshad]. Despite all this, I will still work'. She campaigned for the BJP candidate who ultimately lost to an independent candidate. Not receiving the ticket was a huge blow, but to abandon the party and her social work was inconceivable.

Ananda

Ananda, who gave the articulate account of her social work above, had given a similar length of service to the BJP and social work as Padma, but had not had the opportunity to become Parshad. When she was overlooked for the party ticket for her ward—which was an unreserved (general) seat—a rage arose within her that made campaigning for the party as inconceivable for Ananda as was the idea of abandoning it for Padma. The first time we formally interviewed Ananda was just after her self-nomination as an independent candidate and her subsequent expulsion from the party.[4] 'I have been involved in the party for a very long time, since childhood I have been connected with my heart to the party…and this is how I am treated'. The reasons why Ananda was overlooked for the ticket further fuelled her anger and determination. 'I would never had stood for election if the party had not taunted me that because I am a *pahardi*, I cannot win the seat. They said that this area must be ruled by either a Bania or a Punjabi. *Pahardi* cannot rule the area because they are too meek and too soft'. *Pahardi* refers to people from the mountains. In recent times, Bania and Punjabi (peoples from the plains) have become politically assertive groups; their political ascendency in Dehradun reflecting population shifts following massive migration from the plains to Dehradun. The put-down, that Pahardi are too meek and soft for politics

---

[4] Ananda, like other BJP members who were expelled for running as an independent against the party, were confident that they would be invited back to the party after the local level elections, especially as the BJP required their ability to mobilize supporters for the upcoming Lok Sabha elections.

(of course also perceived as 'feminine' traits) was the additional inspiration that Ananda needed.

It was not, however, the only or main motivation. The show of support from the people in her locality *moved her* away from self-pity to put up a fight. Since not being nominated, people had come to her home to both console her and to express support for an independent run. These conversations revolved around the good work that Ananda had done and the injustice of the party decision, affirming both Ananda's sense of herself as a political leader and her resolve to contest. Her personal feelings of hurt, anger, and disbelief prompted her to think of herself as more than a social worker, and as someone with declared political ambitions. As these feelings were shared with and reaffirmed as legitimate by others, this idea of the (relational) self became imaginable, indeed almost inevitable.

The next three weeks of campaigning further reaffirmed the sense of who Ananda could become. By week two, she had upwards of fifty men and women joining her for door to door campaigning on any given night. Supporters held sticks, atop of which was stuck a kettle: the symbol of Ananda's campaign.[5] They moved from the main road to a side street, their chants becoming louder: 'Vote for *Kettlie*', and 'Victory to Ananda'. To be the centre of attention, surrounded by a large group of people working for her election, was uplifting and humbling at the same time: an unforgettable experience that further sparked self-imaginaries. The extent of Ananda's support was most evident during her motorcycle rally, held on the second to last day of the campaign. A main thoroughfare was taken over by approximately 500–700 men and women on motorbikes and scooters, many holding kettles atop of sticks. A rickshaw was packed with women yelling chants into a loud speaker. At the front was Ananda in an open jeep, garlanded and showered by love and support. She was smiling and looking composed, yet I had goose-bumps imagining what she was feeling at that moment. What a great turn out. Her victory seemed assured.

It was therefore a huge shock when she lost by just over 300 votes to the BJP candidate. We came to see her four days after the announcement. In sharp contrast to the days of the campaign when her house was a hive of activity, the rooms were now empty, seemingly stripped of energy; the silence

---

[5] Each candidate has a symbol that is placed on the ballot paper to assist illiterate people in selecting a candidate. One of the biggest challenges for independent candidates is the need to make people aware of their symbol, which is confirmed by the electoral commission only a couple of weeks prior to the election. As Padma is known as a BJP party worker, she was at risk of people selecting the lotus (the symbol of the BJP) assuming they are giving her their vote.

was deep. Without pleasantries, she immediately started talking about the election result. Ananda would surely had won had she been given the party ticket, as a 300-vote margin would easily be overcome with votes from loyal party cadre. 'While I was campaigning, I was confident, and I was thinking about all the work that had to be done, and that I would do in my area. After I lost, I was not in a good state of mind. I was very sad in my heart and I felt a little lost. I could not take in what had happened. I could not understand what happened'. There was mostly anger in her voice and eyes but also an acute sense of lost. Campaigning had been a whirlwind of emotions; the anger of not getting the ticket and then the great shows of support that encouraged Ananda to affectively invest in the idea of becoming a Parshad. She was already visualizing this future self, planning out her actions after winning the campaign. Now there was a loss of that self.

The show of public support nonetheless seemed to reaffirm her sense of self as a valued and prominent social worker. During our conversation her eyes softened as she spoke about this support, 'I am very *aabhaarii* [meaning grateful and obliged] for the support that I received during the campaign, I am grateful to the entire team'. This support, the affection she felt during the campaign, seemingly furthered her determination to do social work; that is, being a social worker became an even more important part of her sense of self, the part of her self-imaginary that was still realizable. The remainder of our conversation centred on how PRAGATI could help her do more for the people now that the position of Parshad was no longer a possibility. While Ananda tried to find a way to recuperate a lost sense of self as someone who makes a difference in the lives of others, I detected (or perhaps projected) a frustration: a latent self with much greater ambitions but without the opportunity for enactment. Her personal circumstances within a topography for self returned her to the initial stage of possibilities.

Return

Although Ananda was livid with her party, even more so given her loss by a slim margin, she foresaw her return to the party. When I asked her just after the election how she felt about her expulsion from the party due to her running as an independent candidate, she replied:

> It is we who have created so much support for BJP in this area, that have made BJP so dominant that there is nobody here who supports Congress.

So the party will call us back when they need us for the Lok Sabha elections. They won't get the votes in this area without us. And we will also go back to the party, because we have love for the party. We have had this love since a very young age, and so when they call us back, we will go back. Also we women are a little emotional, so we will easily melt when they come. We tend to keep things in the past in the past, and look for a happier future'

Barely six months later in April 2019, Ananda did indeed campaign for the BJP during the 2019 Lok Sabha (national) elections.[6] Her anger had cooled. Ananda states that it is on account of women typically being emotional that they tend not to hold grudges long, yet the strength of feeling is less import-ant than the types of feelings that one has. I suggest that emotional repertoires lead to affective trajectories of love and forgiveness for the party, rather than the persistence of anger and a sense of betrayal. Their capacity to be affected is seemingly gendered, in that certain feelings arise more easily, while others do not persist.

Similarly, despite the strong feelings of anger, frustration, and disappoint-ment expressed at the time of the municipal elections, Sadhika, Marava, and other women party workers campaigned for their respective parties in the Lok Sabha elections. As early as December 2018, weeks after the Dehradun municipal elections, Marava said that she would return to the party that had betrayed her. 'Yes, obviously I will go back, that is where I belong. Had it been anyone instead of us, they would not have been okay working for the party again. All the problems are at the local level, at the state level. At the higher level, it is okay. Modi is a good leader'. Marava's sense of belonging, and I would go further and say her self-understanding, is tied to the BJP; she cannot conceive leaving, so 'obviously' she will return. Marava says had it been anyone else instead of *us*, they would not. By 'us' she is referring to herself and her fellow women party workers in her locality, and the ways women 'get over' disappointment and betrayal. She makes such a betrayal palatable by locating problems with the local level leadership, allowing her to remain loyal to a party she loves, and in which she *is* herself, providing another outlet for the anger she cannot contain. We saw her at the BJP headquarters within a week of the municipal elections, celebrating with her fellow party workers the election of the BJP mayor.

It is not only the capacity to be affected that is gendered, so too is the capacity to affect. Appeals to be given the party ticket are often emotional, appealing to

---

[6] Lok Sabha is the 'House of the People', India's lower house at the national level in its bicameral Parliament.

party leaders' sentiments as much as the rationalities of electoral advantage. The most obvious case of this was with a sitting Parshad, Devani, and her husband, Praveen. Devani and Praveen had a large base of supporters, and had both proven highly adept at getting things done during the five years of Devani's first term. Party leaders had assured her the party ticket to contest an unreserved seat, yet on the final day of nominations, the ticket was given to a male party worker who was relatively unknown in the area. Rumours circulated Dehradun about people paying money for tickets, yet the gossip around this candidate was that he had threatened suicide if he was denied the ticket. He appealed to party leaders that due to his age this was his final opportunity to become a Parshad that he saw as the first step in his political career. He was barely two years older than Devani (early 40s), yet her own appeals as to the importance for her political ambitions to be Parshad again fell on deaf ears. They offered her a token post that she refused. They were not responsive to the expressions of hurt and betrayal that accompanied this refusal; they were unaffected. I suggest that women party workers' capacity to affect, to engender empathy or understanding in male party elites, is relatively less than male party workers: an overlooked factor in women's ongoing under-representation in politics.

Conclusion

The trajectories of women political workers demonstrate that the sense of who we are, and who we are becoming, is dynamic. The self is punctuated by biographic moments that can lead to new self-imaginaries for becoming, followed by processes of responsiveness that define and limit possibilities. What is clear through reading the narratives of women Parshads and non-elected social workers is that reservations for women in local politics (see Chapter Two) has an expansionary impact on women's sense of who they are and who they can become. Even if women do not contest or win elections, that this is a possibility can spark an imaginary that leads to a different trajectory of becoming. As Bedi (2016: 22) notes in relation to Shiv Sena women in Mumbai, reservations provide the potential for 'women who desire political visibility and formal political opportunities'. I would add that such potential includes new social positionings, self-imaginaries, and opportunities for self-enactment. As such, reservations are empowering by expanding the possibilities for self.

The self that one can become is, however, delimited by the topography for self. Women draw on the resources within this topography in their self-making projects; the differential availability of these resources makes certain selves (im)possible. The capacity to be affected is central to our occupying socially recognizable subject positions from which we can act. Without affective responses to social cues, we would fail to develop the dispositions that enable us to move through, and have agency within, social worlds. This responsiveness is both a product of and productive of gendered affective configurations. The ways women respond depend on their affective training, the way their social positioning (as women, high-low caste, and so on) attunes them to feel in particular ways (Ahmed 2010): to gain satisfaction from social work, to be shamed by gossip, to feel the elation of accomplishing real change despite one's prior status and the barriers one has faced. In Dehradun, the capacity to be affected and responsive to the social worlds in which they dwell, encourage women to cultivate themselves as social workers, and to be rewarded by positive affective responses for ambitions and behaviours that conform to this gendered political identity.

The topography for self that shapes the possibilities and foreclosures for self strongly influences Indian local level politics. At stake are not only gendered differences in political expression and styles (Ciotti 2017; Singer 2007; Witsoe 2011), but the *types of selves who are formed in the process of becoming a political leader*. While I have focused on women, men's processes of self-formation—their own possible selves as political leaders within a topography for self—are arguably, due to male dominance, more influential in shaping the characteristics of Indian politicians and hence the character of Indian democracy. Descriptions of politicians generally fail to ask why they share similarities, or else imply that shared characteristics are due to the types of people attracted to politics. The self of the politician is presented as static, an individual rather than a self in a constant state of becoming in relation to others within a socio-historical context. The topography for self helps us to understand why politicians are the way they are, with implications for how, and for whom, politics works in practice (see also Chapter Six).

While affective regimes may reinforce unequal gender relations through the gendered possibilities of becoming (both the capacity to be affected in particular ways, as well as the opportunities for affective experience), affect also escapes power. There is always the possibility that 'experience exceeds itself' (Throop 2018: 204); that is, that the world may impress upon us in ways that are unexpected and that break with the taken-for-granted background in which we dwell. Elections, as heightened emotional experience, offer moments when women push against the boundaries of possible selves (see also Bedi 2016). Experiences such as cross-party discussions among women engender emotions that break with convention. In Dehradun collective anger leading up to the 2018 elections gave licence to women to think of themselves as more than social workers, as having their own political ambitions. Rather than being the prompt for new ways of being (that is, the moment of new potentialities), I suggest that these events are indicative of new horizons that are already dimly perceived and which are now becoming more prominent (Throop 2018). They speak to the potential for new models for becoming a female political actor.

At stake are overlooked strategies to increase women's political ambitions and representation in politics. With PRAGATI, we have attempted to create situations in which unqualified feelings can be articulated as emotions that animate action (see Jakimow 2017b). The above mentioned workshop is just one example of how this might be achieved. The experience of holding a microphone may seem minor for some people, yet for others might be a bio-graphic moment in a new trajectory of self. New solidarities that allow repressed feelings to bubble to the surface may change not only an individual's affective responses to their environment, but the broader possibilities for 'feeling' and 'becoming' within the topography for self. Enactments of self and concomitant affective experiences are therefore critical, yet overlooked aspects of empowering women (and men).

In empowering women through an expansion of the possibilities for self, we also encourage local development agents to make affective investments in this sense of who they are or are becoming. There is a great deal at stake in these projects of self-fashioning, so that their loss can be painful, even unbear-able (Berlant 2011). In Chapter Three, I demonstrated how these affective investments in self were a factor in the reproduction of programme rationali-ties. In this chapter I have examined how an attachment to an idea of self is an accomplice in the exploitation of women's labour (see also Huang 2017 for the link between empowerment and exploitation of local development agents). A sense of self as a social worker motivates women to undertake activities that generate good will for political parties, while discouraging them from being disgruntled when they are not rewarded for the political capital they generate. Some women credit who they are, their very core of being, to the party. To then abandon the party becomes inconceivable, or at least too painful, as it would also entail a loss of self. Political elites take advantage of, or at least benefit from the willingness of women to work towards certain self-imaginings without having to share power with them. Affective investments in self thereby have the potential to trap women in relationships that are ultimately harmful (Berlant 2011). But many women do become Parshads, such as

Meera, experiencing a transformative moment of the election followed by a term as Parshad characterized by new affective experiences and re-attunement to a (different) self-in-relation. The journey of becoming is critical to how they perform their role as we will see in Chapters Six and Eight.

Chapters Three and Four have examined the processes of self-formation in two different development contexts, demonstrating how local development—whether it be in a state-led community development programme or in local governance—can provide possibilities for an expansion in the possibilities for self. The capacity to be affected in ways that are aligned with one's sense of who one is, or is becoming, is critical to these possibilities: a capacity that is unevenly enjoyed. As these self-imaginaries may be nascent and emergent, they are also precarious and particularly susceptible to being affected in ways that threaten this sense of self. I have demonstrated how this leads local development agents to be particularly responsive to the new worlds in which they dwell: be that to the discursive regimes of community development in Medan, or to the gendered ideologies of appropriate feminine political styles in Dehradun. Local development agents affectively invest in these ideas of self; the stakes of these projects are high. That is, they seek out experiences that reaffirm this sense of who they are, are responsive to the affective impulses to be a particular way within social worlds, and become attached to, and protective of, their selfhood. These high stakes are both a consequence of development that 'empowers' people to expand their sense of self, as well as shaping how development is practised. Yet becoming is not 'accomplished', it is an ongoing process (Biehl and Locke 2017). One's durable sense of self is therefore constantly susceptible to being threatened. In Part II, I examine the collective conditions that make both volunteers and women Parshads particularly susceptible to threats to their sense of self.

PART II
COLLECTIVE CONDITIONS

5

The 'Feel Good' Event

The first time we met Pak Anto—the volunteer introduced in Chapter Three—was at an *acara* (programme or event) to mark the completion of a PNPM project. The local BKM had organized tailoring training for a group of women, and then provided loans for them to buy sewing machines to start a small business. Their first order was from the BKM to sew over a hundred school uniforms for needy families in the area. On successful completion of the order, BKM Maju held a formal ceremony to hand over the uniforms. They closed off the street in front of the one-room BKM office and arranged plastic chairs and a tarpaulin to shade attendees from the sun. Government officials and other dignitaries were called, who each gave a speech before presenting the assembled children with new uniforms. The women entrepreneurs and parents looked on. After the completion of formalities, food that the BKM members and their families had prepared was laid out on a table, with Pak Anto encouraging us all to fill our plates.

During my months following several BKMs, I attended numerous such occasions. They had a similar pattern, including an overall purpose of marking the successful completion of a discreet project, the participation of government officials who partook in the distribution of benefits, and people who were, or could stand in for, *penerima manfaat* (the recipients of benefits). The *acara* can be understood as a 'ritual of verification': a performance arranged to support the story of project success (Mosse 2005). Government officials oversee the proceedings and verify the worthiness of 'beneficiaries' because 'the government wants to know the real situation, the truth, do we help the people or not' (Ibu Sharma, BKM member). To consider the scene only for what it achieves for the project, however, ignores the less expressed meanings for participants of the enactment (Trundle 2012) and what it achieves for them personally. As seen in Chapter Three, affective experience is necessary for the accomplishment of self through the enactment of doing good and the positive feelings such actions engender that reaffirm that such action is right for them, that is, aligned with their *jiwa*. *Acaras* are key opportunities for affective experience that reaffirms the sense of who they are and who they are becoming.

Susceptibility in Development: Micropolitics of Local Development in India and Indonesia. Tanya Jakimow, Oxford University Press (2020). © Tanya Jakimow.
DOI: 10.1093/oso/9780198854739.001.0001

The ways those opportunities translate into possibilities for becoming are not fixed, however. We are dependent on human and non-human others for the ways we feel. As Jackson (1998) notes, emotions and consciousness are extra-psychic processes that arise in relation to the external environment. In order to feel gratified from social work, one needs to interpret pleasure or gratitude from the recipient of that work, and be affected by it. Put differently, the capacity to be affected in ways that reinforce one's sense of self depends on the capacity of the other to affect. As noted in the introduction, these capacities are not an attribute of either individual, but are engendered in the encounter between them (Ahmed 2004). The relative force and intensities of engendered affects is shaped by the forms of relationality between objects (Fox 2015). Part II of this book (this chapter and Chapter Six) examines the collective conditions in which these forms of relationality arise, and thereby the differential capacity and susceptibility to affect and be affected.

Attention to affect as a '*collective condition* that mediates how life is lived and thought' (Anderson 2014: 18) helps us move beyond a reading of power based solely on the attributes of individuals. Rather 'bodies [are] formed through *relations that extend beyond them*...bodily capacities express and become part of those relations' (Anderson 2014: 9, emphasis added). That is, the body's force in an encounter with another is shaped by the affective dimensions of the worlds in which we collectively dwell, while those encounters charged by bodily affects produce this world. Anderson (2014: 107) notes that collective affect conditions life in ways that may be overwhelmingly present, or barely perceptible; 'collective affect can be at once operative in giving an "enigmatic coherence" across life whilst also subtending life by persisting in the background'. In phenomenological approaches, collective affect is part of the world in which we dwell, that impresses upon us, pulls our attention towards particular horizons in ways that are pre-cognitive and unbidden (Throop 2018).

Affect shapes the collective conditions in which we dwell in multiple and layered ways. The properties of affect—how it is produced, transmitted, contaminates, infects—determines affects' structuring effects, the way it produces anew, reinforces or disrupts power. Understanding these properties requires us to address a central problem in affect theory: what Wetherell (2013: 222) describes as the 'duality of affect'. Is affect unbidden, impersonal, something that overtakes us in a way we cannot control? In this case, affect is the active agent and emergent. Or are humans able to produce and control their affective responses? In this sense, affect is accomplished, an act of management. The former has greater potential for disruptions to power configurations, while the latter is more likely to reinforce the status quo and existing forms of privilege. Wetherell posits Anderson's (2009, 2014) affective atmosphere as an example of unbidden affect without agency, and Hochschild's (1983) feeling rules as an example of self-management and control of affect. She proposes 'affective practice' as a way to navigate between these positions in order to recognize the human contribution to collective affect, while also recognizing affect's potential for creativity and disruptions.

I have found affective practice exceptionally useful to analyse BKM activities, including the *acara*. At the same time, hanging over these practices was often an atmosphere—what I call drawing upon (Anderson 2014) a moral atmosphere—that was in tension with these affective practices. I examine affective practice and moral atmosphere as two forms of collective affect—layers that swirl, collide yet are distinct and at times separate—that engender differential capacities and susceptibilities to affect and be affected in the everyday work of the BKM. Wetherell (2013: 232) also recognizes that 'affective atmospheres are not singular, consistent, static or, indeed, always effective', and that understanding this 'plurality and variability of subject/object entanglements is crucial to understanding the power of the event' (2013: 232). Examining tensions between affective practices that reinforce certain forms of privilege and a moral atmosphere that poses a challenge to them, help us to understand power and its possibilities.

This chapter examines the collision between a moral atmosphere of *bagi-bagi* (everyone taking a share) with the affective practice of gratifying social work in the everyday experiences of community volunteers. I present two lines of enquiry into collective affect to understand power in local level development. The first is to pay attention to the ways different forms of collective affect shape the differential capacity and susceptibility to affect and be affected. These capacities are realized in encounters between bodies, with important implications for development practice as examined in Part III. The second line of enquiry is to examine the differential capacity to shape these collective conditions. My analysis of an *acara* focuses on this second line of enquiry, considering how the localized event speaks to larger issues of power configurations in 'development' *writ large*.

The Moral Atmosphere of *Bagi-bagi*

'*Bagi-bagi*', said an elderly woman with a smile as I approached her with a clipboard in hand, soliciting me playfully to give her a share of whatever I was offering. '*Bagi-bagi*' was the demand of a government official asked to sign documents so funds sanctioned for an infrastructure project could be released. Development as a share, *bagi*, or something which is distributed, *bagi-bagi*, has emerged as a moral logic shaping development in Medan. *Bagi-bagi* refers to the sharing of resources that flow from the state and other development activities, and the way people are expected or assumed to 'take their part'. Citizens, or *warga*, manoeuvre to receive their share by becoming a *penerima manfaat* (recipient of benefits), while development agents (officials, contractors, volunteers) are expected to skim a share of the funding that passes through them. *Bagi-bagi* is a moral logic, that is, the 'normative configurations which influence actors' strategies' (Olivier de Sardan 1999: 44), and that shape the legitimacy and moral acceptability of acts that are otherwise pathologized. *Bagi-bagi* frames state-led development in Medan, reflecting, reproducing and being the basis of resistance of unequal social relations (Harrison 2006; Shah 2009). As a social preoccupation, it envelopes and permeates people's orientation towards development.

I use the term 'moral atmosphere of *bagi-bagi*' to denote it as part of the collective conditions of life in Medan (see Jakimow 2018c for a full elaboration). I use the term 'moral' to note the way that affect is imbricated in moral logics, involving but extending beyond signification. The word atmosphere is taken from Anderson's (2009, 2014) notion of affective atmosphere to capture the way affect radiates between individuals in encounters, but is not reducible to them. *Bagi-bagi* may be part of the national mood, or structure of feeling that orients the population's evaluations of development, yet what I am most interested in is how *bagi-bagi* envelops bodies within an encounter, or the way it hangs over an *acara*. Atmosphere provides a sense of enclosure, a spatiality that envelops those within, while also having an outside (Anderson 2009). Bodies attune to *bagi-bagi*, and it is through the way they are affected, as revealed through feelings, that the atmosphere becomes charged with its presence. The charge becomes palpable; people are infected by its possibilities. An atmosphere envelops and impresses upon life, but is not something to which people are necessarily consciously attuned.

To say that the development arena in Medan is shaped by a *moral* atmosphere of *bagi-bagi* is to draw attention to the force of ideas, values, and discourses that animate, mobilize, and affect individuals within that arena. As an affective force, *bagi-bagi* recruits individuals to be moved in particular ways, shaping people's horizons, orienting them towards certain cares, concerns, and perspectives (Desjarlais and Throop 2011). The moral atmosphere is an inescapable presence, tension, or energy that infects encounters between 'local development agents and 'others': *penerima manfaat* (recipients of benefits), *pejabat* (government officials), and *orang biasa* (ordinary people). The sensations and resonances of practices such as asking for or giving *bagi-bagi*, or observing and talking about it, arise from an engagement of self within one's social world. The moral atmosphere of *bagi-bagi* engenders feelings processed as guilt, shame, foolishness, or satisfaction when engaged in activities in which the possibility of taking a share, or the sense that one is expected to or assumed to have done so, hangs in the air. The moral atmosphere of *bagi-bagi* predisposes people to being affected in particular ways, frames people's expectations of others, and against which people respond.

Elsewhere (Jakimow 2018c) I have examined this moral atmosphere and the way it shapes urban sociality in Medan. Here, I focus on how this atmosphere influences the power configurations of community development in particular. I argue that the moral atmosphere of *bagi-bagi* shapes the differential capacity/susceptibility to affect/be affected within everyday development in four ways: (a) disrupting the affective experiences that reaffirm volunteers' sense of self; (b) increasing volunteers' susceptibility to engender feelings in others, such as suspicion and cynicism that are counter to their self-representations; (c) increasing the force of complaints and accusations made against volunteers, and; (d) increasing volunteers' susceptibility to be affected by these complaints and accusations.

'I am offended'

Chapter Three outlined how the sense of self of community volunteers in Medan was based on the satisfaction they received from helping others with sincerity. Volunteerism, that is working without a salary, is important for these self-making projects. BKM members emphasized that they did not need a salary to do social activity because they gain pleasure or satisfaction from work oriented to helping others (Jakimow 2017a): 'We work for the needs of the people, and actually this makes us happy' (Pak Henri, BKM coordinator). The representation of BKM members as *relawan* (volunteer) is a point of differentiation within a moral atmosphere of *bagi-bagi*, in which it is perceived and expected that people gain financially from being an agent of development. The rejection of the logic of *bagi-bagi* is a part of their self-representation and self-narrative. Similar to Gibbings' (2013) figure of the 'ethical citizen', many BKM members position themselves as part of the *rakyat kecil*, or little people, in opposition to, and (for some) charged with making sure that elites and government officials remain accountable. This moral capital of 'doing good' for the people with no expectation of reward is critical to the social recognition that volunteers desire, and that is a central motivation for, and benefit of, their work.

The rejection of *bagi-bagi* is important for BKM members' self-making projects, at the same time that *bagi-bagi* envelops and infects their work. In Indonesia, people's assumptions that anyone involved in the implementation or distribution of development resources is taking their share can be traced to national discourses against *Korupsi*, *Kollusi*, and *Nepotisme* (KKN, corruption, collusion, and nepotism) that today are prevalent in the media and everyday conversation. The World Bank's attempts to drive out the 'cancer of corruption' globally, in part through initiatives that promote good governance, have arguably exacerbated perceptions that corruption is widespread, while also inculcating norms that reject these practices (Harrison 2006; Tidey 2013). The pervasiveness of the related, but distinct logic of *bagi-bagi* in Indonesia can likewise be traced to trans-national anti-corruption discourses (Harrison 2006), a political history of pervasive state-corruption and nepotism (Robertson-Snape 1999; Budiman et al. 2013), and IMF-imposed institutional reform associated with good governance (Tidey 2016). Further, as in other parts of the global South, recurrent failures of development to live up to its promises (Fechter 2016), alongside the relatively high salaries received by development practitioners from the global North (Roth 2015), results in perceptions that the main beneficiaries of development are its implementers. Shutt (2012) points to a moral logic in aid-recipient 'communities', where local people assume that implementing agents do, or even should benefit (see also Pigg 1992).

Such logic is prevalent in Medan, affecting and infecting the work of community volunteers. Chatting with people in coffee shops about their views of the PNPM, it became clear that most people assumed BKM members received a salary or other form of payment. For example, one man with minimal knowledge of the PNPM told us: 'It is impossible that people will work without salary, so we know that they mark up project costs'. Sometimes BKM members are directly confronted as to what they gain through their participation. A friend of Ibu Muslimah (BKM coordinator) asked her about an initiative to install sceptic tanks: 'How much money do you make doing this'? When Ibu Muslimah replied none, the friend was disbelieving: 'Impossible you do not get money'. Rather than an altercation, the friend was seeing if she too could benefit from becoming a volunteer in the PNPM. In her account of the incident, Ibu Muslimah did not reflect on her friend's question, but rather

her own response: 'Who is going to pay us? Why do we want to do it? I am also amazed, why I want to do it'.

The sense of being exceptional through the desire to do social activities without payment is, as mentioned above, part of volunteers' understanding of self. Encounters with others that call attention to this exceptionalism can be reaffirming. At the same time, the (mis)perception that BKM members do, or should receive a share of programme money lingers in the air, engendering feelings of doubt and foolishness among BKM members themselves. As noted in Chapter Three, Pak Alrasyad (BKM coordinator) admitted that, initially, after joining the BKM, he was surprised by the lack of salary: 'My wife asked me why did I join something like this. I said "to help the [PNPM] facilitator". She said "but they receive payment, while we are not paid; they fooled you". Many people said this.' Further, being a BKM member was for many a costly expense, requiring money for phones and transport. Out of pocket expenses had encouraged some BKM members to lobby the city government for a small honorarium, although other BKM members rejected this move as detracting from their volunteer status. Whether or not a honorarium was appropriate, the payment of some development agents over others (government contracted facilitators but not volunteers) results in ambiguity as to what is right and wrong, with attendant feelings of being fooled, or alternatively working selflessly. In other words, *bagi-bagi* influenced how they were affected through their work, with consequences for their sense of self.

Bagi-bagi also influences the way that other's perceive them, and hence the affective relationality between BKM members and *penerima manfaat, orang biasa*, and *pejabat*. In the introduction, I drew upon the work of Sara Ahmed (2004) to note the ways that certain objects, including human actors, evoke emotions in others. When coming into contact with an object, there is an evaluation as to whether it will be beneficial or harmful, and this engenders a particular reaction. Some objects are 'sticky', in that they excite certain emotions. They are, to use my framing, susceptible to affect—that is, engendering affects and emotions in others in ways that are unintentional, and can be harmful. While Ahmed (2004) and others (Fanon 1967; Pedwell and Whitehead 2012) have examined the susceptibility to affect in relation to race, here I examine how development workers awaken cynicism and suspicion in others. *Bagi-bagi* pervades social encounters, is present in the evaluations that one makes of another, incites feelings that are not directly and cognitively attributable to the logic of *bagi-bagi* itself: guilt without wrong doing, suspicion without evidence, defensiveness without accusation. An individual is predisposed towards feeling suspicious; another individual is marked as an object of suspicion.

The susceptibility of BKM to engender suspicion or distrust even influences official evaluations of the programme. Precise targeting, or *tepat sasaran*, to reach the most needy and worthy is a key basis for evaluation of the PNPM (World Bank 2013: 10). BKM members claim to be more accurate than other government programmes, as they go to the people directly, and are pure in their intentions (as opposed to other government appointed officials, see Jakimow 2018a). BKMs in Medan have nonetheless been criticized. In one example, academics from a local university presented an unpublished evaluation of the PNPM in Medan at a workshop for PNPM facilitators. They concluded that the identification of beneficiaries was 'subjective': a conclusion based on the opinions of members of the public. Recipients of micro-finance loans were, they claimed, geographically concentrated around the homes of BKM members, and included friends and family members. Several government contracted facilitators who regularly interact with BKMs were incensed by the report. They complained that the researchers had spent barely ten minutes with each BKM, used aggressive tones to demand access to documents, and made generalizations about the whole programme from one example. Nonetheless, the report and its conclusions were lodged.

Unpacking how the researchers reached these conclusions reveals how the moral atmosphere of *bagi-bagi* shapes perceptions of the PNPM. First, the accounts of members of the public were seen as authoritative (even though, as we saw earlier in this section, opinions were not always based on direct experience), while those of BKM members were seen as intrinsically untrustworthy. I too am often accused of being naive by taking at face value the accounts of volunteers by academics who are predisposed to being sceptical of all *local* development agents (see Chapter Two). Second, the interactions between researchers and BKM coordinators were aggressive, seemingly based on an assumption that the latter are involved in taking a share of resources. The interactions engender fear in BKM coordinators, as the moral atmosphere of *bagi-bagi* hangs over them. I have seen this susceptibility to fear and defensiveness firsthand. When we met BKM coordinators for the first time, many assumed we had come to look over their books, and were armed with various forms of evidence to convince us of their sincerity. We had to work hard to break the tension, to reassure, that is to change the relationality between us so that it was not infected by the moral atmosphere of *bagi-bagi*.

These two forms of susceptibility—susceptibility to engender feelings such as suspicion, scepticism, and cynicism in others, and susceptibility to being affected by these involuntary incitements—are in direct relation to the capacity of others to affect. The moral atmosphere of *bagi-bagi* makes it easy for others to accuse them of wrong doing. Pak Alrasyad narrated one incident:

> The people in neighbourhood A asked us 'why did you do [infrastructure project] in neighbourhood B, why not in A'? And the problem again is sometimes there are people who are *pintar* [smart, with a connotation of cunningness] and who ask, ask…they can make the situation difficult.… I am worried that it will provoke other people. Later they will say that 'Evidently the BKM plays favourites, wherever their family lives, they only work in that locality'. A situation like this scares us, because later it will influence other people.

The force of the complaint in this case is not due to its accuracy, but its plausibility. The moral atmosphere permeates BKM activities, casting them in a cloud of suspicion. At the same time, BKM members are susceptible to becoming afraid in such circumstances, in part due to the ongoing effects such an accusation would have.

This account demonstrates how the moral atmosphere of *bagi-bagi* increases residents' (*warga*) capacity to affect. The impact of the forcefulness of the accusation are several. As noted, members of the public, or *orang biasa*, are able to engender feelings of fear, and perhaps guilt or defensiveness, in BKM members due to the threat to their reputations and self-making projects. This fear may have material consequences if they are able to effect a reallocation of resources (this possibility is explored in more detail in Chapter Eight in Dehradun). By engendering suspicion in others, the accusation can also arrest any enhancement of BKM members' social status as a result of their activities, thereby impacting the relation between volunteers and the general public. We encountered many such instances where accusations have been made against BKM members that are forceful, that stick, and have material and affective consequences. Most of the BKM coordinators we spoke to had been accused of corruption, either directly or through the media. Such incidents can be frightening, and insulting. Pak Hendri, a BKM coordinator, was exasperated by people's treatment of him and the programme: 'Even if we do our best, and work as a volunteer, the people always think that we are taking money. I am offended by this'.

My point is *not* that there is never any truth to the criticisms of BKMs and their projects, or that the more serious accusations of corruption are baseless. Although all the BKM coordinators we knew had been able to weather such accusations due to the accounting processes in the place through the BKM, we were not looking for evidence in support or denial. What I can say with some confidence is that what I describe as the moral atmosphere of *bagi-bagi* was a shadow and stench that could not be dispersed from their everyday activities, and this atmosphere shaped the differential capacity and susceptibility to affect and be affected. I am also confident that accusations of corruption, or the threat of accusations, place a heavy emotional toll on some BKM members. Anxiety and risk are recurring themes in volunteer narratives. The risks one faces as a volunteer are intimately tied to the importance of their social activities for their idea of who they are and who they are becoming. Hence, as I now show through an analysis of an *acara*, there are efforts to establish different collective affects that are more supportive of these projects.

'Feel Good' Event

The home of Pak Dumadi (BKM coordinator) had a different feel when we arrived for an *acara* to mark a social activity of BKM Timbul. We had sat many times in the guest room (*ruang tamu*), chatting over drinks and snacks. This time there was a sense of anticipation and excitement. The furniture had been removed, and in its place were mats upon which women and their children were seated. We recognized the eight guests as *penerima manfaat*: the recipients of benefits of social activities. They were sitting quietly, waiting, not speaking with one another, and not smiling. They wore casual clothes, but had 'freshened up' for the occasion. Only one of the women wore *jilbab* (veil): the woman who had gone around and collected the *penerima manfaat*. We took a place on the mat, and tried to initiate conversation. They were short on details as to why they were here, only knowing that the woman in *jilbab* had called them and asked them to bring their children. They did not know each other as they live in different *lingkungan* (neighbourhoods).

The BKM members were standing at the front door, greeting people as they came in. Their numbers steadily increased until twelve or so members were chatting and laughing, creating a joyous atmosphere in contrast to the solemnity inside. They were wearing their BKM uniforms that they had each purchased, and which Pak Dumadi told us 'gave people spirit'. Several volunteers came in to shake the hands of the seated *penerima manfaat*, but none lingered inside, and one by one they returned to their colleagues outside. There was some excitement inside the home. Next to the guest room, Pak Dumadi and his son whispered to each other as they placed a large bag in the doorway, inching it forward and backwards so that it remained just out of view of the women and children. It reminded me of a parent playing Santa Claus, delighting in the surprise to come. Pak Dumadi was all smiles when he came into the room, shaking the hands of the women. His playful enquiries into the well-being of the women were met, however, with awkward silence or shy responses. The woman in *jilbab* was the only one to engage him in conversation, but she too retained a nervous laugh.

We sat and waited for the final guests to appear: an official from the *kecamatan* (sub-district) office, and two facilitators from the PNPM office at the city level. We sensed that the patient waiting of the women had turned into annoyance. They looked to the clock, frowned, shuffled on the floor. Finally, Ibu Camat—the head of the *kecamatan*—arrived 45 minutes late with a couple of contracted PMPM facilitators and officials from the PNPM city office.[1] Without apology, she took her seat on the mat with a frown. I caught her attention and the *acara* was further delayed as she grilled me over my research and the relevant permissions. With growing restlessness Pak Dumadi finally started proceedings. After the Shalat Ashar (Islamic prayer), he declared the purpose of the social activity: to give school bags to *anak yang kurang mampu* (children who are less well-to-do or capable). The bag is to be an incentive for learning, Pak Dumadi explained, further stressing that the women and children assembled were only representative of the large number of recipients of bags. The recipients listened in silence, with a 'flat face': that is, without expression.[2]

Before distributing the bags, Pak Dumadi requested that the children sing the Indonesia Raya (national anthem). He was animated, smiling and coaxing the children to their feet. The children were reluctant, but after some prodding from their mothers, finally stood to sing. Ibu Asmira stood up to direct the children: a significant gesture for a woman who outside of BKM activities is shy and timid. Finally the women assembled broke into a smile, some of them singing along with their children. The distribution of bags then commenced, with the children getting in to two lines at the side of the room. Pak Dumadi, the government officials, and this researcher, presented the bags, with each child pressing the hand of the giver to their forehead in a mark of respect. I was surprised at the lack of excitement or curiosity; none of the

---

[1] In Indonesia it is common to call the wife of the Lurah or Camat, Ibu Lurah or Ibu Camat. In this case, the Camat in question is a woman herself, and I am not referring to her as a wife.

[2] A lack of expression is not culturally unusual, and people are restrained to show excitement at gifts. This interpretation was developed along with my research assistants, who felt that the tone was flatter than usual, beyond politeness to a sense of boredom and annoyance.

children opened the heavy bags to see what was inside. Even they seemed a little bored and unenthused. In contrast, the BKM members were watching, smiling broadly.

With everyone back seated, Ibu Camat said a few words. She spoke in a solemn tone about the PNPM, and all the good work it had done in the *kecamatan*. Pak Dumadi requested that one of the women give a few words. After an uncomfortable silence, the woman in *jilbab* who had assembled the group finally spoke. She expressed her unlimited gratitude, '*terima kasih yang tak terhingga*', and her hope that there would be more aid and more concern for the community. The official from the PNPM Medan office told the group that this was one of the best BKM in the city, and that the people should be proud to have this BKM in their *kelurahan*. Formalities over, a group photo was called. Each child held up their school bags, surrounded by BKM members and officials. The majority of *penerima manfaat* left immediately after, indeed so quickly that I did not have time to note their disappearance. The BKM members lingered. They were in high spirits, enlivened by the events. They shook our hands warmly as we left, asking us how we found the event.

As noted, programmes (or *acara*) to mark the completion of PNPM activities were common, and this one followed a familiar pattern: the presence of government officials and *penerima manfaat*, the 'handing over' of goods alongside a show of gratitude, the formality alongside the joviality—serious business, but also a moment of celebration. The 'witnessing' of the event by officials and the members of the community and its capture in the form of photos provide a verifiable record that the activity took place and that money was expended for an appreciated outcome. In this way, the *acara* also responds to the demands for 'good governance' in a moral atmosphere of *bagi-bagi*. The *acara* also plays a role in the 'becoming' of BKM members, providing an opportunity *to feel* the satisfaction of their work, or in the terms described in Chapter Three, to satisfy their *hati* in ways that support their understanding of self. At the same time, the *penerima manfaat* seemingly had a different perspective of the event. While they did not disrupt the possibility of engendered feelings of satisfaction, their body language, gestures, and words did not generate these possibilities. On returning back to my room, I could not shake the sense that the event had two different affective registers: one of excitement and celebration, the other of boredom and perhaps cynicism. The two different affective registers of the programme are a starting point to examine the multiple forms of collective affect present in the scene.

Affective Practice

Ibu Asmira was unrecognizable in the *acara*. In BKM uniform and matching *jilbab* her dress was different to the casual garb she usually wore. But more so it was the lifted chest and high head that oozed confidence. Her smile was constant, yet relaxed, revealing a genuine contentment; she beamed as she led the children in song. As examined in Chapter Three, for volunteers such as Ibu Asmira, the BKM was critical to their self-making projects; their idea of who they are and are becoming is reaffirmed through the emotions they feel (the response of the *hati*) in their activities and encounters with others. As I recall the image of Ibu Asmira on that day, it is like watching the realization of self in real time. The realization of self is, however, susceptible to the impressions made by others. The less than enthusiastic responses of the *penerima manfaat* have the potential to affect her in ways that would conflict with this sense of self. Ibu Asmira is not, however, perturbed. She is seemingly predisposed to being affected in ways that reaffirm, rather than challenge, her self-making project.

The extent to which we can generate, manage or control our responses, or in contrast the ways we are involuntarily moved or impressed upon, has consequences for the possibilities of personhood, including the power or capacity of others to shape these possibilities. The agentive nature of personhood, alongside our innate susceptibility to be impressed upon by others, returns us to the tension between an understanding of a subjectless, unbidden affect, in contrast to the self-management of affect. Wetherell (2013: 221) addresses this 'duality of affect—potential control in contrast to potential lack of control'—directly, aiming to find a middle ground. Examining two extremes, she interrogates Hochschild's notion of 'feeling rules', and the pinch air hostesses feel between how they feel and how they should feel, resulting in the 'regulation of spontaneous and authentic emotional reactions' (Wetherell 2013: 221). Hochschild (1983) describes this self-regulation as 'emotional labour': a concept Fechter (2016) uses to describe the labour of aid workers in remaining optimistic in the face of development failures. Hochschild's theory thus provides one response to the question of the extent to which affective responses are unbidden or alternatively self-managed, arguing that 'Emotion arises, relatively automatically, and people then regulate this unbidden affect so that their behaviour conforms to what is expected' (Wetherell 2013: 226). In this interpretation, Ibu Asmira manages the feelings that arise in her so that her emotions allow her to perform that task, and more critically here, reaffirm her sense of self.

Against this notion of management, Wetherell posits Anderson's (2009) affective atmosphere. While Anderson has built on this idea in subsequent work in ways that address some of Wetherell's criticism (Anderson 2014), her initial critique is useful to draw out the lines of debate. The human agent is absent in this account, as affect is 'an unspecified force, unmediated by human consciousness, discourse, representation and interpretation' (Wetherell 2012: 228, see also Thrift 2008). Human subjects move through atmospheres, they become a 'waiting room' upon which certain affects are realized, with no capacity to manage these emotions. If we apply this understanding to the moral atmosphere of *bagi-bagi*, for example, volunteers are uncontrollably infected by fear and anxiety. This 'subjectless affect', Wetherell argues, ignores the work that goes into creating certain affecting scenes. Using an example of an ANZAC (Australian and New Zealand Army Corps) memorial service in New Zealand, she demonstrates how symbols, practices, and rituals move the participants in ways that turn them into 'patriotic citizens with a specific relation to the fallen dead' (Wetherell 2013: 231). The way people are affected is not natural or authentic, but neither is it a case of self-management or control.

Wetherell (2012, 2013) proposes affective practice as a means to read the memorial service. Building upon Bourdieu's notion of habitus, she examines how a 'feel for the game' is part of one's social dispositions, which encourages a certain orientation and attunement to the scene. Evidence for the learnt nature of affective responses is found in the behaviour of the children, who fail to 'catch' transmitted affect. In the solemn ANZAC memorial service they remain joyful and playful. Wetherell thereby brings affect into Bourdieu's practice theory, arguing that 'affective practices come with a 'universe of ready-made feelings and experiences' when prompted by a familiar situation' (2012: 106). That is, certain social arrangements engender affects in people who have been socialized/attuned to 'feeling the right way' within them. Further, affect solidifies, or in other words 'affective practices sediment' (2012: 115), with one's unthinking repertoire of everyday responses and actions sustaining class distinctions and social hierarchies. In this way, we are conditioned to respond in ways that are an 'accomplice to social reproduction' (2012: 106). The ANZAC memorial service has a 'distinctive affective flavour' (2012: 103), prompting an affective relationship with the 'fallen dead' that is exclusive of the Maori soldiers in New Zealand's settlement wars, for example.

The affective practice of the service thereby reinforces a history that washes over past and contemporary injustices, as an accomplice to ongoing inequalities.

I use affective practice to analyse scenes of local level development. It helps us to recognize how 'affective atmospheres organise subjectivity, and how affected subjectivities with particular histories can also actively work to bring about, alter, maintain, resist and challenge affective atmospheres' (Wetherell 2013: 235). In other words, affective practice is a means through which to interrogate the middle ground between the extreme positions of unbidden affect and emotional self-management to arrive at nuanced accounts that capture the complexity of collective affect and how it informs 'becoming'. Such an approach requires attention to the 'practical methods for performing, re-animating and re-configuring social relations' (Wetherell 2012: 115) through the engendering of affective responses. Below I offer a reading of the *acara* with attention to the symbols, practices, and rituals that engender the feelings commensurate with the idea of self being realized through volunteer activities, and in their relation to others. I also draw attention to the relationships between the various participants in the *acara* to understand how affective practice contributes to the reproduction of social hierarchies in local development, and the accomplishment of social mobility through local development.

Three Timbres

Reading the *acara* as an affective practice reveals three timbres that together create the conditions in which BKM members such as Ibu Asmira are affected in ways commensurate with their self-making projects. The first of these is the sense of celebration. Practices such as the late disclosure of the 'gift' that enables a 'pleasant surprise' for the recipients, asking the children to sing, and taking photos all mark the occasion as something both noteworthy and worth celebrating. The way BKM members occupied space further helped them to generate and safeguard enthusiasm. As they congregated at the front of the house together, they chatted and laughed with each other. Their enthusiasm was contagious, and through the interactions it multiplied. The BKM members who came inside where the tone was much flatter, quickly left, thereby not being affected/infected by indifference or boredom. When the *acara* formally commenced and the BKM members left their place at the front entrance to take their place in the guest room, their high spirits settled over them, maintaining that sense of celebration and dispelling the flat atmosphere that was circulating among the *penerima manfaat*.

Wearing the uniform of the BKM further marks the event as out of the ordinary from day to day activities. Ibu Hanum tells us that the uniform gives a sense of *wibawa*, that is, of prestige or authority, clarifying that she does not mean this in a way to show off, but rather as a way to mark themselves as different and as people with responsibility over development in the local area. To put on the uniform is to enter that different persona or relation with the other. Ibu Citra explains that when she is wearing the uniform, she is *diatas*, that is, above other people in the community, while on other days of the year, she is *orang biasa* (an ordinary person). Most BKM members say that putting on the uniform gives them a sense of pride, and we observe that it also seemingly brings a level of confidence (as seen with Ibu Asmira). A uniform also helps to obscure the socio-economic position of the BKM member. Several poorer BKM members wore the uniform to PNPM events and workshops held in hotels where poor quality clothing would mark the individual as out of place. In the *acara*, it enabled a visible class differentiation between BKM members and the *penerima manfaat*. Visually, it gave a sense of solidarity, of working towards the same admirable goals.

Alongside celebration was a timbre of ceremony, a formality that marked the occasion as part of state development efforts. The singing of the national anthem not only added a joyousness to the event, it also situated the activity within a discourse of national development. The attendance of the head of the *kecamatan* met certain programme requirements, in particular the need for verification. Her presence, in the khaki uniform of officials, alongside her officious demeanour was also critical to bestowing a seriousness on the occasion, and further brought this community-based activity into national development efforts. She was not only there to observe and verify, but also to congratulate and thank the BKM for their national service. The experience of standing beside, and being on the same team as government officials was very affecting for some BKM members, moments of subtle inner transformations where the BKM member becomes a 'development agent', someone with a status in the community, and recognized as contributing to society. The presence of the 'state' manifest in the official 'rubs off' on the BKM members, who share in her authority and are enlivened by their temporary social co-location.

The third timbre, particularly relevant to BKM Timbul's *acara*, is that of care. Ibu Hanum and Ibu Asmira both said that the social area of BKM's work was the most important, directly responding to the slogan of the PNPM, *kita peduli* (we care). Care has been an important theme of feminist scholarship, which has examined its potential to offer a 'radically different way to look at moral and political life' (Tronto 1995: 142). Attentiveness and responsiveness are critical to caring relations, as distinct from the impartial and universal application of welfare associated with an ethic of justice (Held 2006). These themes cropped up in conversations with BKM members, many of whom claimed that their caring disposition makes them attentive to the people, and distinguishes them from local government officials (see also Jakimow 2019 et al.). While some BKM members say that they have a caring disposition, or a *jiwa* that cares, Pak Anto states that it has also been *through* his involvement that he has developed a caring disposition: 'I feel a lot of changes…in the past we had less care [*kurang peduli*]. Lacking care in the sense of the word, that we only cared about what we feel and see [that is, which is of concern to us personally]. Now it is a must!' Care is therefore critical to many BKM members' idea of who one is, and/or who one is becoming.

Care is inherently relational (Butler 2004; Philip et al. 2012), and therefore the reaffirmation that one's actions are acts of care is conditional on the acknowledgement of such by the recipients of care. The *penerima manfaat* therefore play an important role in the *acara*, as grateful recipients of acts of care. They are invited as representatives to directly receive care, enabling the BKM members to feel the satisfaction and warm feeling of having cared for another. If they were to disrupt the scene through an open performance of ungratefulness, it would threaten the affective practice that engenders these feelings. At the same time, the emotional and affective properties of care practices also structure unequal relations between carer and cared for that is neither symmetrical, nor equal (Lawson 2007; Philip et al. 2012).

That the *penerima manfaat* did not disturb the scene therefore reproduces the unequal relations between them and the BKM members. I next examine the affective practices of the *acara* from their perspective.

Flat Faces

Even though not prominent, the moral atmosphere of *bagi-bagi* hung over and lurked in the background of the *acara*. This atmosphere has the potential to engender different emotions and entanglements that are in conflict with the affective practice of the BKM members. As noted, *penerima manfaat* were not 'caught up' in the feel-good atmosphere of the moment, and *bagi-bagi* may provide part of the explanation for their 'flat faces' and lack of enthusiasm. Perhaps they too think that the people to benefit most from the social activity of the PNPM are not the *penerima manfaat* like them, but rather the BKM members themselves. While my own estimation is that volunteers do not benefit in material terms (as they are often accused) they do benefit in terms of the ability to feel good about their activities, and to realize 'self' through affective reaffirmation. In this particular exchange, these 'warm and self-affirming feelings' do seem of more value to BKM members than the school bags laden with stationary are for the children. Considering the cost–benefit of the participation of *penerima manfaat*—over 150 minutes during a busy time of the day—one can appreciate the restlessness, the flat faces, the failure to be infected by the celebratory feel of the event, and perhaps even a conscious effort to reject it.

So why do they come in the first place? I have written elsewhere (Jakimow 2013) about how NGOs and CBOs require a field of practical action in which 'beneficiaries' can be assembled at short notice, and with little, if any compensation. Several practices are required to sustain this field, including holding out the possibility of future benefits, implicit obligations for current participation and micro-finance. These strategies are also (whether con-sciously or not) employed by BKM members. Volunteers rely on their social networks for participants, and most critically, manage a programme of rotat-ing loans through which they have power over people's access to credit. Further, in a moral atmosphere of *bagi-bagi*, where favouritism is assumed to direct the distribution of welfare programmes, it is an astute decision to remain on the good side of people who are perceived as having some power over resources. In the case of the BKM, this includes not only the resources of the PNPM, but potentially other government programmes, as several mem-bers are also *kaders* (see Chapter Two). For this reason *penerima manfaat* come when called. They do not disrupt the affective practices of the BKM that engender a positive feel, even if they do not contribute to a positive atmos-phere beyond their presence. The management of their feelings, and the fol-lowing of a script of conduct that does not disrupt, even if it is not supportive to this affective practice, can be considered a form of emotional labour (see also Feldman 2007).

Read more strongly, we can view the *penerima manfaat*'s failure to contrib-ute to the feel-good atmosphere of the *acara* as a form of resistance. State-directed welfare and community-driven development exacerbate small differences in social status between development agents and 'developees' (Pigg 1992). Particularly for volunteers of community development pro-grammes such as the PNPM, this may result in social mobility. BKM members and local developers in general share a close social location with the beneficiaries of their projects, and indeed, being a development agent is one of the few distinctions between them. The *acara* makes stark these emerging social hierarchies as BKM members sit alongside government officials, wear uniforms that distinguish them from the *penerima manfaat* and make them part of a social collective with power over government resources. Complaints, accusations, and rumours, pull down people who have the potential to become socially mobile by becoming a development agent. Not expressing either verbally or through one's body language genuine gratitude in an event designed to elicit it could be considered a 'weapon of the weak' (Scott 1987). The capacity not to be moved by or contribute to a feel-good atmosphere of celebrations is one of the few powers that these women have.

The *acara* also reveals, however, the limited power of this capacity. The flat faces of the *penerima manfaat* did not seem to affect the BKM members. They were ignored, misread, and avoided. If there was cynicism, suspicion, or a general bad feeling towards the BKM and their activities, these affects were not contagious. The women's capacity to affect the collective mood of the *acara*, even if unconsciously, was limited. The volunteers' own capacity to affect each other, and to be affected in ways conducive to their self-realization was the stronger of the two forces. The effectiveness of their affective practice in the face of countervailing forces (including but not limited to a moral atmosphere of *bagi-bagi*) helps us to 'understand the power of the event' (Wetherell 2013: 232). The heavily orchestrated nature of PNPM *acaras* makes disruption of their affective practice difficult. At the same time, other bodies in the encounter do have a greater affective force. Had Ibu Camat (the government official) refused to congratulate the BKM and instead use the occasion to express some doubt over the effectiveness of the programme, the affective force would have shattered the generated feel of the affective practice. Here then we need to look not only at the differential capacity to affect an 'other', but also to shape the collective forms of affect in which those differential capacities are engendered.

Conclusion

Development occurs within, and shapes collective conditions that mediate life (Anderson 2014). These conditions attune us to horizons, prompt certain preoccupations, engender feelings, demand a responsiveness. We perceive these conditions at first affectively, they operate below consciousness, impress upon bodies in ways that are unbidden and involuntary. Yet there is still human agency in the production of the conditions themselves. Affect in its transpersonal circulations may be transmissible and contagious, yet humans also generate affects through conscious and unconscious practices. The nature, force and content of these generated affects, the effects of these affects, are not determined or wholly controllable however. In this chapter we have seen how the affective practice of 'feel-good' social work does not, in all circumstances, override a moral atmosphere of *bagi-bagi*, which has the potential to disrupt and derail the affective experiences that volunteers desire and need for their ongoing sense of who they are, and are becoming. What happens in the collision or layering of different forms of collective affect is of significance for understanding local level development.

In particular, attention to collective affect helps reveal overlooked aspects of power configurations in development in two ways. First, these conditions engender the differential capacity/susceptibility to affect and be affected. The potentialities of bodies in relation are never solely dyadic, but rather contain numerous elements, histories, ideas, and so on (Jackson 1998; Ahmed 2004). It is the aggregative work of affects that produce capacities and susceptibilities (Fox 2015). In this chapter I have explored how collective conditions shape the capacity to be affected in ways that reaffirm one's sense of self (through the feel-good affective practice of the *acara*), as well as the susceptibility to be affected in ways that threaten that same sense of self (through the anxiety and fear engendered in a moral atmosphere of *bagi-bagi*). I have also shown how collective conditions increase the susceptibility of volunteers to affect others, to engender suspicion, jealousy, cynicism (in a moral atmosphere of *bagi-bagi*), as well as the capacity of others to affect (through the force of their complaints, as well as their potential to disrupt the feel-good affective practice of BKM activities). The consequences of these differential capacities and susceptibilities are examined in Part III.

The second aspect of power configurations that this chapter identifies is the uneven capacity to shape these collective conditions. Collective tones, moods, and atmospheres are dynamic; they constantly shift with implications for people's capacities and potentialities as outlined earlier in this section. Wetherell (2012, 2013) underlines the need to be attentive to these changes, to see these not as neutral or non-agentive transformations, but as reproductive of certain forms of privilege and unequal relations. The *penerima manfaat* have limited capacity to affect the tone of the *acara*. Unequal relations with BKM members prevents them from openly disturbing the celebratory feel. Further, their inability to disrupt the sense of gratification felt by BKM members despite the manifest (yet not verbally expressed) lack of gratitude by *penerima manfaat*, speaks to the ongoing unequal power relations in local level development. At the same time, *orang biasa* do contribute to the moral atmosphere of *bagi-bagi* that seemingly enhances the capacity of 'beneficiaries' and members of the public to affect BKM members. When we get beyond the scripted spaces of community development, potential disruptions and injuries to BKM members' sense of self become more possible, and effective (Chapter Seven). Whether this is a good or bad thing in the specific circumstances of community development in Medan is an open question, but it is in any case significant for what it suggests about enduring power relations or their transformation.

Questions about how collective affect is generated in spaces of local development is of further significance for examining 'becoming' within these collective conditions. As noted in Part I, we are responsive and attuned to a world which we draw from in our self-making projects, and which imposes upon us in involuntary ways. When the broader environment is not conducive to becoming in ways that one imagines or fantasizes, the sense of self is unsustainable; it undergoes what Berlant (2011) describes as a drama of adjustment. Chapter Four examined the self-imaginaries of women political actors who became Parshads. In Chapter Six, we examine how the collective conditions make these 'selves' untenable in certain circumstances, and the dramas of adjustments that follow as a consequence.

6

Servitude

We often sat with Kashi, a Parshad, in her garden on plastic chairs among the flowers. Her home is on a hill leading out of town, and the air is fresh and cool, pleasant even in May. On one such occasion we were deep in conversation when a local woman approached and interrupted our conversation. She said that she was holding a *puja* (prayer/worship) and the local *mandir* (temple) required cleaning. Her tone was polite, but firm enough to indicate that rather than consider this a favour, she expected that Kashi arrange this task without fuss. Kashi nodded. She did not smile, but neither was annoyance apparent in her voice as she replied that she would send someone to clean the hall. As the woman departed, however, Kashi shook her head and in an incredulous tone asked us to observe the expectations of the people: 'They expect that I should do each and every work. If she is the one holding the *puja*, and it is such a small place, then she should clean it herself. Every day people come to me with such petty work, morning to night, expecting me to do each and everything.'

In 2017, Parshads were four years into their five-year term. Many were at the end of their tether, inundated by angry demands to do work they had no power to complete or that fell outside their responsibility. Many were running around undertaking the 'petty' and non-urgent tasks of constituents, while complaining about the lack of consideration shown for their own circumstances. Such everyday experiences are mostly missing in accounts of local level political actors in India who are most often presented as using (overwhelmingly) *his* status, connections and a coterie of party workers and brokers to provide privileged access to state resources in return for electoral support (see, for example, Berenschot 2010; van Dijk 2011; de Wit 2017). While there were some women Parshads who somewhat fit this description, they were the exception. The majority were like Kashi, whose sense of self and political identity was tied to being a *sevak samajik* (social worker), but who were often positioned as a *naukraanii* or servant, there to do the menial work of their constituents.

This positioning is in part a consequence of the collective conditions in which women Parshads 'become'. As in Chapter Five, I consider the

Susceptibility in Development: Micropolitics of Local Development in India and Indonesia. Tanya Jakimow,
Oxford University Press (2020). © Tanya Jakimow.
DOI: 10.1093/oso/9780198854739.001.0001

multiplicity of affective registers, again returning to the analytical frames of moral atmosphere and affective practice. In the worlds of aspiring and current Parshads in Dehradun, these collective conditions arise from the idea and practices of 'democracy', while also producing democracy as inhabited and lived through its subjects. A moral atmosphere of 'clientelism' envelops and permeates Parshads' encounters with others. In contrast to Chapter Five where affective practices offered a counter force to this moral atmosphere, in this chapter we explore the consequences of mutually reinforcing forms of collective affect. In particular, I examine how the affective practices of supplication during the election campaign resonate in the affective configurations between Parshads and constituents long after the votes are counted. The moral atmosphere of clientelism settles in and augments these affective arrangements.

In this chapter I examine how these collective conditions shape the possibilities for the being and becoming of women Parshads, and the differential capacity/susceptibility to affect and be affected in their encounters with voters. I make two arguments in relation to these two points. First I show how processes of attunement to collective conditions does not always align with their durable sense of self as being a social worker (Chapter Four), resulting in what Berlant (2011) describes as a 'drama of adjustment'. Second, affective practices of supplication during election campaigns within a moral atmosphere of clientelism shape the power configurations ordering social encounters between Parshads and constituents. As a consequence, what is seen as a *temporary* inversion of the power relations that occur during election campaigns (Banerjee 2014) have more long-lasting effects. The consequences of these two findings are examined in more detail in Part III. In Chapter Seven I examine how threats to self, and responses to these threats, hinder reflexive development practices; in Chapter Eight, I examine how differential capacity to affect is a factor in the unequal distribution of state resources. In this chapter, I examine what these collective conditions indicate about India's democracy.

Understanding Democracy Affectively

Democracy as an idea, discourse, and set of affects is a constitutive part of the collective conditions in which political actors dwell. These collective conditions, and the ways democracy shapes and is realized within them, are particular to socio-historical conditions, or in Michelutti's (2007, 2010) terms, part of a 'vernacular democracy'. Michelutti (2010: 47) describes the 'vernacularization of democratic politics' as the process in which new values and practices around democracy become locally embedded, taking shape in relation to pre-existing social and cultural practices, as well as potentially modifying those practices. Studies in the anthropology of democracy that have inspired or built upon this idea (Paley 2002, 2008; Gaonkar 2007) examine the contextual situatedness of democracies, their local meanings, discourses, contestations, and everyday practices. Vernacular democracies invite us to go beyond evaluation of formal institutions and practices against a normative model of how democracy should be, to maintain an analytical openness that can reveal its substantive workings and multiple manifestations. Most critically, anthropology has revealed the way that democracy as an idea and set of practices enacts certain forms of power and potentially reconfigures existing social relations (Paley 2002). This chapter examines the configurations of power produced through democratic practices, in particular the ways democratic practices are shaped by, and in turn shape collective forms of affect.

The anthropological literature on democracies has drawn attention to the symbolic, axiological, discursive, and rhetorical. Attention to the affective can augment these understandings. As affects give meanings, ideas, and symbols their intensity, they shed light on how certain expressions of vernacular democracy come into being (Pedwell and Whitehead 2012). Being attentive to affect can also reveal that which escapes power, or offers the potential for alternative or emergent political logics. For example Kunreuther (2018) examines how sound in democratic protest engenders certain affective responses and political subjectivities in Nepal, while Perman (2010) reveals how dances acquire political meaning by engendering emotions that offer messages of resistance without explicit articulation. Although there is a growing literature on this topic, the affective and emotive registers of democratic practices remain an under-studied element of democracy.[1]

Bedi's (2016) book *The Dashing Ladies of Shiv Sena* is one of the few attempts to bring the affective into an analysis of vernacular democracies. Her concept of 'affective grids' is particularly useful to examine the generation of political and symbolic power, and how such circulations shape other forms of power. She describes affective grids as 'performative, material, symbolic,

---

[1] Emotions and affect have not been wholly absent in the political science literature on democracy, but has mostly been used in relation to a normative project. For example, political scientists have examined the 'emotive', 'irrational' and 'unreasonable' elements of democracy as a danger, for example in the guise of ethnonationalist movements. As Markell (2000) argues, however, affect and emotions can also establish the commitments and identifications with liberal democratic values and practices.

embodied and emotive registers' (Bedi 2016: xvii), comprised of political transactions and offering fields of potentialities. Her ethnographically rich account of Shiv Sena women in Maharashtra reveals the ways that narratives and practices of 'dashing' and dangerous transgression, power affective grids in ways that renew symbolic resources and political authority. Their outer self-representations and deeper self-understandings are in part framed by the 'affective and symbolic grids of political obligation that sustain the everyday life of the state and political parties in India' (Bedi 2016: xviii). In other words, the affects generated through their regular practices such as protests and marches, as well as the more exceptional experiences of campaigning, deeply inform a sense of self in relation to others, and the nature of that relationship.

While Bedi's (2016) research reveals the generation of political and symbolic power through these affective grids, my own research in Dehradun was revelatory of the way affective configurations diminish the power of women political actors. While the term 'affective grids' evokes electricity and generative potentialities, I use the term affective configuration to capture the possibilities for ordering through affect. I am particularly interested in the (re)production of affective arrangements, that is the patterning of affects engendered in the relations between bodies within a socio-historical 'micro-relational milieu' (Slaby and Mühlhoff 2019: 1). The relational dynamic between bodies is entangled with symbolic and discursive registers, including those related to democracy. Patterns of affective recruitment (the way bodies are predisposed to feeling in particular ways in social encounters) are bound to, and can be reproductive of power, while also having an openness that means there is always the possibility of disruption. I examine women political actors within these affective configurations, not only in terms of how they enhance their power (as in Bedi 2016), but also attentive to the possibilities of diminishment in their encounters with other bodies.

I examine the patterning or ordering within affective configurations through the concepts introduced in Chapter Five (see the section 'Affective Practice'). Wetherell's (2012, 2015) useful concept of affective practice high-lights the way that affective configurations/arrangements come to be repro-duced, or produced anew. As seen in Chapter Five, affective practice refers to the ways individuals are predisposed to feeling particular ways, and repro-ducing those affective patterns through collective social practices. Affective practice is thus 'a moment of recruitment, articulation or enlistment when many complicated flows…entangle and intertwine together to form just this affective moment, episode or atmosphere' (Wetherell 2015: 160). Affective responses, as manifest in practices, produce the socio-historical context, and in this way, 'affective activity is a field of open and flexible patterns' (Wetherell 2015: 147). I am interested in the patterns, or affective configurations that are produced anew through democratic practices. In particular, I examine the affective practices of local body elections in Dehradun, arguing that they produce affective configurations that resonate long after election day. The second element, moral atmosphere, refers to the inescapable presence, tension, or energy that infects encounters between local development actors and citizens, which relates to, but exceeds a moral logic. In Dehradun, the moral atmosphere infecting the work of Parshads is that of clientelism.

A Moral Atmosphere of Clientelism

India is often described as a patronage democracy (Chandra 2004; Piliavsky 2014; Manor 2016): a continuation of pre-colonial institutions in which personal connections to leaders are important to people's access to opportunities and resources (Witsoe 2011; Piliavsky 2014). In democratic post-colonial India, patrons are most often those with access to state resources, obtainable by being elected into a position with authority over those resources (Pattenden 2011). Over time, the durable relationships of patronage have been replaced by a more short-term clientelism: 'the distribution of patronage (goods, services, funds, and favours) through networks of clients to selected social groups in the (often vain) hope of winning their votes' (Manor 2016: 244). As a consequence, 'elections have become auctions for the sale of government services' (Chandra 2004), with a vote exchanged for the provision of goods such as security and the smooth processing of claims made on the state. While these can be short-term transactions, the party-centric nature of India's clientelism in comparison to, for example, Indonesia, means that enduring relationships between party supporters and their cadre are also part of the moral idiom of Indian politics (Piliavsky 2014; Aspinall and Berenschot 2019). Clientelism frames the mutual obligations and expectations between representatives and voters.

The moral logic of clientelism is productive of a certain breed of politician, and cultural interpretations of their practices. Piliavsky argues it has led to the creation of 'legions of elected and informally acting politicians, whose work consists primarily of helping citizens access the state.... But in both popular imagination and politicians' rhetoric these efforts appear as *personal* favours and gifts' (Piliavsky (2014: 7, emphasis added). In scholarship, the media, and everyday conversations, politicians are seen as being purely driven by electoral calculation and material gain, and as 'shrewd operators...and "political entrepreneurs"' (de Wit 2017: 164–5). Any suggestion that they are driven by other motivations, such as genuinely wanting to do good, are met with cynicism. In Chapter Five, I outlined how a moral atmosphere of '*bagi-bagi*' (each taking their share) led to a preoccupation with the possibility of immoral practices, making community volunteers susceptible to engendering cynicism and suspicion in others in Medan. The stink of potentially corrupt and immoral practices is perhaps even more pungent among Indian local level politicians, fuelled by a scandal hungry media.

In part this susceptibility to affect (engender feelings in others) is due to voters' expectations that politicians bend rules and act in potentially corrupt ways, with moral character a second order priority compared to getting things done for their constituents. Piliavsky and Sbriccoli (2016) argue that such characterizations of India's politicians are not necessarily negative, but rather are part of an 'ethics of efficacy' that values what one can achieve more than the type of person one is. While male political actors (and they only talk about men) may engender a sense of awe in others through their ability to get things done regardless of the moral rights and wrongs of such actions, women engender different affects in others when they operate in the same way. Although there are always exceptions (Bedi 2016), generally women are punished politically if they are seen to be engaged in 'dirty politics' (Rai 2012). That is, while both men and women may engender certain suspicions in others on account of them being political actors, the evaluation of these is shaped by gendered ideologies.

While the moral atmosphere of clientelism hangs thickly around politicians, it also infects voters. Much of the literature still describes a vertical relationship between these two actors (Berenschot 2010; van Dijk 2011), but in pockets of India, these hierarchies seem to be flattening, if not reversing. Increased political competition due to the electoral demise of Congress and the rise of caste and regional parties has led to a growing assertiveness of a citizenry who make demands on politicians (Manor 2016). Politicians in Bihar refer to ' "corruption from below," the feeling of entitlement that a voter has to make concrete demands of the politicians that he or she helped to elect' (Witsoe 2011: 626). There are now several accounts in which voters verbally abuse politicians, or else mobilize caste or familial identities as a means to get them to do their specific work. These changing power dynamics can be understood as both a shift in the terms of trade (in particular, the value of a vote against the perceived ease with which a politician can secure resources), as well as a moral idiom of clientelism that intersects with others markers of identity, most importantly caste. These explanations are centred on a direct relationship between the voter (who may share a caste or clan identity) and the politician (come patron). I argue that an additional explanatory factor are changes to the 'micro-relational milieu' (Slaby and Mühlhoff 2019: 1), producing a new relational dynamic and affective arrangements between voters *in general* and politicians *in general*. That is, the collective forms of affect that pattern the recruitment of bodies to feel in particular ways in social encounters (in this case between politician and voter) have changed.

The moral atmosphere of clientelism helps us to understand these dynamics by drawing attention to the affective conditions ordering political encounters. A voter standing before a politician has a bravado, emboldened to make demands based not on any actual prior transaction between them, but based on a sense of entitlement, itself made manifest and intensified through ideas of democracy. Such bravado is relational with the micro-charges of the body of the politician. Within a moral atmosphere of clientelism, the politician is susceptible to engender cynicism, disdain, scorn: the politician's susceptibility to affect makes possible the voter's capacity to feel emboldened. Politicians are sticky with affect, not as the body's characteristic, but 'as an effect of the histories of contact between bodies, objects, and signs' (Ahmed 2004: 90, emphasis removed). That is, the socio-historical context, which includes a pervasive sense of clientelism, establishes the conditions of the social encounter, its potentialities and probabilities, before the encounter takes place. The moral atmosphere of clientelism already hangs over political actors and is a constituent force in the affective arrangements between them and others. In this way, the force of clientelism exceeds its actual practices, becoming a background or setting in which individuals dwell and encounters take place.

Emotionally Charged Elections

Elections are a series of encounters between would be elected representatives and constituents. They are a critical time for the establishment and communication of expectations between voters and politicians, and as such, elections make evident and produce power relations, particularly in local level politics (Lama-Rewal 2009). Elections have been studied as rituals that establish or show commitment to an understanding of power, the role of leaders, and their relationships with constituents (Hauser and Singer 1986). As events that are rich with symbols, myths, and meaning-laden practices (Paley 2002), they are also generative of affects. The emotionally charged atmosphere of elections can intensify social encounters, with heightened responsiveness to the cues of the other. Examining election 'rituals' as affective practices (Wetherell 2013) reveals their potential to shape the affective configurations between candidate and voter. Affective practices reverberate in the social encounters between elected representatives and constituents throughout Parshads' five-year term, in some cases solidifying what are often seen in the literature as only fleeting reversals of social hierarchies.

Numerous studies point to the significance of elections for poor people as moments when their subordinated positions are inverted (Banerjee 2014). Campaigns are times when otherwise neglected and discriminated against individuals and groups can demand an audience with politicians. For this reason, door-to-door campaigning and constituency visits are important in the electoral strategies of candidates as well as expected by voters (Singer 2007). Carswell and de Neve (2014) underline the emotional importance of the act of voting, which provides an opportunity for marginalized people to receive recognition and respect and to assert themselves as members of political communities. Poor people mistreated during ordinary times are equals on election day, and hence voting is a valued right (Ahuja and Chibber 2012). For all citizens, the act of voting can engender feelings of entitlement among constituents, and is thereby generative of a particular democratic logic that results in an assertive citizenry (Witsoe 2011). Indeed, it is my contention that the political subjectivities made possible through the experience of being equal and of receiving respect do not simply disappear after an election, but continue to inform one's sense of self within a social imaginary.

While a great deal of literature examines the emotional significance of elections for voters, and especially poor voters, there are few studies of the experiences of candidates (see Mahler 2006 for an exception). Elections are emotionally charged events, full of tension and excitement for candidates who have a great deal at stake. Candidates invest financially, as money is necessary to fuel campaigns and create relationships (Björkman 2014), and affectively, in that they make an affective investment in a sense of their present and future self. As seen in Chapter Four, for women in Dehradun this self often included a self-imaginary of being a social worker, appreciated and loved by the people. Elections are moments when this sense of self is reaffirmed, or even made possible, through their encounters with a supportive constituency. But as Zigon and Throop (2014) remind us, acts that involve the making of self through the forming of relations with others also puts at risk the relational self that becomes in and through these experiences. During elections the attempt to forge a new sense of self or public identity tests the secure self (as social worker), quantified by the number of votes one receives. It is therefore not surprising that candidates in the 2018 Urban Local Body elections in Dehradun described the campaign as emotionally gruelling, exacting not just a physical toll, but a psychic one as well. Campaigns are times of heightened susceptibility for candidates with much at stake.

Door-to-door Campaigning

Aditi is a seasoned campaigner; the 2018 municipal elections were her third as a candidate, and her first as incumbent Parshad. Each day of the four week campaign she stood before voters to be evaluated. The most important strategy in local elections is door-to-door campaigning, described by candidates as 'the most powerful weapon that women have'. Unlike men, women can enter the home and sit with the women of the household, developing bonds. Prior to the start of the campaign, these door-to-door activities were described by aspiring candidates as entailing long discussions over tea in the kitchen. Once the campaign started, however, the pressure to get round the entire ward of around 5,000 voters several times makes it difficult to linger. There is a subtle politics that determines how long Aditi spends at each house. The majority of visits are less than a couple of minutes, and sometimes barely long enough to give a leaflet and 'show their face' to the people. But other residents are able to demand more time, and successfully insist on making candidates stay for tea and just one more sweet.

Visiting poor and lower caste households has a particular symbolic significance. Aditi, a high-caste Hindu (Brahmin), moves quickly through the Valmiki colony (Valmiki is a *jati* that is a Scheduled Caste, or Dalit), but is sure to take drinks from at least a couple of households. The woman we approach is prepared with plastic cups and her son hastily purchases some cool fizzy drink from the nearby shop. Such practices help Aditi circumvent norms of untouchability that would be directly contravened if she were to drink tea made in the kitchen and served from the household crockery. There is some discomfort, but it is necessary. As she said later, 'If you want people to vote for you, then you need to sit with the people. I am a public figure, and so I need to do this'. She does not speak of the discomfort of the Valmiki household, who know these rules of engagement and do not hesitate to comply with what could be read as insulting modifications to a campaign ritual. Aditi brags that Valmiki people used to vote Congress, but now they all support her party.

Aditi's political training prepares her for such encounters; the training includes an affective counter-pedagogy. Highmore (2010: 136) argues that our 'affect horizons', our sensorial attunements to the world, 'are the result of a deep pedagogy'. He uses the example of an Anglo English man eating a fiery curry that suggests a willingness to transform one's evaluative judgements: what is disgusting, or delicious, the (dis)comfort of the chilli burn. The man undertakes an affective counter-pedagogy, that is, he learns to have different bodily responses to sensations, which Highmore (2011) argues can be the start of an affective politics. Likewise we can see Aditi's lack of disgust at taking a drink from the Valmiki household as a form of affective training. While her response is in many ways offensive, as she is still practising a form of untouchability, it is nonetheless remarkable given her upbringing. I have seen others (not political actors) shy away from the touch of a Dalit person, and Aditi's family continues to admonish her for entering their homes at all. Aditi claims that she would happily accept tea in Dalit homes were it not for her family's feelings. Whether true or not, she showed no hesitation, no involuntary response to being in the Valmiki home. This counter-affective pedagogy (Highmore 2011) is critical to seasoned politicians such as Aditi, an important affective practice that establishes relations between her and Dalit households. Aditi credits this (affective) practice as more effective than acts which bring material goods for garnering support in the area.[2]

Each day of campaigning, Aditi was joined by around fifteen supporters, with roughly a quarter to a third being men. She is a stunning woman in her *saree*, covered by a cardigan, with somewhat incongruous joggers on her feet. The latter are crucial for the amount of walking to be done, as well as to navigate the alleys with broken tiles, mounds of garbage, and pools of water. When encountering these obstacles Aditi simply hitches up her *saree* and marches on, with only a slight hint of distaste. Her supporters are more vocal of the perils involved in their work, complaining about the sight of garbage and how the untidiness of the area reflects on residents. For Aditi these materialities engendered different feelings. As a person responsible for the collection of garbage and the fixing of roads, each flaw in the ward is a subtle indictment of her record.[3] Being an incumbent gives these failings a visceral

[2] In a contrasting affective experience, we followed Kashi, a Dalit, as she campaigned for the BSP in a seat reserved for SC. The reactions of some voters who pulled away from her, would not open the gate, and her training to remain at the threshold, not enter the home of higher caste households, was a repetitive affirmation of her low status.
[3] Her term had finished in May 2018: six months before the elections were held. Administrators were appointed by the state in the interim to undertake the functions of the Parshad, yet when they did not perform these tasks adequately, it was the (now former) Parshad who was seen as being at

charge. Walking through the wards with other incumbent Parshads, their eyes were drawn to roads not fixed, lights not working, areas where water flooded, mounds of rubbish. These problems demanded, engendered, an attentiveness that would not be as urgent during non-campaign periods (see Throop and Duranti 2014).

Door after door, Aditi greets the occupants, acting as warmly as she can while repeating an election spiel for the umpteenth time that day and that campaign. She is particularly attentive to the signs of deference required. She touches the feet of elderly men and women, holds the hands of the infirm, and gives 'pranaam' (a greeting that signals obeisance) to people who are upper class or in other ways demanded respect. There was a different tenor of these greetings as opposed to her day-to-day interactions as Parshad. Through tone and gesture she communicated her supplication. The voter would nearly always respect the limits of the supplication, that is, accept Aditi touching their feet and only then laughing and taking her hand to gesture that it is not necessary. The act allowed Aditi to signal her suitability as Parshad without losing her stature as a high-caste, middle-class woman. Elderly and not so elderly men and women would call her *beti* (daughter), or *bahu* (daughter-in-law). Other people she would greet in more status-neutral terms, evoking friendliness, similarity, and warmth. These voters would for the most part return such gestures with genuine affection, or at the least in a tone that did not disrupt the tone of the encounter.

Such relationship building demands that one give oneself fully in encounters in which one is also susceptible to rejection. In the times we joined Aditi, there were only small slights: the person who did not hear her out before closing the gate, the failure to return a smile, a coldness in the greeting. Often after such occasions Aditi's supporters would laugh and make fun of the voter, thereby neutralizing or softening the insult. Aditi would carry on, usually without comment, perhaps with a raised eyebrow. Although fleeting, each slight had the potential to inflict a small affective mark, a small dent in Aditi's confidence, engendering uncertainty and anxiety. After one day of largely positive encounters with voters, I was surprised by the anxiety in Aditi's face. I asked how confident she was: 'Yeah, I am confident...but I am worried. One never knows what the people are thinking. They can say one thing, and then vote another'. Such anxieties were repeated by other candidates, including

---

fault. Most Parshads therefore continued their work in the six months leading up to the elections, as any failings would damage their re-election campaigns.

those whose support and track record made their re-election seem guaranteed. Aditi was one such candidate and she won by a large margin.

Supplication

The modes of relationality shaped through the campaign influence Aditi's work following her election. This is perhaps a mundane observation, as the exchange of symbolic and material resources during election campaigns create mutual bonds of obligation (Hauser and Singer 1986; Witsoe 2011; Björkman 2014). What has been less remarked upon in the literature are how the affective practices of elections are generative of certain affective configurations, with consequences for inchoate and barely perceptible forms of power. The routines and rituals of the campaign are like other social encounters and come with 'affective slots for actors already sketched (in this situation you do superiority, I do abasement and deference, or *vice versa*)' (Wetherell 2012: 125). Candidates and voters alike are recruited into these affected slots; the former is in a dependent and hence inferior position, needing the votes of the latter, while the voter in this affective configuration is in a commanding position, perhaps emboldened, assertive, superior. The rituals of the campaign, particularly going door to door, are an affective practice that (temporarily) inverses enduring social hierarchies between them based on other positionings, related to caste and class for example.

I describe these affective practices as supplication. In order to address the unequal relations between researchers and subjects of research, England (1994) advocates supplication for feminist researchers. Supplication 'involves exposing and exploiting weaknesses regarding dependence on whoever is being researched ... [thereby] explicitly acknowledge[ing] his/her reliance on the research subject' (1994: 82). England's approach is an ethical strategy, part of a feminist politics in which solidarity is the basis of research, requiring a flattening of hierarchies between what is (usually) the privileged researcher, and the marginal 'researched'. Supplication can also, however, ease the research process by gaining the trust and openness of the research subject. Similarly, I suggest that women political candidates endear themselves to voters when they over-emphasize their dependence on them. They downplay and potentially inverse social hierarchies in which the candidate is in a superior position in relation to the voter, while at the same time, they over-emphasize the hierarchies when they are in encounters with their social superiors. These acts of supplication are not, I suggest, a purposeful or conscious strategy.

Rather the affective practices of the campaign produce the affective slots of supplication that women candidates inhabit. Each knock on the door entails a repeat of this supplication, producing anew the affective configuration that arranges the relations between candidate and voter.

In affective practices of supplication, the individual is the site of transformation and pattern-making. A person's 'affective history...the ongoingness of a particular subject, their repetitions and continuities' are critical to the ways they are affected, their predisposition to affective slots, and how they are transformed in these encounters (Wetherell 2012: 125). In this way 'present [affective] practice intertwines with their past practice' (Wetherell 2012: 125). Dispositions to be affected in a particular way shape practices that then go on to sediment and produce anew the patterning of affect in encounters. The campaign itself is a form of affective training in which candidates and voters develop the susceptibility and capacity to be affected in particular ways. Aditi's affective pedagogy to not feel uncomfortable in a Dalit home is the most obvious example, but such training occurs in more subtle ways. The repetition of the act of supplication trains one to occupy the slot of deference in relation to a range of actors that are otherwise one's social inferior or equal.

Gendered affective biographies influence this affective training. In part this is due to the division of political and emotional labour of the campaign. As noted, women are able to, and responsible for, door-to-door meet and greet, and are therefore more subject to the repetitions of supplication. I only campaigned with women, and it was a UNSW male student intern (Lennon) who generated empirical material from the campaign of a male candidate.[4] The only two women in the entourage accompanied the male candidate to the door while the large number of male supporters waited some distance back. On one occasion a female voter started to complain that the street floods during the monsoon. The candidate quickly promised that he would fix the problem immediately after being elected. An English-speaking supporter explained to Lennon what was happening in the encounter. He described the candidate as needing to be manipulative: 'You have to make promises, but promises are made to be broken...as a candidate you have to make promises that you know you will not be able to keep'. He continued that the candidate

---

[4] I am indebted to Lennon White for these observations. Lennon joined the campaign of one man on three occasions, with no comparison with other male candidates. He informed all the people he spoke to of the research, and the potential use of his observations as part of my research. The empirical material he was able to generate as a young white man, was distinctly different to what I would have been able to generate as a middle-aged white woman, even given access to the same campaign.

would not help this woman post-election, but would talk himself out of it: 'These people get enough things, the government gives them so much, and so they expect all of these things, all this "individual service" from the Parshad'.

As we will see, women Parshads often had to accede to the demands for individual service from constituents. Further, I never heard any woman candidate act or speak as flippantly about the promises made to voters. That is not to say that they did not or would not break promises made during a campaign, but the intentionality to do so could never be discussed, and I believe not even countenanced. I suggest that the practice of making promises has a different affective force for women candidates that make their blatant disregard difficult. The heightened susceptibility of the candidate during the election campaign when their sense of who they are is tested before the voters, makes an affective pedagogy of supplication particularly effective for women. Their senses are attuned to be highly responsive to voters and sharply self-critical. The physical evidence of past failures or current deficiencies by way of rubbish, the social gestures that communicate a lack of conviction, or outright hostility impress upon the candidate, and have a weightier force during the campaign. Relational to this susceptibility is the greater capacity of voters to affect through subtle gestures of rejection, outward displays of anger, or the engendering of anxiety by describing deficiencies. Voters, too, are undertaking an affective pedagogy in inhabiting superiority and a sense of entitlement, in their social encounters with candidates.

Demands

These two conditions—a moral atmosphere of clientelism alongside the affective practices of election campaigns—resonate in the experiences of women Parshads far into their electoral term. These conditions are productive of an assertive citizenry (Witsoe 2011) who make demands on their Parshad regardless of the actual transactions between them during campaigns, and whether or not they voted for them. That is, the sense of entitlement to the Parshad *exceeds* the moral logic of clientelism in terms of who is bound to its norms, and the limits of en*force*ability of mutual obligations. I argue that the collective conditions of affect *embolden* the voter to make demands: an emboldening that is only possible within the affective configuration that shapes encounters with Parshads. Furthermore, this affective configuration augments the force of their demands, and the susceptibility of the Parshad to be affected in such a way that they meet them despite their unreasonableness.

Citizens may be assertive, but as outlined in Chapter Two, the capacity of Parshads to satisfy their demands is low. They lack discretionary funding and, for many, the social and cultural capital to work through other mechanisms to get things done. The need to work through Members of Legislative Assemblies (MLAs) not only restricts what they do, but also their ability to get credit for their accomplishments. It was not unusual for women Parshads to develop proposals based on the people's needs and oversee the completion of work, only to see that it is the name of the MLA that adorns the signboard marking the success of the project. Their financial dependence on others to get things done therefore frustrates the women's 'politics of presence' (Bedi 2016) required for successful politicians. Further, unlike men, women cannot hang around tea shops bragging about their accomplishments. Such occupation of public space is not socially acceptable and most are busy with household chores during the evenings when men are in the streets chatting. Voters often do not know or care about these external constraints to their work, and rather attribute women's failure to 'get things done' as being due to incompetence or lack of suitability for the job.

Many Parshads therefore devote energy to tasks they can achieve, in particular, helping constituents access entitlements. The importance of Municipal Councillors (MCs) in facilitating the flow of information between citizens and the state and connecting the former to entitlements is well-known (John 2007; Berenschot 2010; van Dijk 2011; Shekhar-Swain 2012; de Wit 2017). What is less remarked upon is that this type of work may be one of the few things that MCs can actually achieve. Many women Parshads in Dehradun presented the number of pensions or ration cards obtained in the ward as their biggest, if not their only achievements. For this reason, many Parshads go out of their way to complete all the formalities on behalf of the constituent. As we walk with Parshads through their wards, we are introduced to people who now receive pensions or ration cards and who profess their appreciation and, presumably, loyalty. Beyond votes, these acts engender affects in Parshads, which animate them to continue this work. Devani introduced us to one elderly man who she and her husband had helped to receive a pension. Speaking to the man at the front of their one room home, it was hard not to be moved by his account of what a difference the small pension had made in his life. Work that engenders these small satisfactions are one of the most straightforward outcomes to achieve. I examine these animations in more detail in Chapter Eight.

In this chapter, I examine how the nature of many of the demands voters make on Parshads signal a different kind of relationality. Like Kashi in the opening scene, in 2017 many Parshads complained about the unreasonable demands made by voters and the relentless amount of work they had to do as a result. There are several aspects to these demands that make them distinct from claims based on mutual obligations between patron and client. First, what voters are often demanding is the *devolving* of the task of engaging with a burdensome state. Government procedures to obtain entitlements are incredibly burdensome, demanding patience not only of citizens (Auyero 2012), but also of MCs. Even a simple pension has convoluted processes, requiring multiple signatures, each entailing travel to a different office. In contrast to the literature on MCs (Berenschot 2010; Van Djik 2011; de Wit 2017), the Parshads I knew did not have a coterie of party workers helping them to undertake these everyday tasks. They spent much of their time engaged in these types of activitives, as well as money from their own pockets. As Parshads do not receive a honorarium or 'sitting fee',[5] many depend on their husbands or children to financially support these activities. Simple constituent demands can therefore exacerbate women's financial dependence within the household.

The voter, unaware of or uncaring about these difficulties, devolve the financial and opportunity costs of engaging with the state to women Parshads. For some voters, the Parshad is obliged to undertake the work of engaging with the state. Devani told us of another man she helped get an old age pension. She provided the form, wrote a letter of support, and took this documentation to various government offices to be verified. To complete the application, the man only needed to visit the welfare department so that they could verify his age in person. He refused, saying 'this is not my work, this is your work, as you are the Parshad.' He only relented when Devani's husband agreed to accompany him. Another Parshad, Ananda, complained that engaging with the state has become a significant task: 'People do not go to the Nagar Nigam [city municipal office] themselves. They think that I am the representative, and so it is your work and you should go. We do not even receive a honorarium, yet we have to pay for our phone, *aanaa, jaanaa* [transport, coming and going]'.

The second aspect to these demands is that voters do not *depend* on the Parshads to meet them. Contra the relations between patron and client in which the latter *needs* the help of the former to gain access to services, for

---

[5] Women Parshads attempted to pressure the Dehradun Nagar Nigam to provide an honorarium. After several years of campaigning, they were offered an amount considered insulting, and therefore rejected by the Parshads. The issue was left pending at the time the new cohort of Parshads were sworn in.

voters in Dehradun, the demand is made in order to make their lives less burdensome. The old man in Devani's account was capable of visiting the welfare office, but perhaps anticipating delays and wishing to reduce his inconvenience, demanded to be accompanied. The expectation that Parshads should reduce or bear the inconvenience of dealing with a convoluted state, is most stark in Indrani's complaint. On meeting a man from her ward in the Nagar Nigam arranging his *Aadhar* (biometric identification) card, he demanded to know if Indrani had eaten lunch yet. He complained that he was having to wait in line without eating while she had a full stomach. The man had significant cultural and social capital and was perfectly capable of doing this task. Nonetheless, he made it sound as if it was the Parshad's responsibility. 'People have such mentality that the Parshad should stand in a queue and get their work done' Indrani complained.

Indrani also complained about the third aspect of these demands: they were made without regard for the Parshad:

> Today someone was knocking at my gate at 6 am. I was not well and still resting....He said, 'I want your signature for electricity clearance.' I told him that my timings are on the board on the gate. He yelled at me that since I am the Parshad, I should do his work....For people, what matters is their convenience and their work. They totally ignore others' convenience and don't value their time.

It is not unusual for voters to approach MCs at any time of the day across India, particularly if there is a perceived emergency or if a matter is sensitive (Berenschot 2010; van Dijk 2011; de Wit 2017). Parshads in Dehradun do not resent 24-hour availability but complain that people come at any time for work that is petty and not urgent. Gender plays a role in these expectations. Women are more likely to be found at home, and thus prone to interruptions. While such availability is an advantage for women political actors as they are able to form relations with constituents (Bedi 2016), for many women Parshads in Dehradun, it meant they had no time for themselves and their household work.

A final aspect of these demands is that they often fall very much outside the purview of a Parshad's role. MCs often do work that falls outside of their official responsibilities to build political capital and demonstrate competence (Ghosh and Lama-Rewel 2005; Berenschot 2010; van Dijk 2011; de Wit 2017). The list of demands in Dehradun seems to border on the absurd however. Aditi told us:

This lady called to ask for a plumber. This was a personal problem and not the area's issue. They expect that first I should give the contact details of the plumber and then negotiate the rate. So it is the responsibility of a Parshad to arrange a plumber for you! They expect so much. They don't have time for themselves.

Other demands we heard about or observed included booking hotel accommodation, arranging furniture for a private event and constructing covers over drains to the driveways of private residences. As Aisha exclaimed: 'Their expectations are so high, they think the Parshad should even sweep their homes. They think we are a free *naukaar* [servant].'

Servitude

I suggest that casting the Parshad as a servant is possible due to the affective configuration between Parshads and voters. The supplication of the Parshad, a lingering after-*affect* of the elections resonates in future affective arrangements, so that the voter cum constituent is emboldened to make demands on the elected representative that exceed the moral norms governing their relationship. At the same time, Parshads are susceptible to being affected by these demands, at times compelling them to meet them despite their unreasonableness. I examine the circumstances in which Parshads do, or do not accede to these demands in Chapter Eight. Here I examine how these demands are indicative of a relationship between Parshads and voters based on servitude. 'Servitude' is not a moral idiom, but rather a non-normative relationality based on, and supportive of, patterns of potentialities to affect and be affected. Within these affective configurations, voters are slotted into the role of entitled citizen, while Parshads are cast into a role that is akin to a servant, or *naukraanii* in Hindi.

I use the feminine form for servant, *naukraanii*, rather than the more common masculine *naukaar* for two reasons. First, as noted above, there are indications that it is a positioning more likely to be inhabited by women. Second, there are parallels between the tasks Parshads undertake and a gendered division of labour in the household. *Naukraanii*, is analogous to the 'tedium of daily household chores [that] still falls largely on the woman's shoulders' (Munshi 1998: 580). The devolving of household tasks to Parshads may be in part due to changes in the family structure in urban areas from joint to nuclear families, with a consequent loss of feminized labour in the household.

Sushma, a two-term Parshad, says that the problem of being called on to do petty tasks is because '[e]very single person is disturbed with their work and responsibilities', while Aditi noted above that voters 'expect so much. *They don't have time for themselves*' (emphasis added). The changes are most stark for middle-class families, as poor women have for a long time worked outside the home. Indeed, it is the demands from 'posh areas' that are seen as increasing and/or most unreasonable. This is also the class who do not face 'social handicaps' (de Wit 2017) and hence are not dependent on Parshads for access to the state.

The positioning as 'servant' has parallels with the familial relations that women Parshads claim as part of their political identities—but with important differences. Ghosh and Lama-Rewel (2005: 131) found in their study of women MCs across India, that it was not unusual for women to present themselves as being the surrogate housewife of the ward:

> Comparing a constituency to a large household has long been a favourite figure of speech for women politicians, by presenting themselves as superhousewives. In other words, they make themselves acceptable in a domain where women's presence is an exception, by likening it to the domain that is defined by women's presence.

Parshads in Dehradun also use such rhetorical strategies. Devani described herself as 'a daughter, daughter-in-law, of the whole ward'. Her husband, with evident pride adds 'her nature is that she speaks very softly to people whosoever comes to our house, so she has earned praise from everybody that their daughter-in-law's nature is very good'. The cultural-symbolic demeanour of the daughter-in-law is one of servitude, to be responsive to the demands of her new family in recognition of her expendability and without expectation of prestige or honour (Ross 1961; Munshi 1998; Lamb 2000). Devani is not a submissive or unassertive woman, yet she and her husband draw on an ideal of North Indian womanhood that highlights her subservience.

Although women Parshads may gain some political mileage out of being a 'daughter-in-law', I argue that this positioning is more effective as a euphemism for the actual relations between ward member and constituent, rather than an effective 'style' that can garner support. By treating 'daughter-in-law' and 'housewife' as a political style (see Price and Ruud 2010), we are reading at face value politicians' claims that their political identities are a case of self-authorship. In revealing the ways Parshads are cast in the position of *naukraanii*, attention is drawn to the power of constituents to shape these identities as well as the limitations of Parshads' own self-authoring. For this reason, I avoid a second Hindi equivalent for servant: *sevak*. In part this is because *sevak* has been appropriated by Hindu nationalist organizations to describe 'servants to the Hindu nation' (see Beckerlegge 2015). However, the reason for rejecting the term here is rather different, in that *sevak* is also a political 'style'/self-representation, and perhaps more critically, a core part of many politicians' self-imaginary (Ciotti 2012). *Naukraanii*, in contrast, is neither politically advantageous, nor aligned to self-understandings; it is a threat to both.

The fantasy of what life will be like as a Parshad, as well as their pre-existing sense of self as social worker, can therefore radically differ from their experiences after they win the election. Devani spoke about the sharp transformation that occurred: 'Earlier, they [people in her ward] used to ask me about me, my family and how am I doing. But now they are contacting me only to get the things done.' Almost immediately people whom she had known for years stopped asking how she was when they came for work. Invitations to special events had hidden agendas, with expectations that she would ensure that there are no electricity blackouts, the roads are clean, and that she will arrange the disinfected powder to be laid out on the road that gives events a festive feel. People's interest is not in her as a person engendering affection or love, as would be expected by an actual daughter or daughter-in-law. Nor does she have the authority as might be expected of someone of her status. Instead, the encounter between Parshad and voter is business-like, stripped of its friendly or familial affections. While Parshads continue to describe themselves as social workers, this imaginary is not always sustainable in their relational encounters.

Dramas of Adjustment

Returning to the scene with Kashi with which the chapter opened, we can read her annoyance as having deeper roots than the mere inconvenience of having to accomplish an unwelcome task. What is at stake is not solely her time, but also her positioning within an affective configuration. The desires and imaginaries of the role, tied to a sense of self in occupation of that role, is of someone who engenders awe, affection, gratitude in others, and who in return experiences satisfaction, love, even power. On being elected, women Parshads are treated as merely a tool of convenience, and in return, they feel exploited and taken for granted. The affective slots sketched out for them in social encounters with voters are the opposite of what they had expected:

feelings of obligation or compulsion land on them, while voters seem infected by a sense of entitlement and emboldening.

Read alongside the affective investment that women make in a sense of self as being a social worker, loved and respected by the people (Chapter Four), being cast as a servant of only instrumental value can be wrenching. Women Parshads' fantasies of the 'good life', the ordinary everyday of their *being* a Parshad, are discordant with the actual conditions of life (Berlant 2011). I suggest that for many women Parshads, such incompatibilities between who one thought one is and who one is in actual relation, entails what Berlant (2011: 3) describes as a 'drama of adjustment'. Like the protagonists in *Cruel Optimism*, the ordinary becomes a space not for realizing the self of one's affective attachments, but rather of adjusting to the actual possibilities of being within the topography for self (Berlant 2011: 3). The dissolution of these optimistic scenarios do not necessarily lead to the abandonment of these ideas of self, but rather require a re-telling that can cause Parshads to double-down on these fantasies. Parshads invest even more in relations that are ultimately cruel, redefining them as familial relations even though they lack affection. Complaints about voters presented as singular instances also help to maintain the fantasy. Parshads avoid questions as to what unreasonable and aggressive demands signal about the self-in-relation to a singular encounter, thereby protecting their imagined relationship to constituents in general.

Comparison with the volunteers in Chapter Five indicates how the layering of different collective forms of affect shapes the becoming of development agents and their relations with others. Unlike in Medan, where volunteers engaged in affective practices that counteracted the moral atmosphere of *bagi-bagi*, in Dehradun, the moral atmosphere of clientelism and affective practices of supplication are mutually reinforcing. These collective forms of affect are part of the conditions that make certain selves (im)possible, and (im)probable, as we are responsive to the world as it impresses upon us. In Medan, affective practices made the becoming of someone doing good possible; in Dehradun, affective practices of supplication made Parshads' becoming a 'servant' probable. These are not their only sense of self or self-representation. We are multiple selves as we move through different 'worlds' to which we belong (Biehl and Locke 2017). The possibilities for becoming that I have focused on are important as they pertain to the motivations, beliefs, and values of local development actors. As Fechter (2012a) notes, the personal is important as it shapes development processes and the possibilities for change (see also Jakimow 2015), as we explore in Part III.

The collective affective conditions of life explored in Part II are also significant for the ways they order the differential capacity/susceptibility to affect, and be affected. As we saw in this chapter, social encounters between Parshads and 'voters/citizens' carry the traces of past iterative affective practices, enveloped by a moral atmosphere. The affective configuration governing their relational capacities have affective slots that recruit bodies: the deference of the Parshad, and the superiority and sense of entitlement of the voter. Reading the encounter between Kashi and the women in the opening paragraph, we can see how the latter has the capacity to be emboldened, entitled; such feelings arise in her encounter with the Parshad. At the same time, Kashi is susceptible to engender further affects in the woman, a sense of disdain perhaps on account of her being involved in 'dirty politics'. The collective conditions also engender differential capacities and susceptibilities to affect. The woman can charge the scene with her demand, intensified through a barely perceptible yet still effectual moral atmosphere of clientelism that implies the right of the woman to make demands, reinforced through affective practices that elevate her position in relation to the Parshad. Kashi is susceptible to being affected, in ways that compel her to meet those demands. The ways in which such differential capacity to affect and susceptibility to be affected influences the distribution of resources in Dehradun is explored in Chapter Eight.

PART III

ENCOUNTERS

7

Injury

Ibu Veronika was a shy woman before she joined the BKM. When she describes herself, she goes beyond the usual modesty to display an uncomfortable level of self-deprecation. She volunteers as she believes that 'in our life, we should live *bermasyarakat* [socially, in and with the people], respectful and with mutual affection'. She used to tremble when she met people, but since joining the BKM she has changed. She now sits at the front in meetings and talks to other women with confidence. She has also built new relations: 'I have more friends. I feel like I am meeting with my new family, maybe we are the same age...so she is like a sister for me. For those who are older than me, I feel as if I have new parents. I have a new family, so I enjoy it'. Ibu Veronika has built these relations through her work as a finance officer for the BKM, in charge of distributing loans and collecting repayments. She sees this work as a caring act, helping poor women to access capital that can lead to brighter futures. In return, she enjoys their hospitality, their friendship, and the affirmation of her belief that they need her.

Not all encounters with the 'beneficiaries' of the PNPM are positive, however. One day she was walking along the road when she encountered the father of a young woman who had taken a loan. Ibu Veronika had been visiting the woman since she stopped making repayments, imploring her to resume using a 'strong intonation, so she can feel it'. Upon seeing Ibu Veronika on the street, the father started calling her names, such as *retenir* (usurer): a word with particular affective force as *riba* (usury, or benefiting from exploitative gains in trade) is *haram*, or forbidden in Islam. As Ibu Veronika is Christian, the force of the comment is augmented by her minority status within Medan that is majority Muslim. The man, who was also a *kepling*, kicked her bicycle, and abused her when she fell. It was not an isolated incident. Alongside the encounters with people that reaffirm her self-understanding as someone doing good for the people, are incidents that challenge this self-understanding. People accuse her of benefiting from a government programme, and refuse to repay government money that they perceive as their 'share', or *bagi* (Chapter Five). Tears stream her cheeks as Ibu Veronika tells us about these disparate encounters: 'Sometimes I cry when I get back home,

Susceptibility in Development: Micropolitics of Local Development in India and Indonesia. Tanya Jakimow,
Oxford University Press (2020). © Tanya Jakimow.
DOI: 10.1093/oso/9780198854739.001.0001

sometimes I feel happy, I can laugh.... So many things happened since I join the BKM. From all the experiences, I have only a little sad feeling, but it is still kept in my heart.'

I start with this encounter to introduce the themes of Part III and how they relate to the discussions around self and collective conditions examined in Parts I and II. Ibu Veronika is much like the other BKM members we met in Chapter Three who have been able to cultivate a 'better' self through the BKM. These projects of self-making are reaffirmed through the affective experience of engaging with the recipients of benefits (in this case loans), which further increases Ibu Veronika's affective investment in this sense of self. Their relations are also, however, shaped by the moral atmosphere of *bagi-bagi*. Ibu Veronika is sticky with suspicion that she is benefiting by taking *more than her share* from a government programme, while she must insist others repay government money. As a consequence of these collective conditions, some of her relations are not mutually affectionate but rather antagonistic. In Part III of this book, I delve into the how these circumstances—self-making projects with much at stake and collective forms of affect—shape the interactions and relations between local development agents and others. In my analysis of the affective life of local level development, I pay particular attention to the differential capacity/susceptibility to affect/be affected emergent in *encounters*.

Encounters are the moments in which bodily capacities and susceptibilities are made manifest. There is an immediacy to encounters, but with reference to the past. In this way, the encounter is not only that point in time, rather '[s]omething of the past exists in an encounter, any encounter contains references to past encounters, and encounters are made through accumulated relations, dispositions and habits' (Anderson 2014: 87). Encounters are thereby mediated by discursive and signifying forces, as seen in Part II. At the same time, because affects are 'expressed in a specific person or specific thing' (Anderson 2014: 102), affective patterning and arrangements that reinforce particular social relations can be disrupted. These disruptions manifest in encounters, the analysis of which can help reveal emergent forms of power (the capacity to affect), as well as the pre-conscious responses by the 'Other' within the encounter to reduce their susceptibility to be affected. In this chapter I interpret how my interlocutors experienced various types of encounters, and analyse their own narratives of them as a means to reveal the differential capacity/susceptibility to affect/be affected of actors in community development initiatives in Medan.

In particular, I focus on encounters that make manifest local development actors' susceptibility to be affected in ways that threaten their sense of self.

In the above scene, Ibu Veronika suffers what I call an 'affective injury': an affective dissonance between the self she feels herself to be, and the one that can be sustained in the encounter. Similar to the women Parshads in Chapter Six who were cast in the position of servant, threatening their sense of self as social worker, Ibu Veronika is cast as a loan shark: an identity incompatible with a sense of self as someone who does good. The importance of Ibu Veronika's self-making project amplifies the impact of the charge that she is *retenir*, while the moral atmosphere of *bagi-bagi* (as collective affect) enhances the plausibility of the man's claims, and thereby his capacity to affect. The encounter is the moment when these latent susceptibilities and capacities are realized. As we will see, however, human actors are not impuissant in such encounters. Conscious and unconscious responses allow Ibu Veronika to at least partially recover from the affective injury.

Resilience to susceptibility, including recovery from affective injuries, has implications for development practice. As susceptibility is a condition of our responsiveness to the world and our dependence on an 'Other' for the I, adjustments to our sense of self should occur when confronted by situations in which former imaginings are untenable or unsustainable (Zigon 2009). This reflexive practice of self-cultivation (Foucault 1986) transforms the 'self' of the development actor, their relations with others, and thereby development practice. Giri and Ufford (2003: 254) argue that this aesthetics of ethics can lead to the 'reconstitution of development as a shared human responsibility, and as a shared human possibility' and the 'the establishment of a non-domineering relationship between self and other' (2003: 259). This normative ideal about how development should be, however, comes up against the unconscious and quotidian efforts to protect durable understandings of self, and to double down on affective investments in self-making projects (see Berlant 2011; Laidlaw 2014). Rather than opening up reflexive possibilities and new relations, susceptibility may lead to a hardening of prior convictions. When, and under what circumstances local development actors are susceptible in ways that challenge their sense of self are important questions for understanding the possibilities of reflexive practice.

Second, examining differences in the degree of susceptibility, and the circumstances in which susceptibility arises, and how these sediment into durable affective configurations, deepens our understanding of power. I aim to reveal the patterns of adjustment and resilience, who can and cannot withstand affective dissonance, and how these shape the relations between local development actors and others. In Chapter Eight I examine the consequences of these patterns for citizen entitlements (people's uneven access to resources).

In this chapter, I examine the possibilities for transforming these configurations from an upward responsiveness that reinforces prevailing power relations, to a downward responsiveness based on care that inverses them. Through attention to encounters, I aim to provide a different understanding of power relations between local development actors, the targets of development activities, and other development agents higher up in the 'aid chain'. Encounters thereby help us to assess the *actual potential* of susceptibility to result in more fair, just, and effective development.

Rethinking Power in Development

Development is characterized by unequal power relations: between donors and recipients, parent NGOs and community-based organizations, and implementers and the targets or so-called beneficiaries of development. Local development agents occupy different positions within multiple sets of relations. BKMs are in a hierarchical relationship with the PNPM facilitators and officials who evaluate their work, with non-governmental organizations (NGOs) which fund discrete projects, local level government officials (such as the Lurah) who sign off on documentation, and of course, the local people, divided into *warga* (citizens/residents) and *penerima manfaat* (the people who directly receive benefits). It is the latter sets of relationship that are often assumed to be hierarchical in favour of local development agents. Indeed, becoming someone who implements development, rather than someone in need of development, may be the only point of differentiation between individuals who otherwise share a similar socio-economic location (Heaton-Shrestha 2006; Pigg 1992; Chapter Two). In Indonesia, becoming a development agent can often be a route to social mobility, and community development is hence productive of unequal social relations at the local level.

Power differences are shaped by access to and control over material and ideational resources. Early and ongoing critiques point to the ways control over money structures relations. For example, large international NGOs may withdraw funding from local level partners, resulting in upward accountability and survival pressures for small NGOs (Fischer 1997; Ebrahim 2003; Jakimow 2010). At the local level, elites may divert funds so as to benefit their own family, supporters, and clients, reinforcing patronage and shoring up their own political and economic status (Lund and Saito-Jensen 2013). In Indonesia, *kaders, ketua RT/RW, kepling,* as well as various types of brokers command power and respect by channelling development resources to individuals (Berenschot and van Klinken 2018). Other development agents, including BKM members, have control over access to loans, establishing another means through which hierarchical relations between them and people in need of credit are established and maintained (Jakimow 2013; Kar 2013). Control over material resources is translated into other forms of capital, structuring relations

As post-development critiques have revealed, immaterial and ideational resources can be equally productive of unequal power relations (Ferguson 1990; Escobar 1995). Being fluent in 'development speak' establishes a regime of expertise in hierarchical relationships with the 'ignorant', while discourses order whose interpretations and knowledge counts (Hobart 1993; Kothari 2005). Knowledge is also a 'good' or resource, with preferential access being a point of differentiation with others (Pigg 1992).[1] Knowledge seems particularly central in Indonesian development, which under the New Order regime was characterized by *pembinanaan*, or guidance (Suryakusuma 2011; Robinson 2014). Knowledge followed lines of authority, and trickled down to the grassroots through various intermediaries (including *kaders*). Tania Li (2007: 4) captures the centrality of knowledge in her characterization of development agents as 'trustees' 'a position defined by the claim to know how others should live, to know what is best for them, to know what they need'. Becoming a trustee puts one in a hierarchical relation with 'deficient subjects', the target group in need of improvement.

Volunteers often spoke of the benefit of having access to knowledge/information and being in a position to educate others, even if they were less candid about how this structured their relations (see also Chung 2015). Ibu Rosa, BKM coordinator told us: 'there are a lot of blessings from the PNPM, one I have received is knowledge…I cannot pay for it, I cannot buy it. With my *ilmu* [science/ knowledge] I face the people (*masyarakat*)…with my *ilmu* I face officials…already I have received so much, I have guidance'. Knowledge is the basis for her relations with the people and officials, enabling her to stand before and face people, despite her limited education. For Pak Anto, sharing knowledge with others so that they too can improve their situation is part of how he has found meaning in his life. He describes how he learns with his fellow BKM members and is then able to share this knowledge with people less fortunate. BKM members become inducted into the group of 'trustees', positioned alongside state agents in a common agenda, while also having

---

[1] As Pigg (1992: 506) notes in the context of Nepal, frequently it is not so much access to knowledge, but the absence of 'locally instilled belief' that provides developers with a higher social status.

access to information and knowledge considered a desirable resource. As a consequence, they are differentiated from the targets of that knowledge, establishing or reaffirming a hierarchy between them and other *warga*.

Hierarchical relations are counter to efforts to realize bottom-up development that is—if not responsive to—then at least benign for the poor and marginal.[2] Considerable effort in academia and practice has been invested in reversing these power relations (Chambers 1997), but markedly less has been put towards extending our understanding of them, and if need be correcting our assumptions. Questions as to how relations in development are structured and the types of ordering apparatuses that govern them are seemingly resolved. There are partial exceptions. Kar's (2013) insightful ethnography of microfinance institution loan officers in India reveals the complex relationships that these local development agents have with the recipients of loans. In what should be a straightforward hierarchical relationship in which loan officers have cultural capital and power over financial resources, borrowers display a surprising ability not only to resist these unequal relations, but to reverse them. Borrowers greet loan officers by pouring water over their heads, locking them in their homes and calling them names. Loan officers do not feel empowered over borrowers, but are often uneasy, susceptible to challenges to their relative position.

The reasons for loan officers' susceptibility are critical to the arguments in this chapter. First, the loan officers often have ethical concerns about their work and ambivalent feelings about whether they are doing good. Kar (2013) describes the emotional labour to control such feelings in order to persist in work that often entails demanding money from a poor person: labour that is exploited by financial institutions and used to benefit their own interests (Hochschild 1983). While emotional labour is somewhat relevant in the case of BKM members, I am more interested in how the maintenance or recovery from particular feelings engendered through their work enables them to sustain their own self-making projects. The moral ambivalence of their work makes such projects precarious. Second, microfinance has come under increasing public criticism in India, and loan officers were therefore stigmatized as money lenders. Just like Ibu Veronika in the introduction, they were susceptible to engender scorn, while the borrowers had a greater capacity to affect loan officers within these collective conditions. Here then the capacity and susceptibility to affect shape the relations between borrowers and loan officers in ways that turn conventional hierarchies on their head.

---

[2] See Li (2007) and Bernstein (2005) for 'practical political economy'.

I suggest that the failure to take seriously a core element of the human condition—namely fundamental impressionability and dependence on the 'other' (Butler 2015; Throop 2018)—has led to these affective dimensions of power hierarchies being overlooked in development. Ibu Veronika and the loan officers in Kar's (2013) ethnography are involuntarily impressed upon in their encounters with others. Experiences exceed expectations (Throop 2018), so that one's prior self-narrative of doing good may break radically from the feelings engendered through such actions. Rather than reaffirming one's sense of self-in-relation, the 'Other' may create the conditions in which such a self is unsustainable—can neither be logically nor affectively aligned with the prior evaluation or narrative of self. Being called a loan shark may create in Ibu Veronika an affective dissonance, causing 'actionable critiques' or 'radical swerves' in her becoming (Biehl and Locke 2017). Such instabilities in the ways local development agents 'dwell' in the world, their responsiveness to its affective patterning, *as well as* its unpredictable deviations, disrupt understandings of hierarchies based purely on material logics or discursive regimes.

Care as an Ordering Logic

Recent moves in feminist scholarship to revive 'care' as an alternative framing to moral and political life (Tronto 1995; Butler et al. 2016) aim to take this fundamental responsiveness and dependence as part of a normative project to neutralize power relations and arrive at more just futures. Rather than foregrounding persons' autonomy, an ethics of care 'characteristically sees persons as relational and interdependent, morally and epistemologically' (Held 2006: 14). Our everyday lives and sense of self can only be achieved through our relations with others (Sevenhuijsen 2000; Butler 2004; Philip et al. 2012). Rather than prioritizing equality, impartiality and non-interference as per an ethic of justice, an ethic of care prioritizes 'trust, solidarity, mutual concern, and empathetic responsiveness' (Held 2006: 16). Emotions and relational capacities are not something to be overcome in the impartial administration of development, but rather valued for the way they 'enable morally concerned persons in actual interpersonal contexts to understand what would be best' (Held 2006: 12). The susceptibility to be affected lies at the heart of responsive, caring relations: relations that can be seen as amenable to bottom-up development.

Affective practices of care are not neutral, however, but rather productive of (unequal) relations (Held 2006; Philip et al. 2012).[3] Lawson (2007: 5) argues that 'caring involves complex flows of power in which the carer exercises (often unwittingly) control and influence over the cared-for'. Care does not reverse power hierarchies, it produces different (and arguably more positive) outcomes from unequal relations. The way caring relations *produce and reinforce* unequal relations between BKM members and the *penerima manfaat* is evident in the use of certain terms to describe their work. It is common for BKM members to describe their meeting with the people using terms such as: '*kami turun* [we descend] so that we see the poor directly' (Ibu Asima). Ibu Hanum tells us 'we feel grateful, that even though we are only a little above (*diatas*) them, we can understand the people below (*dibawah*)…we indeed have one heart that dives down [*terjun dibawah*]'. She put it differently on another occasion, saying: '*saya senang mengayomi masyarakat*' (April 2015). The literal translation is 'I am happy to protect the masyarakat', but the term *mengayomi* draws heavily on the symbolism of the banyan tree: an image evoked to describe a somewhat paternalistic relationship between the protector and the people.[4]

When 'care' is not *only* an ethical position, however, but *also* core to who one imagines oneself to be or becoming, caring acts can, I argue, disrupt and even reverse unequal relations. In the literature on care, vulnerability is a condition of the cared for, which makes the carer responsive and responsible to them. As seen in Chapter Three however, BKM members need affective affirmation from an Other that they are a caring person. Ibu Veronika is dependent on the recipient of care (loan recipient) for the affective cues that reaffirm or confirm that she is engaged in an act of care, or of doing good. Ibu Veronika is therefore also vulnerable (or I would say susceptible) to being affected in ways that are in conflict with this belief. It is this susceptibility and the capacity of the *penerima manfaat* to affect her in ways counter to her self-understandings that has the potential to disrupt hierarchical relations in development. I am not suggesting that other aspects of power inequalities—that is control over material resources or access to 'expert' knowledge—are not equally important in the structuring of relations between local development actors and others, but that it has been the susceptibility to be affected

---

[3] An observation as relevant for caring relations between the Global North and South, as it is in the family (Raghuram et al. 2009).

[4] The interpretation of the symbolism of the banyan tree with paternalism was that of my two research assistants, both of whom are local to Medan.

and capacity to affect that have been overlooked, and which can augment our understanding of development hierarchies.

This understanding also needs to take account of differential susceptibility and responses to affective dissonance. Phenomenological approaches to becoming often focus on unreflective responsiveness and attunement to the world, the ways that moral experiences may prompt re assessments and self reflexive practice (Zigon 2009; Desjarlais and Throop 2011; Zigon and Throop 2014). Indeed affect can be an intensity that 'energizes, contradicts, and overwhelms the narratives through which we live' (White 2017: 178), prompting new self-imaginaries (Moore 2011). At the same time, while impressionability is a part of the human condition, the extent to which individuals are modified in these moments, their defencelessness to being shaped through encounters, is perhaps over-emphasized. Quotidian practices of maintaining a relatively durable sense of self, an 'ongoingness in the world' (Berlant 2011; Laidlaw 2014) are also part of the human condition, particularly when there is much at stake: no less than one's sense of self. Resilience to impressionability and recovery from affective dissonance are the other side of our 'innate vulnerability' (Butler et al. 2016). For this reason I speak of differential *susceptibility*, arguing that local development actors may be innately impressionable, but in ways that are uneven in terms of their force and the potential for recovery. Susceptibility does not, therefore, in itself lead to a reversal of development hierarchies. Rather we need to pay attention to the moments of susceptibility (when and in relation to whom) and the acts of recovery that follow.

Injury

Ibu Hanum was showing us around her neighbourhood in Medan. Walking up and down the narrow lanes she pointed out the work of the BKM as manifest in new drains and sealed roads. Every so often we met people in the street and Ibu Hanum would introduce us to the happy recipients of loans. '*Saya dekat dengan semua*' (I am close to everyone). The tour provided visual proof of what she had narrated to us about her work and social status, as someone 'doing good' for her community. The usually reserved and humble Javanese housewife, Ibu Hanum was evidently proud as she showed us the outcomes of this labour. The physical imprints of her work, and the expressions of gratitude from the local people we encountered enabled the sense of satisfaction that was evident on Ibu Hanum's face. We turned into a wider street to examine a drain that had been built by the organization. 'This whole street used to flood regularly, but we have not had a single flood since', she told us. 'The people themselves contributed the labour', taking further pride in the ability to mobilize the community in the development works they implemented.

The street adjoins a large field and we turned the corner to walk alongside the shacks that bordered it. We walked past some people who did not greet us, nor did Ibu Hanum introduce us. An elderly man was loading wood into a cart but seeing us he pointed at Ibu Hanum and yelled: 'Because of this lady, water comes into all of these houses here. They built a drain, and now the water does not disperse, instead the flooding is concentrated in this area. This lady is involved in building this drain'. Almost as soon as the man started to talk to us, Ibu Hanum took two steps away and turned to the side. The spell of the 'feel-good' tour was shattered in that moment; we were acutely embarrassed at having heard a complaint that contradicted Ibu Hanum's account of the same project just moments earlier. More so, as people who had listened to Ibu Hanum speak at length about the significance of her volunteer activities for her self-understanding, we became a little protective. As she turned her back we shielded her with our bodies from the gaze of the man and tried to turn the conversation back to the process of building the drain. Ibu Hanum answered in a distracted way, her shoulders slumped. The man eventually turned his back and continued to load wood but the altercation had emboldened another woman to come out of her home who repeated the man's complaints.

As we walked slowly away, Ibu Hanum said that the elderly man only rents 'dia cuman menyewa', and as he is not the owner he has no right to complain. 'This old man is "orang yang agak gimana" [a person who always has some complaint]....People feel satisfied, but then they become comfortable and spoilt'. As we walked further from the scene, I raised the courage to ask her how she felt when people make complaints like this. She replied that for her it is okay, 'because although one person may complain [mengeluh], ten other people are proud [bangga]'. While we continued the tour, however, the atmosphere emanating from the encounter followed us around like a stink. Ibu Hanum's sunny mood turned flat.

The encounter lays bare the susceptibility of Ibu Hanum to be affected in ways that were counter to her sense of self and her self-making project. The tour of the neighbourhood as a form of affective practice (see Chapter Five), had until then engendered feel-good sensations. Encountering the material objects and human beneficiaries of the BKM's work aroused satisfaction and pride in Ibu Hanum and admiration in myself, Ibu Yumas, and Ibu Aida. However, unlike the affective practices of the *acara* in Chapter Five where BKM members selectively interpreted the emotional cues of the *penerima manfaat*, the incident with the elderly man left no room for misreading. The charge of the man's complaints was clear, with its accusation that Ibu Hanum was doing harm rather than good.

I describe such moments when the response of the 'other' impresses upon or affects the BKM member in ways that are counter to, rather than aligned with their emergent or durable ideas of self, as an affective injury. The term affective draws attention to the centrality of senses and impressions for one's ongoingness in the world (Ahmed 2004; Wetherell 2012), while also capturing the uncontrollability of affective forces, the ways they recruit and impress *upon* individuals (Butler 2015) in ways that may confound, threaten, or be at variance with self-making projects. The term injury aims to capture the consequences of this derailment, experienced as hurt or discomfort that requires affective management to recover from the threat to self. Pain is caused by something that impresses upon us, resulting in an intensification of feeling (Ahmed 2004). These injuries are *affective* as they occur below the level of consciousness, and involve an unexpected impulse and response inconsistent with the emotions and senses required for an ongoing idea of self. Affective injuries are therefore a result of and make stark our dependence on others for the affective experiences that are self-reaffirming, as well our susceptibility to be *impressed upon* 'in ways that are radically involuntary' (Butler 2015: 7).

The 'in-betweeness' of affect, which arises in the midst of 'the capacities to act and be acted upon' (Seigworth and Gregg 2010: 1), is important here. One is impressed upon in an encounter. In the passage between affect to feeling and action lies a not-yetness, a potential to be other than ourselves. From the force of the encounter, to feeling, then action, there is a rupture, so that the intensities generated lay bare the potential that one is other than what one thought. Ibu Hanum is susceptible in this scene. The scene also, however, points to the capacity of *warga* (residents), *penerima manfaat* (beneficiaries) and the material environment (such as a failed drain or incomplete bridge) to affect 'local development agents', engendering negative feelings such as doubt, guilt, embarrassment. I am not suggesting that the man in the above scene *inflicts* an injury; he is not the subject in the harm *done to* Ibu Hanum. Rather the emotions Ibu Hanum feels (doubt, embarrassment, guilt,) arise from the contact (Ahmed 2004) between the man (beneficiary recast as wronged party) and the BKM member (social volunteer recast as harm-doer).

I suggest that such affective injuries are a common yet unrecognized aspect of development and humanitarian work. Their ordinariness is in part due to the impossibility of development agents' missions (Fechter 2016), as well as the importance of their work for their sense of self. Roth's (2015) account of 'passionate professionals' is full of people susceptible to affective injuries for these reasons. For example, a development practitioner woman working in Palestine explained her feelings when fired upon by a Palestinian man. '[F]or me this was the most difficult thing to overcome. Because I accept being shot by the Israelis.... But if you are shot by the people that you think you are helping, that's terrible. I remember. I just thought I could never go back' (Roth 2015: 97). It is the lack of gratitude, the rejection of claims that she was 'doing good' that has an affective force: a force all the greater as it questions her self-understanding. The woman escapes the physical injury, yet sustains an affective one so severe that she feels she could not return to her work. Yet Ibu Hamun is not like the practitioner in Roth's (2015) account. She responds to the involuntary impressions caused in the encounter in ways that minimize their harm. She is susceptible to them, but not in ways that threaten her sense of self and her evaluation of her practice in any durable way.

Recovery

In part, Ibu Hanum's resilience to the affective injury is due to the affective practices of the BKM, as explored in Chapter Five. The production of the collective conditions in which BKM members dwell predispose them to being recruited into affective slots of 'doing good', and to read the emotional cues of others in particular ways (Ahmed 2004; Wetherell 2012). While the world may *impress upon* the subject, individuals are *impressionable* in personal ways. For example, a couple of weeks after the above incident, we asked Ibu Hanum in a formal interview about the recognition she receives as a BKM member:

> Now we have real evidence of our good works. They [the people] are happy, they feel they are cared for. They do not say it like this, 'you are good', but from their gestures we feel that we have helped them.... For example where the flood used to come, every day when I pass that road people say 'we are lucky to have her, we never have floods anymore'. They recognize me, and I don't think they are being false; the language is sincere.

Ibu Hanum refers to the same drainage project that was the subject of the man's complaint: the significance of which I return to below.

Before doing so I draw attention to the way Ibu Hanum describes how she expects to be impressed upon in her encounters with the people as a BKM member. She responds to their gestures in ways that reaffirm her belief that she is doing good, 'from their gestures we feel that we have helped them'. Her reading of gestures, tone, language, are aligned with, and indeed reaffirming of her self-perception; she occupies the affective slot that reaffirms her understanding of self. Concomitantly, 'Emotions in their very intensity involve miscommunications' (Ahmed 2004: 10). The psychic need to feel the satisfaction of gratitude, for example, may result in (mis)readings of the gestures of others. While Ibu Hanum and others often reflected on the gratitude they received through their work, our readings of these encounters often arrived at different interpretations, for example as seen in the *acara* in Chapter Five. Her (mis) reading is important in enabling a particular understanding of self, and the nature of her relations with others.

As noted, however, there could be no misreading of the emotions of the elderly man in the felt immediacy of the encounter. Ibu Hanum's face dropped, and I felt the charged atmosphere where the accusation hung in the air. She quickly recovered, however, as reflected and achieved in her narration immediately following the event. Her explanation and counter-accusation that the elderly man is 'someone who always has some complaint' overcomes the threat to her secure self, allowing her to re-inhabit her being in the world as an ethical person. Recovery encompasses the way the experience is cognitively processed, reflected upon, and represented. This may immediately follow the event, such as when Ibu Hanum gave us her impression of what had just happened, or it may be a memory recalled days, years, or decades later, such as when she returned to the incident in her description of people's gratitude in a discussion several months later. The first temporal scale of lived immediacy can be a moment in which one's lack of self-authority and inability to control aspects of life becomes conspicuous. Processing these experiences later through stories 'enable[s] people to renegotiate retrospectively their relation with others, recovering a sense of self and of voice that was momentarily taken from them' (Jackson 1998: 23). Attention to people's narrations of affective injuries reveals the effort taken to undo some of the damage caused by experiences that threaten one's durable understanding of self.

These initial responses and modes of recovery are distinctly different from the moral dilemmas faced by development workers (Arvidson 2008; Fechter 2012b; 2016; Shutt 2012). As seen above, an aesthetics of ethics

(Giri and Ufford 2003) invites practitioners to change in response to the moral uncertainties that they face in the field as a means to reconfigure development relationships. In this case, the incident with the man would be followed by Ibu Hanum's conscious acknowledgement of the moral tensions implicit in her work, reflection on her own moral position, and consequent self-(trans) formation. Moral dilemmas can be considered a companion to an ethic of care that demands an openness and a responsiveness to the other, a vulnerability. I argue, however, that while Ibu Hanum is susceptible, she is not vulnerable (see Chapter One, section 'Vulnerability' for the distinction). She resists the pull to be transformed in the encounter; that is, she engages in acts of recovery after experiencing an affective injury that protect her from the need for self-reflection. These quotidian efforts protect durable understandings of self or investments in self-fashioning projects by supressing nagging doubts, ignoring uncertainties, and recovering from affective injuries. These acts of recovery, a form of affective management, are therefore not a *prompt* to reflection, but rather subconscious responses that *prevent* it. They entail a refocusing of attention away from the hurt, or a conjuring of emotions that re-reaffirm one's self-understanding. Such acts of recovery sustaining an idea of self are, in my observations, more common than breakdowns leading to transformations in self.

The response to similar incidents suggests a pattern in the way developers supress doubts and quell anxieties in development work. Schwittay (2014) follows the blogs of Fellows in Kiva's microfinance programme: volunteers with a firm belief in the power of microfinance as *the* solution to poverty, and who often have future ambitions tied to this belief and the desire to do good. One Fellow describes feeling as if he had been punched in the guts when encountering a situation that questioned this faith (Schwittay 2014: 148). Rather than reflection, such experiences circumscribe the questions they ask. Their blogs show both the reflection on the moral dilemmas they face, as well as the 'limit of reflexivity' (2014: 164); 'Fellows hang on to these ideas, not wanting to pierce the Kiva veil even when it starts to rip' (Schwittay 2014: 166). This suppression of thought is due at least in part to the affective investments they have made in the programme. The term 'affective injuries' aims to make explicit these experiences of development and humanitarian practitioners and to draw attention to their consequences. Analysis of the affective injuries endured by BKM members and the ways they recover from them, tells us much about the hierarchical relations within the development arena, as well as the everyday experiences of local development actors.

Differential Susceptibility

Significant in the scene near the constructed drain was the low intensity of Ibu Hanum's susceptibility to be affected and the low generative force of the man's complaints: his capacity to affect. The differential susceptibility to be affected and capacity to affect of the two bodies in the encounter are generated in the relations between them, within collective conditions. That is, they reveal the relative lack of affective capacity of the man already marginalized by his age, his status as a poor renter, and as a migrant. The force of his complaint is perhaps magnified by our witnessing it, as demonstrated in Ibu Hanum's reference to it in a later interview. Yet it seemingly lacks the force to significantly derail Ibu Hanum's general sense that she is doing good, or to prompt reflection on the work of the BKM. Yet encounters between other bodies within scenes of local development reveal different patterns of differential susceptibility to affect and capacity to be affected that are revelatory of the subtle dynamics of power.

We witnessed one such encounter during a site visit of Pak Anto's BKM Maju by the PNPM city level office. The evaluation visit was arranged in order to select the top five BKMs in Medan who would be awarded a special prize by the mayor. We toured the locality, visiting a couple of 'beneficiaries', who performed their expected roles of gratitude. We arrived at an alley (*gang*) that had recently been paved. A group of women called out to Ibu Citra (a BKM member) and complained loudly: 'I am a poor woman, only washing people's clothes. Yet I did not get Raskin or Jaskesmas'. The woman was referring to two government schemes providing subsidised rice and healthcare respectively. BKMs have no role in administering either and Ibu Citra calmly explained: 'The data for these programmes does not come from us. We only look after the BKM'. But the women were now having fun, teasing Ibu Citra, 'We also have not received any benefit from the BKM. I know all about this PNPM, and we have received no benefit, only this *gang*'. Ibu Citra replied by drawing attention to the benefit of the alley, 'A lot of money has been spent on this *gang*, and now you do not have to walk in the mud'. Going nowhere with this line of teasing, a third woman reverted back to what are common complaints in a moral atmosphere of *bagi-bagi*: 'People who get Raskin, they have a good house and a motorcycle'. Ibu Citra lost her patience: 'Please talk to your *Kepling* about this, not me'.

The scene was light. The women were speaking in a half-joking fashion, not as a way to soften their complaint, but as if playing a game as if nobody takes these things too seriously. Ibu Citra was *seemingly* unaffected by the scene. It was not the composure of emotional restraint; her voice was strong as she returned the banter and she too had a joking cadence in her voice. She made no effort, then or later, to explain the incident to any of the government officials or to us. We came to know Ibu Citra well. She had joined the BKM as a favour to the facilitator, and was not committed to the activities. She never described herself as someone with a *jiwa sosial* and within a year of this incident she had left the programme altogether.

Just outside the scene, however, watching but not interacting with the women, was Pak Anto. I turned to the government officials to catch their reactions, and caught sight of him to the side. His face dropped; he turned away from the women. For the next few minutes he avoided our eyes and those of the officials. At the time it was only the second occasion I had met Pak Anto, but even so the affective force of the complaint, the lack of gratitude, and the will to embarrass, was evident. While the other participants continued to chat, maintaining the atmosphere associated with celebrating good work, Pak Anto was noticeably more subdued. He hid his face and lost the skip in his step. The moment of pride and satisfaction of showing government officials what the BKM had achieved was tainted.

The more we came to know Pak Anto, the more painful such incidents were to witness. Pak Anto was one of the most committed BKM coordinators who repeatedly stressed the importance of the programme for his life, and who he had become (Chapter Three). It is this 'achieved self' that is threatened by complaints, accusations, and failures of gratitude. Pak Anto has weathered multiple instances of all three, and not all have the same affective force. He is most threatened when he is made to feel foolish for his work instead of receiving public recognition. The above complaint of the women is not forceful for the implied accusation of wrong doing so much as the contempt displayed for the project, seen as lacking seriousness. The half-joking nature of the taunt, the connection to other government programmes that are notorious for failing to reach the right recipients, feeds into a narrative that the PNPM is *ecek-ecek*: a mocking term, suggesting a lack of seriousness, only doing things for appearance in order to get a share (*bagi*) of government money.

Pak Anto often talked about such encounters. Indeed, one of his recurrent narratives involves a *kepling* who uses similar language to dismiss the work of the BKM. The following is taken from one of the transcripts in which he talked about this incident. Pak Anto set up the story by giving an account of what I have called the moral atmosphere of *bagi-bagi* (chapter five), so that we understand the context of what he said next.

The people's thinking is still old-fashioned. They think... 'This is a project, there must be a lot of money'. The old paradigm is fixed in their heads, '*bagi-bagilah proyek*' [share the project]....It is not only common people, government officials also have the same thoughts. When we meet them, they say, 'where is my share'? One time a Kepling said to me 'it is *ecek-ecek* [not serious]'...'*Ecek-ecek* Dah? We will prove it whether it is *ecek-ecek* or true'. Finally he felt embarrassed. It turns out, this is a real project. We made a mail box for people to complain....We are audited. I told them that this is my life journey until now, and I have found what I have searched for.

Pak Anto relays the procedures such as the audit and complaints box to demonstrate that the BKM is not *ecek-ecek*. In doing so he not only counters the complaint, but in his narrative to us, regains his sense of self as someone engaged in serious work for a good purpose. The affective injury is not entirely healed, however, as evident by the way Pak Anto repeatedly tells us about this incident. Each time he tells it he is agitated, outraged, emotional. The memory still engenders negative feelings; the retelling perhaps helps to soothe those feelings.

Our conversations and formal interviews with Pak Anto have other similar accounts. Reading through them, the accusations and dismissing of their work as 'not serious' is more forceful when it comes from a person in a position of authority and when it relates to the procedural aspects of the BKM. Pak Anto did talk about the difficulty in convincing members of the general public to take their work seriously, but there was not as much hurt as frustration in his voice. He dismisses such opinions as being related to their bad attitude, and the mindset of the people, which he believes the BKM should try to change. That is, his relative position on account of being a 'trustee' with the knowledge of how people should live (Li 2007) makes him less susceptible to their opinions or complaints. 'Deficient subjects' are thereby less able to engender the capacity to affect Pak Anto in their encounters with him. On the other hand, as seen in Chapter Three, Pak Anto desires to be useful and competent in the managing of the BKM. His insecurities are therefore heightened in encounters with officials, and those who enjoy greater social status or cultural capital.

In the above scene with the women in the alley, it is therefore not their words that engender an affective injury. Rather I suggest that it is their display of scorn in front of the PNPM officials that makes Pak Anto's face drop, his body slump. Pak Anto is relatively less susceptible to being affected by isolated complaints by members of the general public, but this susceptibility increases in situations where his sense of self is evaluated by people he respects. In this particular encounter, he was most susceptible in front of the PNPM facilitators and government officials whom he tried so hard to impress. His susceptibility increased as he lacked conviction that he was actually performing his role well. Constant reference to his poor education and his nervous manner betrayed his insecurities. We barely knew Pak Anto at this stage, and my sense is that we were a minor bodily force within the affective configuration, although I cannot completely dismiss our influence. What is significant is that within the encounter, the affective configuration seemingly enhanced the capacity of some bodies' in comparison to others. In this instance, this differential capacity to affect reinforced existing power relations.

Downward Responsiveness

Not all affective configurations reinforce conventional development hierarchies. In a nearby *kelurahan*, BKM Kesatuan offers an example where responsiveness to the people made them resilient to the complaints of an NGO. The BKM was funded by an international organization to deliver business training to would-be women entrepreneurs. The members of the BKM visited the women who had taken small loans to assist in their businesses, such as running a small shop, producing tempe or crackers for sale in the market, and making cakes for order. After catching up on news, volunteers invited would-be-participants to take part in the five-day training. A woman from a local university took the training, admonishing everyone around her, telling the women they were stupid for how they packaged their products, making fun of the BKM members, and telling me off for being Australian. The women participants loved her, indulged her admonishments, laughed at her jokes and her quips at others. They were enthusiastic about the training afterwards, not so much for the usefulness of the lessons, but for the fun in being together. Most importantly they became a close-knit group with strong relationships with both volunteers and the woman trainer, who went out of her way to support the women entrepreneurs far beyond the five-day programme. The project seemed to be a success.

It therefore came as a shock to Pak Alrasyid, the BKM coordinator, when he was visited by a representative of the NGO. She yelled at Pak Alrasyid for not meeting the selection criteria that required that women participants be under the poverty line of 1.7 million rupiah a month. The poverty line is recognized as being too low to accurately capture people living in poverty in a city as expensive as Medan. The idea that someone could be under the poverty line and have a small business, let alone take five days off from work, is nonsensical. Pak Alrasyid listened to the complaints, but he was not moved. He explained to us later:

> When people come to see if someone is 'poor', then they only look at income and houses. They do not look at the real condition of the people, how many dependents they have, whether the house is inheritance or reflective of actual wealth. But we really know the situation of the people.... Further, everyone knows that no one can live on 1.7 million rupiah.... Ibu [NGO] said that we are wrong. But I can take responsibility for every person in that training, that even if they did not meet the strict criteria, it was a good programme for them.

Pak Alrasyid was exasperated by the encounter, yet it did not spark an affective injury. He was secure in the way that he and his fellow BKM members recruited the participants, based on their attentiveness to their circumstances and a responsiveness to their needs. Pak Alrasyid is the only man in the BKM, and he and the women BKM members formed close relationships with the recipients of loans. Pak Alrasyid stated that women are more caring than men and are able to build closer relations with the *masyarakat*. Indeed care was a strong theme in the women BKM members' accounts of their work. For Pak Alrasyid, being involved in the BKM made him acquire a caring disposition. He told us: 'this feeling of humanity, of caring for society arose from being in the BKM'. This care for the people, as encompassing attentiveness, concern, and responsiveness seemed to be an affective disposition within this particular BKM, and is not common through all BKMs in the city.

Most critically, seemingly this affective configuration made Pak Alrasyid less susceptible to being affected by the NGO manager. That the NGO did not seem to have the capacity to engender anxiety in Pak Alrasyid, or a sinking feeling that the BKM had done wrong, is significant. As seen in Chapter Three, Pak Alrasyid was of a low socio-economic status, potentially susceptible to claims of wrong doing in similar ways to Pak Anto. But he was not; he dismissed the claims as nonsense and remained confident in the work of the BKM and his own convictions that he was doing good. I suggest that the openness to the people that this entails, particularly in the context of community development, provides a resilience to claims of wrong doing by others. Caring relations provide a conviction of doing good that shields someone against being impressed upon in ways that could otherwise contradict that self-understanding.

Complicating Hierarchies

The intensity of the above encounters between volunteers with other people in the locality suggests that it is inadequate to understand relations in community development as hierarchical in any straightforward way. Each incident demonstrates the capacity of the other to affect the volunteer in ways that threaten their self-understanding, or alternatively of the volunteer to be resilient in the face of such threats. Their susceptibility to be affected is on account of the importance of 'doing good' to BKM members' sense of who they are or are becoming, and their dependence on the other to reaffirm this understanding through appropriate affective cues (Part I). Not all BKM members suffered affective injuries, however. Some, like Ibu Citra, had little investment in the programme; others, like Pak Alrasyid, were more confident in their convictions that they were doing good. The biographies and self-making projects of volunteers are critical to understanding how social encounters in development impress upon and affect them.

For other BKM members like Ibu Veronika, Ibu Hanum, and Pak Anto, affective injuries are frequent due to the weight of doing good through development activities for their emergent and durable understandings of self, as well as their insecurities that they are doing good. The affective and emotional dimensions of their encounters with others are critical to reaffirm this idea of self, at the same time that the qualities of the encounter may affect volunteers in ways that threaten it. That is, many volunteers are susceptible to being affected in their encounters, engendering discomfort, anxiety, doubt, and stress. While these are negative emotions, I am not suggesting that affective injuries are something to be avoided altogether. Indeed affective injuries are indicative of the new opportunities BKM members have to enact possibilities of self (Chapter Three), while also suggesting an openness and responsiveness to the other. Susceptibility to be affected by others provides the conditions through which development agents can engage in reflexive practices of self, seen as necessary for an ethical development (Giri and Ufford 2003).

The acts of recovery to affective injuries demonstrate, however, that while BKM members are susceptible to being affected, they are not always vulnerable in their relations to others. BKM members did not, on the whole, engage in reflexive practices of self. Instead they quickly sutured the wound, containing the hurt to the specific encounter, not allowing it to challenge their sense of self. Even when this first aid failed and the wound reopened, it was managed through self-assurances rather than self-reflection. Ibu Hanum did not take the complaints of the old man seriously. Pak Anto did not ask how he could be more responsive to the needs and desires of people in his locality. The rotating loans continued in the same fashion led by Ibu Veronika. BKM members were not open and responsive. They were defensive. The response to affective injuries has practical significance in the development sector. The impulse to suppress doubts, divert objections through actions or remembrances that prevent the derailment of self-fashioning projects is a 'limit of reflexivity' (Schwittay 2014: 164). Volunteers will be unlikely to critically reflect on, much less openly challenge the modality of development through the PNPM, when to do so threatens the idea that they are doing good and their affective investments in self.

The unevenness of the force of and the ability to recover from affective injuries in relation to different bodies has further implications for power hierarchies in development. As noted, even the most marginal of 'beneficiaries' have the capacity to affect: a power that is generally overlooked in the development studies literature. But this capacity is uneven and often reaffirms rather than disrupts existing hierarchies. BKM members such as Pak Anto are more susceptible to being affected by the disapproval of the PNPM officials than the people living in the locality. Volunteers such as Ibu Hanum are most resilient to the affective injuries arising in encounters with the most marginal people in her neighbourhood. We therefore need to be attentive to the moments of affective dissonance when volunteers are moved in ways that confound their expectations. That is, when can the affective configurations that sustain certain forms of privilege be disrupted; what are the forces of particular bodies in relation, and within particular scenes. The differential capacities/susceptibilities to affect and be affected within these configurations become manifest through close attention to encounters.

A body's force is always contextual, generated in encounters between particular bodies, within collective conditions and histories. Attention to these forces helps us to move beyond an understanding of hierarchies as established and effectual in relations, to see how they are produced by particular affective configurations. As affective capacities are not a quality of the body, but rather the body in relation, it stands to reason that in order to enhance the capacity of the *masyarakat* to affect community volunteers requires changes to the terms of that relationship. The implications are twofold. First, attention to the differential capacity to affect and susceptibility to being affected is an important component of relations between actors within development, and second, affective configurations ordering these are varied, and dynamic in local level development. In the next chapter I examine in more detail why this matters. Beyond reflexive development practice, the differential capacity/susceptibility to affect and be affected has consequences for the distribution of resources, and hence, life and livelihoods.

8

Compulsion

Devani was sitting at home when a man approached the door looking agitated and angry. He did not greet Devani before he launched into an account of how his wife had run away two days ago, demanding that Devani deal with the situation immediately. Devani was occupied with her household chores and was looking after her son. She did not know this man well as he was not a supporter, and she did not want to become involved in a domestic dispute where the wife could have had good reason to flee her home. Furthermore, he was making demands that fell outside her formal role of Parshad and she was already feeling harried by the constant stream of demands on her time by constituents. She pushed back replying 'Why are you telling me this? You should go to the police station to report it'. The man would not budge, and screamed: 'I have voted for you and you are the ward member and until you accompany me to the police station then I will not leave this spot'. Devani was annoyed, another disruption to her day to help someone who was unlikely to be grateful. The scene was making her uncomfortable however, forcing her either to return the man's aggressive tone with an angry dismissal of his claim to her assistance, or to surrender to his demands. She called her mother-in-law and asked her to look after her son as she pulled her scooter out to go to the police station.

In Chapter Six I examined the affective configurations between Parshads and constituents that I characterize as 'servitude', which emboldens the latter to make unreasonable demands on the former. The man in the above scene demands that Devani undertake work that falls far beyond her responsibilities and Devani feels compelled to accede to those demands despite them being unreasonable and inconvenient. The man has the capacity to affect Devani, engendering feelings of compulsion, while Devani is susceptible to being affected in such a way. Chapter Seven explored variations in the capacity to affect and susceptibility to be affected that are produced in different types of relationships between local development agents and Others and the consequences of this for development practice. In this chapter I explore this differential capacity/susceptibility to affect and be affected between Parshads

Susceptibility in Development: Micropolitics of Local Development in India and Indonesia. Tanya Jakimow,
Oxford University Press (2020). © Tanya Jakimow.
DOI: 10.1093/oso/9780198854739.001.0001

and constituents and the consequences for the distribution of resources and livelihood outcomes.

Attention to the different affective forces that compel Parshads to accede to demands, and the reasons why Parshads are particularly susceptible to the demands made by some citizens over others, makes two critical interventions in the literature. First, I argue that the capacity to affect is an important factor in a citizen's ability to gain access to resources and services from the government, or their 'entitlements'. Entitlements are distinct from rights. As McFarlane and Desai (2015: 3) explain, whereas 'rights generally take the form of legally binding statements, entitlements are produced through social relations and based on people's experience and perceptions'. An individual may have a legal right to a certain resource but not be able to access it; other individuals may draw upon sources of legitimacy—for example social norms of sharing—to make claims that exceed legal or formal rights. The personalized nature of Indian bureaucracy (van Dijk 2011; Gupta 2012) coupled with the state's low infrastructural power, results in 'gaps between both the formal-legal channels of entitlement actualization (and informal channels) and differently positioned places or collectivities' (Van Dijk 2011: 307). Municipal Councillors play an important role connecting citizens to government resources and services in the context of scarcity (Berenschot 2010; Van Dijk 2011; Shekhar-Swain 2012; de Wit 2017), that is, in the production of citizen entitlements.

The prevailing understanding of the relationship between Municipal Councillors and constituents (see Chapter Six), suggests that entitlements are based on moral claims to resources based on a moral relationality of 'patronage' (Piliavsky 2014), or on the instrumental logic of clientelism (Berenschot 2010). Without denying the importance of these factors in determining citizen entitlements, as seen in the case of Devani, these explanations do not exhaust the possibilities through which citizens can demand and access resources and services beyond their legal rights. Devani feels no moral obligation to help the man as he is not a known supporter. Frequently Parshads meet the demands of people they suspect, or know did not vote for them, and are unlikely to vote for them in the future. Electoral calculation is therefore unlikely in itself to encourage Devani to inconvenience herself to the extent she did. Rather it is the affects engendered in the scene through the display of anger, made forceful through Devani's susceptibility to such affects, which animate or even compel the Parshad to meet demands. The relationality between Devani and the constituent is not solely moral, it is also affective, with consequences for the ability of the latter to secure entitlements from the former.

Not all encounters where constituents make claims on Parshads are successful, however. Examining when a Parshad is animated or compelled to respond positively to the demands made by citizens, and when they are unmoved and unresponsive to claims reveals how the *differential* capacity to affect and susceptibility to be affected is an overlooked element of citizen entitlements. The second intervention I make in the literature is to reveal the ways these differential capacities/susceptibilities reinforce or disrupt power hierarchies, forms of privilege and disadvantage. These capacities and susceptibilities are produced in the relations between Parshad and 'voter' and hence are not immune to the moral relationality of patronage. At the same time, the capacity to affect is determined by factors beyond patron–client relations to include a larger set of relational possibilities shaped by gender, class, caste, age, and so on. Furthermore, Parshads are not susceptible in identical ways to bodies marked by these identifications; they are differentially susceptible in encounters with others based on their personal biographies and characteristics. While susceptibility is therefore in one sense individual, shared experiences and ascribed identities create patterns in the ways that Parshads respond to constituents. These patterns of differential capacity and susceptibility to affect and be affected thereby map onto other modalities of power that govern 'who gets what' within the political economy of Dehradun.

Love

Although being compelled to accede to the 'unreasonable demands' of voters was commonplace among Parshads, many were also animated by positive feelings. Devani describes being confronted by people in a *basti* (slum) whom the government refused to help.

> These are my people, and they come to me with their problems, and I being their public representative, I have to solve their problems. And these are the people who do not have proper roads.... See we must fight for these people. When the party gives us a target to collect so many people to make a crowd, this is our responsibility

The animation to take on the fight for them is a mix of her concern for the people, her feelings of responsibility for their problems, and political calculations. For Devani and her husband, the first two are not necessarily the subordinate factors; rather elections and political support seem to be important as validation for their good works and the building of their social networks. The importance of these became clear when Devani's husband spoke about getting through a difficult period when their son was sick: 'See, when my son had surgery, and the doctors said that there was no chance of survival, then we had the wishes of so many people, and [as a consequence] our son is with us today'. The election becomes a demonstration of the relationships that they have formed, the love of the people towards them. Devani told us 'Even if we do not run for election next time, then these relationships are still important for us'.

Three years into her term, Devani's account of affection highlights how the experience of the election comes to be reinterpreted and reinscribed with meaning later. As noted in Chapter Six, election campaigns are characterized by affective practices of supplication, in which the Parshad over-emphasizes their dependence on the Other. The experience of supplication is not absent in their accounts of their work, but what Devani (among others) emphasize is the affection that they feel in relation to the people. In the literature the ways in which elections influence the behaviour of Municipal Councillors is usually limited to an instrumental exchange: entitlements in a return for a vote. For Parshads like Devani, however, these relationships mean more than just her ability to obtain the position of Parshad. The election is a moment of reaffirming one's standing, one's commitment to the people, and the mutual bonds of affection that are established through the act of getting one's vote and then repaying it. These feelings animate Devani's work later, the ties established through the election are reinscribed with affection that continue to motivate Devani to be particularly responsive to the constituents' claims.

Rather than a relationship based on instrumental electoral logic, many Parshads consider their relations with the people as familial. In Chapter Six we saw how women Parshads often adopt kinship terms to describe their relations with their constituents: Devani describes herself as the daughter-in-law of the ward, voters described Aditi as their daughter during the election campaign, while Padma talks about her motherly qualities. Familial ties are often used across India to invoke the obligations of state actors including politicians towards citizens. For example Gupta (1995) notes how people refer to local state actors as *maap-baap*, or mother, father; Witsoe (2011) observes that caste membership in Bihar encourages constituents to call local politicians *bhai*, or brother, with commensurate expectations. These familial relations are, I suggest, valued by women Parshads for the mutual affection that they imply, and not solely for electoral gain. Their reading of relations as familial engender concomitant feelings that animate them to help their constituents.

While Chapter Six revealed that these familial representations were often a euphemism for actual relations based on servitude, these are not incommensurate possibilities. The affects engendered by both may circulate within the same scene. While the sense of 'servitude' may embolden a voter to make an 'unreasonable' demand, it may be with a feeling of sisterly love that the Parshad fulfils it. There are slippages and excesses across affective configurations; these are patterns that can arrange potentialities but never determine outcomes. Likewise, one's sense of self as a social worker also animates Parshads to help constituents, going above and beyond their formal duties. Parshads experience positive feelings (or feelings qualified as positive) when undertaking work that reaffirms their sense of self as a social worker (Chapter Four). In the encounter with citizens, they are susceptible to being affected (moved by sympathy with someone's plight and an ability to do something about it). The Parshad's susceptibility to be affected is in direct relation to the capacity of the citizen to affect. This relational capacity to affect is a power overlooked in accounts explaining resource distribution.

One such encounter demonstrates how this capacity to affect and susceptibility to be affected motivates actions that defy electoral logic. We were sitting with Padma (whom we met in Chapter Four): a second-term ward member elected into an unreserved seat. She was looking exhausted from having to care for her sick mother throughout the night. As we spoke, Padma received a phone call from a man living in the adjoining ward. Several minutes later, he was in the front room requesting Madam-ji to write a letter for an electricity connection. It was not the first time he had come to Padma about the connection. The Parshad from his own ward had delayed writing the letter and requested 500 rupees to complete the work promptly. Once the man had the hand-written letter, he found that the electricity department would not accept it because it was illegible. He then came to Padma and asked her to add a line verifying what the letter said, adding her own stamp. The electricity department did not accept this and requested a new letter. In desperation, the man went to the mayor who told him that any ward member, not only his own Parshad, could write a letter verifying his address and need for connection. He had returned to Padma to get this work completed.

Exceptionally polite to 'madam-ji', the man directed anger at his own Parshad. 'We voted for him so that he can do our work. But after becoming elected, he does not do any work at all'. The voter is Muslim, and voted for the Congress Parshad, who was now in power. He admitted that he would not vote for the BJP—the party to which Padma belongs, and which has an Hindutva ideology that discriminates against Muslims. If he was in Padma's ward, however, 'I would vote for her because she is a good human being'. After the man left, Padma discussed the payment demanded by the other Parshad from a poor man.

> Some ward members ask for some money for every small thing they do, like arrange a ration card or write a letter. Perhaps for this ward member it is his livelihood or way of earning money. But I am of the opinion that if you are doing social work, you should not be bothered with earning money. If you want to earn money then you should be in some other profession.

Padma's actions are seemingly not without electoral calculation. The BJP's ability to mediate between different groups and the state has enabled them to build support among groups (such as Dalits and Muslims) whose interests are counter to its ideology and policy positions (Berenschot 2014). Electoral considerations are not, however, the only or even primary factor. The man does not live in Padma's constituency, and would therefore not be able to vote for her. By his own account he would not vote for the BJP: a trend reported across the state, where the BSP is the second choice for Muslim voters unsatisfied with Congress.[1] Nor did our presence make a difference, as she had helped the man on a previous occasion. Instead, I suggest that Padma's sense of self as a social worker animated her to help the man as best she could.

After Padma completed the task, she pulled out a large book from under the table. In it she wrote the details of the work just completed. She was visibly pleased when we asked her to show us the book, turning large pages full of inscriptions of the everyday work of the Parshad. The tome is impressive for what it represents: hundreds if not thousands of people who have received her assistance. The actual instrumental purpose of the ledger is not clear, but its emotional effect on Padma is evident. Writing up each entry reinforces her competence as a ward member with her own processes for getting things done. The large volume has its own affective presence, communicating the quantity of the tasks she has completed through its weight; I can barely lift it on to my lap and cannot help but be impressed. Each inscribed task also represents the warm feeling of doing good. While the entries are prosaic, for Padma re-reading them invites a memory of people such as the Muslim man

---

[1] http://timesofindia.indiatimes.com/city/dehradun/muslims-dalits-hold-key-in-11-seats-of-haridwar-district/articleshow/57152119.cms and for a similar trend in Uttar Pradesh, see http://timesofindia.indiatimes.com/elections/assembly-elections/uttar-pradesh/news/myths-of-muslim-dalit-and-jat-votes-busted-numbers-show-1st-two-groups-backed-sp-and-bsp-while-the-3rd-stood-by-bjp/articleshow/57639878.cms

and the positive impact she has had in his life. She is animated by her act of doing good, making her susceptible to being animated on occasions when she can do a small act. Correspondingly, Padma's susceptibility is related to the Muslim's man capacity to affect her. The other Parshad who perhaps does not feel the same 'high' from being competent is not susceptible to being affected in ways that animate him to help. In relation, the Muslim man has limited capacity to affect. I return to the gendered nature of this differential susceptibility below.

Anger

The opening scene was not one of affection, however, but rather anger compelled Devani to complete the work of an agitated voter. It was an almost everyday occurrence for Parshads to be on the receiving end of angry tirades. As Massumi (2015) notes, a performance of anger demands a response, even if the response is to refuse to be provoked. As this section explores, displays of anger have a strong affective force in the encounters between Parshads and constituents. Padma, however, was not susceptible to being affected in ways that compelled her to act (as a negative response), rather she interprets this anger in ways that animate her (as a positive response) to help the constituent:

> People do come to me very angry, but it is in the form of family anger, that means, in a possessive manner. My relation with my people is like children coming to their parents to get something. This is their love so we cannot take it in a negative way. So I don't feel bad for the people who come to me in anger because that's their way of showing love.

The position of the ward member, as a mother who looks after their children, provides a different affective hue to the interaction, one in which anger is reinterpreted as love. Her sense of self as being a social worker adored by the people results in her (mis)interpretation of the affective bonds that animate the display of emotion, and shapes her capacity to be affected in ways that reaffirm the sense of being adored. As a two-term Parshad, with decades of experience in social work, this sense of self is secure enough to interpret scenes in such a way.

Only experienced Parshads interpreted anger in this way. Most women Parshads found such encounters disturbing. We were introduced to Bimla in

Chapter Four: a first-term Parshad elected into a seat reserved for scheduled caste women. Being screamed at was a common occurrence in her work.

> People scream at me to get their work done and if I am unable to do their work, then again they shout at me and say that we have voted for you, so do our work....We keep a little fear in us, no. The government officer will not have any fear. People talk politely and with good manners with the officers, like we do too. Towards me it is like *ghar kii murgi daal baraabar* [the house hen is equivalent to lentils, or 'familiarity breeds contempt']....[Parshads] don't get any money from anywhere. If we are making phone calls we are using our husband's money....Still people keep on pressing us....We feel that these things happening to us are wrong. What have we done? You have given us a vote at one time, but we are serving you for five years (Bimla).

People would use harsh and sometimes derogatory language towards Bimla, even in front of her family. She told us that the people are never satisfied. If you do seven things out of ten for them, then they will forget what you have achieved and scream at you to accomplish the other three.

Contained within Bimla's account are various clues to understanding the affective configuration that both emboldens voters to make demands angrily and that compels Bimla to accede to them. The first clue is the reciting of the Hindi version of 'familiarity breeds contempt'. Parshads spoke about their familiarity with the people as making them approachable and therefore close to the people, particularly compared to other politicians such as MLAs. While this familiarity can be an electoral advantage (Bedi 2016) it also makes unnecessary certain formalities and politeness, so that voters feel uninhibited to speak rudely and with ingratitude to Parshads. Many women Parshads complained that people spoke to them in a manner that they would never address an MLA or government official. The people who approached Bimla with the most anger were people of her own caste (Valmiki, a Dalit caste) with similar low socio-economic status. As seen in Chapter Four, becoming a Parshad under these conditions was a source of pride for Bimla. At the same time, her relatively lower status—that is similar to her constituents—makes her familiar in an additional sense, of being someone 'like' them, and potentially susceptible to arousing resentment or jealousy in others on account of her increased social status. Hence social cues of deference are not shown. 'Voters' consequently have the ability to display anger (if not become angry), and thereby have the capacity to affect Bimla by this display.

Bimla is susceptible to being deeply affected by this anger. She had little experience prior to becoming a Parshad, and spent the first eighteen months struggling to cope with her work and the people's expectations (Chapter Four). The phrase 'We keep a little fear in us, no. The government officer will not have any fear' is telling. I suggest that Bimla is highly susceptible to becoming fearful due to her uncertainties about her role, her responsibilities, and the desires of her party. Lacking a secure sense of who she is as a Parshad, social encounters that make possible a reading of ineptitude or incompetence easily affect Bimla in ways that further increase her insecurity. Bimla qualifies these feelings as fear, with the Hindi construction 'hamen to thoda dara ke rakhte hain na [We keep a little fear in us, no]', suggesting that there is always some fear inside that is easily brought to the surface. She cannot read the anger as familial affection as Padma does, rather she reads it as an indictment of her record. Bimla was the most open about the fear she feels when people are angry with her, but her experience of failing to perform her role effectively in her first few months is common. I suggest that these experiences linger on beyond the period of incompetency, to make women Parshads susceptible (to fear, anxiety) far into their first term.

Even experienced women may respond to angry constituents in order to dispel any perception that they are incompetent. Indrani is also a first-term Parshad, but as a long time social worker, is confident in her work. She is frequently yelling at people to get work done, responds to what sound like polite requests with sharp barbs and seems unfazed when people speak to her in anger. She was not, however, completely unmoved by angry outbursts. After taking a phone call during one of our lazy afternoon conversations, she was quickly animated, launching into a tirade against the caller:

> He does not have light [electricity] in his home. He asked me if I had light in my home, and if I was sitting under a fan comfortably. I told him to call the electrician but he is deriding me, telling me that I should go myself and climb the pole and fix the problem....I told him he can call the authorities himself. We are just the means to reach the solution. But some people are so arrogant.

Indrani did not seem to be a woman easily swayed, but as I turned to say goodbye, she was already getting on her scooter, ready to yell at someone in the electricity department.

Indrani often complained about the unreasonableness of demands made on her as seen in Chapter Six. Frequently, however, she complied with the demands, raising the question as to why. Her pathway to becoming Parshad provides some clues. When her seat was reserved for women, Indrani requested the party ticket but it was given to a female relative of a man high up in the party hierarchy. Indrani ran as an independent, won the election, then shifted her allegiance back to the party. She told us that some people from her own party continued to undermine her, taking credit for her work, and questioning her ability to get things done. The perception that women lack the capabilities to be a ward member hangs over female Parshads in Dehradun and India more generally (Ghosh and Lama-Rewel 2005; John 2007). The man's demands can therefore be interpreted as provocations, teasing Indrani about her lack of ability, engendering a sense of insecurity. Indrani knows she is capable, yet feels compelled to demonstrate it again and again. The 'common sense' (in the Gramscian sense, Crehan 2016) that women become Parshads only due to reservations not their own capabilities makes female Parshads susceptible to being affected by any hint that they are not competent. At the same time, when they have the opportunity to display this competence, women Parshads may feel an affective high, as we saw with Padma above.

The display of anger also seemingly affects women Parshads in ways that make them highly responsive to constituent's demands. Devani is explicit about how anger prompts her to respond differently to her constituents:

> First we need to remain calm in front of them, because if we answer then a fight will ensue so it's better to stay quiet. I just listen to them and do their work…we first try to complete the work of loud people and then take up the work of people who are sitting quietly. And many people are aware of this fact, that if they are loud, then the Parshad will complete their work first, and so they purposefully become loud.

The claim that Devani responds calmly to angry constituents is part of her self-representation. In the words of her husband: 'her nature is that she speaks very softly to people whosoever comes to our house, so she has earned praise from everybody that their daughter-in-law's nature is very good'. Perhaps as a consequence of this sense of self that does not allow an angry response to an angry scene, Devani works quickly to de-escalate the situation by completing the task as soon as possible. She described other situations, in which people have come to her house, threatening suicide, screaming at her in front of her children. These scenes engendered strong feelings in Devani of fear, discom-fort, embarrassment. She did not argue the details as to what was a legitimate demand but sought to end, or not escalate the feelings engendered in the encounter.

The literature mentions angry and assertive citizens in passing (Berenschot 2010; Witsoe 2011; de Wit 2017), but does not delve into how the affects and emotions engendered in their encounters with elected representatives shape their ability to command resources. It seems that displays of anger are an effective way for voters to mobilize women Parshads to get their work done. Whether this is equally the case for men I cannot answer from my own empirical material, but Parshads such as Kashi believe this to be the case. She tells us that voters are more likely to talk angrily with a woman as 'they think, she is a lady, so by speaking loudly we can get our work done by her'. Kashi suggests that voters take advantage of the greater susceptibility of women to being affected by angry scenes, and perhaps they also feel particularly emboldened to display or feel anger in front of a women, compared to a man. Kashi, Padma, Devani, Indrani, and Bimla all had slightly different responses to this anger, and there was no uniformity in how women were affected. It does seem, however, that their affective biographies and gender ideologies do result in a relatively greater susceptibility to be affected by anger, with consequences both for them, and their constituents.

Class and Caste

Not all people are able to display anger, and anger does not have the same affective force in each encounter. Class positionings and caste identities influence the differential capacity of voters to affect the Parshad, and the differential susceptibility of Parshads to their claims. Class and caste difference is not a simple equation, in which higher class/caste residents compel lower class/caste Parshads to meet their demands. Rather, in my observations, it is a closeness in socio-economic standing that has the potential to engender discomfort or embarrassment in the Parshad. The difference between how rich people interact with Bimla compared to her neighbours is instructive. Bimla is rarely the recipient of angry demands from middle-class constituents, who tend to come to her only if they need a signature: 'when they have work for me they will talk nicely, and once their work is done, if I pass by their house, they will refuse to recognize me'. Bimla did not suggest that she is offended by what could be considered a snub. Rather she put this down to a simple calculation that they do not need much from her and so there is no need to maintain close relations. Unlike her 'familiarity' with people of lower socio-economic class, she is not familiar to the middle-class constituents and the transaction remains business like.

For other Parshads, however, it is 'people who live in posh areas' who are the most assertive and who make the most unreasonable demands. That they do so is further evidence of the limitations of electoral calculation as an explanation for who Parshads are responsive to and why. Middle-class people across India consistently fail to turn up to the ballot box, and Dehradun is no exception.[2] Nonetheless, many expect better services and infrastructure to support middle-class needs (such as driveways to park their cars) and for Parshads to do their menial tasks as seen in Chapter Six. The lack of electoral calculation or moral basis for their claims raises the question as to why Parshads accede to their demands in the first place. Furthermore, many middle-class residents were seemingly able to command a *greater* share of resources than poorer residents. It is useful to examine who did not give in to the demands of the middle class. Aditi, a middle-class Brahmin refused to give in to what she perceived as unreasonable demands. Padma, who was in her second term in an unreserved seat was confident in her abilities. She claimed that most demands came from the poor, while middle-class people assisted her in her work. Aditi and Padma's class and caste background seemingly changed the nature of the demands made on them, or alternatively the way they were affected in such encounters.

Rachna, in contrast, was part of the aspirational lower middle-class. She had a relatively poor education, attaining only tenth standard. She was far from shy. I personally felt intimidated by her assertiveness, magnified by her loud voice and formidable physical presence. Rachna nonetheless complained that she was constantly having to run around after middle-class residents.

> There are more complaints from posh areas. Residents expect me to go to their homes to hear their complaints, rather than coming here. They expect me to cater to everything that they ask for.... Rich people are more distempered/upset if the work will not be done. They are eager and quick to complain.... They are aware and they know that their demands will definitely be fulfilled if they talk to us in a particular manner, whereas the poor people are unaware and give us respect.

---

[2] The greater tendency for the poor to vote is a widespread phenomenon across India (Banerjee 2014). For recent anecdotal evidence from Dehradun, see http://www.dailypioneer.com/state-editions/dehradun/poor-rich-divide-in-voting-approach-also.html (accessed 3 May 2017).

Rachna described the qualitative difference in how rich and poor residents approached her. We saw several examples of the latter. People would sit on the veranda and wait for Rachna to finish what she was doing, and then meekly ask for her signature. Rachna's own response displayed her occupation of the affective slot of 'superiority' to their 'deference' (Wetherell 2012), reinforced through her use of the diminutive verb forms: '*Ha, bol*' (yes, speak), her tendency to make them wait, and her quick dismissal of claims that fell outside her responsibility. She was positioned as a 'servant' (Chapter Six) only in relation to some, mostly better-off, constituents.

What compels such an assertive woman to go to the houses of better-off residents and meet their unrealistic demands? The question is perhaps best pondered when going to her home that also serves as her office. Our driver sets us down on the main road before driving off to find a place to park in this congested part of town. We walk under the hot sun, needing to ask directions even on our third visit to find her home through the tangle of lanes. Her family occupies the second story of a small brick house; the staircase is very steep, and my colleague pauses for breath. I present these details to give a sense of how unlikely it would be for a constituent of high socio-economic class to come to the home of Rachna. There are no caste barriers here, just class ones. Does this create a level of embarrassment that prompts Rachna to visit the home of richer constituents? If so, she did not share this with us. Indeed, she could not give a reason why she goes. She was adamant that rich people do not vote, so she was not courting their political support. She was compelled for reasons that remained unclear to us, and perhaps impenetrable to her own self-understanding. I speculate that the class difference between Rachna and people in posh areas has an affective force that influences her response. They were able to engender embarrassment or insecurity in Rachna in ways that lower-class people could not.

People who are poor, lower caste, or lower class, have a different affective force. Kashi was particularly responsive to people who were in need, her heart was stirred when she heard their stories. She spoke with tenderness of families that she had helped, and was persistent in fighting for their entitlements or any other support they could receive. These affective responses are tied to her sense of self as a social worker. Bimla too went out of her way to help people in need, saying that she understood what it was like to experience poverty, and to have a small bit of help that could make such a difference. She did so even when there was no electoral advantage. For example, Bimla said that she always helps Muslim people, even though they will not vote for the BJP, and despite the strong objections of people in her party. 'I have to work cautiously, with fear, as many people in my family tell me not to go out with Muslims. But I think, aren't they also human beings'?

The ways people are affected are rarely straight forward, and the animation to help others is often entangled with other aspects of lives and being. Leaving aside the possibility that Bimla is over-stating her willingness to help Muslim people, there are seemingly other factors that mobilize her. As noted above, as a first time ward member with low education, Bimla underwent a sharp learning curve. Becoming competent has been life changing, and getting things done in a competent manner brings an affective charge. We have observed the way she lifts and swells when she accomplishes something, even the act of filling out a pension form. Helping a Muslim person is another opportunity to experience this high. I am not discounting her empathy towards poor Muslim people, but rather I aim to highlight how these animations are entangled with other emotions emanating from the biographical details of her life, and her sense of who she is, or is becoming.

The Vote

Although I contend that electoral calculations are not the only factor in the distribution of government resources, they are one factor in the emboldening of constituents, and the response of Parshads to their demands. As noted above, Bimla said: 'they shout at me and say that we have voted for you, so do our work', suggesting an implied moral obligation to the voter in return for the vote. I suggest that this emergence of an 'assertive citizenry' (Manor 2016) and a responsive cohort of Parshads is not only (or even) on account of trans-actional politics based on clientelism. As seen in Chapter Six, affective practices of supplication during the campaign also create the conditions in which certain affects can be engendered (a sense of entitlement, or obligation): conditions that last throughout the Parshad's term. While the vote has a power to compel Parshads to do their work, I suggest that it has an affective force beyond its exchange value. The excess is found in the ways non-voters and non-supporters draw upon the imagery of the vote to get things done, and in the demands of voters that far exceed what could be considered a just return for the vote. As Bimla said: 'We feel that these things happening to us are wrong. What have we done? You have given us a vote at one time, but we are serving you for five years'.

Voting is often considered a gift within the moral economies of electoral politics. Voting is called *matdan*, or the *dan* (gift) of the *mat* (vote, also means belief). This is not the *dan* of the 'free gift': the giving without an expectation of return that has religious significance for Hindus and Buddhists (Bornstein 2012; Parry 1986). Rather in the context of patronage democracy (Chandra 2004), the gift of the vote is reciprocated by the leader through access to state resources. The challenge that Parshads such as Bimla face, is that there is no guidance, no set rules outlining when it is reasonable to consider that debt to be repaid. Her status as a political novice engenders uncertainty (as to what is a reasonable expectation of return) and fear (of not upholding her obligations). These emotions, rather than a moral obligation, are the mobilizing force that compel Bimla to do all she can to meet the myriad of claims made upon her. That is, the '*dan*' in '*matdan*' is not the free gift without expectation of return, but rather its opposite, a gift that can never be repaid.

The gift of the vote thereby establishes a relationship of open-ended obligation. As long as the 'debt', or obligation is not repaid, it enables domination (Bourdieu 1990). Bimla complained that '*phir bhii log hamen itna daba ke rakhte hain na, ki chhotii-chhotii baat ke lie hame dabaate hain* [still people keep pressing down on us, even for small things, they keep pressing]'. The use of *dabaana*, to press, gives a sense of being under the thumb, to use an English phrase, or to put it more succinctly, dominated. The evocation of the vote is an affective prompt to (re)occupy the slot of deference, of servant, established through the affective practices of the campaign. From this positioning, one cannot argue against the legitimacy of claims. Parshads are compelled to meet them, regardless of their feelings as to their unreasonableness.

The power of the vote is not fixed however; it is one ingredient of negotiations over expectations. Meera, another Parshad elected into a seat reserved for SC women, also came under pressure from people who demanded entitlements on the basis of their vote:

> They say that you have to sort out problems of the area as we have voted you. Then I said that voting is everyone's right…you must not taunt us like this.…We know our responsibility. The people who have voted for us will say I have voted for you and the people who haven't voted for us will also say that we have voted for you. Now it's our responsibility to help all our community members.

Meera's bravado in this interview is not as evident in her encounters with her constituents. She aims to please and is responsive to voters' claims. Rather she seems to be letting out a frustration in our recorded conversation at the unreasonable demands, and potentially at her inability to meet the ones she considers valid. She reduces the affective force of the vote by pointing to a different moral logic, her responsibility as an elected representative to help all the people in her area.

The 'vote' nonetheless maintains its affective force, particularly in the lead up to fresh elections. Meera, and her husband Kapil, have been particularly hamstrung in the Nagar Nigam as they belong to a minor party and lack powerful contacts in government. The unmet expectations of her voters in return for their *matdan* hangs heavy in her final months as Parshad and during the campaign, making Meera highly susceptible to criticisms. On one day of campaigning in the November 2018 elections, Meera suffered what I called in Chapter Seven an affective injury. We were walking up a narrow gully that Meera and Kapil had made *pukka*, that is, improved the dirt path into a concrete ally. On such a sunny day the road looked resplendent, evoking a sense of satisfaction through the material form of their achievement. The occupants of one house backing on to the lane were not so impressed, however. On hearing Meera and her supporters approach, a husband and wife came out of their home and started abusing her. They said that as a consequence of the problems with the construction of the road, water pools outside their house. They had therefore raised part of the road themselves, but this created a dip in the road from which water flowed into other people's houses; that is, their solution created a problem for their neighbours further down. The consequence was ill will among neighbours.

The man of the house was drunk and started to shout very rudely at both Meera and Kapil, asking how they could expect their votes when they had not performed their job well last time. His wife was verbally abusing Meera, being very disrespectful in the tone of her voice, its volume, and the words that she used. The scene quickly escalated, as Meera became livid. She yelled at both of them, and could not be calmed by her team. The altercation was heated, and only after ten minutes could Meera's campaign team pry her away from the scene. We doubled back the way we came and went to the home of a supporter. Meera sat on the bed, visibly still extremely irate, trying to calm down. She said that the couple did not appreciate that before they started working in this area, there was no road here, and that the problem was created by these people building a platform. 'I have helped that lady in so many ways. She is head of the Aaganwadi, and I have had to sign so many documents for her, and done so many other things for her and then she has treated me like this, shouting and using harsh words'. Meera was shaking, deeply affected, and only very slowly started to regain her composure.

Meera's response, her white hot anger, was no doubt intensified by her physical and emotional exhaustion this late into the campaign. Yet it is remarkable at what it betrays about her sense of reciprocation or obligation of the gift of the vote. Here, her anger was directed at the lack of gratitude, the sense that one can never give enough as an elected representative, that people will always demand more, and demand in a way that ignores the Parshad's humanity. The incident did not come out of nowhere. The husband and wife were emboldened by Meera and Kapil's greater susceptibility during the time of campaigning. Meera was easily incensed as the five years of tolerating people making demands, being ungrateful when they were fulfilled and angry when they were not, had built up inside her. Meera did not suppress her emotions, I did not think she would be able to contain them, her body was taken over by how she felt.

Meera's outburst speaks to the different flows of affect that shape the configurations between Parshads and voters during their five-year term and beyond. While Meera had seemingly reached her limit and responded angrily towards the woman, this was only after having served her for five years, and in a context in which she had no power to meet her demands. The voter still pushed, and indeed used the campaign in order to press further demands, making Meera feel as if she had failed and that she should respond. The campaign is a period when the affective force of the vote is most evident, but its force is always present, to varying degrees, during Parshads' five-year term. Indeed many supporters refused to take money during election campaigns even though this was common practice, as it would reduce the force of their claims later. As one woman said, if she comes to Meera later when she is in need to support, 'they will say to me, "but you took money to support me"'. That is, rather than strengthening a relationship as Björkman (2014) found in Mumbai, money turns it into a transaction, where the debt is repaid. The affective force of the vote, or the support during elections, is greatest when the debt remains outstanding.

Differential Susceptibility

Within the encounters between Parshads and voters or citizens, affects are engendered that animate, mobilize, or compel the former to accede to the demands of the latter, or alternatively, to ignore them. Voters' capacity to affect in these encounters is neither even, nor constant. Poor voters may have a diminished capacity to affect Rachna compared to voters who live in 'posh areas'.

The reverse was true in voters' encounters with Padma, where sympathy for the poor was more of an animating force than class embarrassment. Lower-caste voters may feel more emboldened to make demands on Bimla on account of her familiarity and closeness compared to higher caste voters. It seems likely, but still unproven, that voters are more prone to anger (have the capacity to become angry, and/or affect others through performances of anger) in encounters with female Parshads in comparison to male Parshads.

This differential capacity to affect has material outcomes. Middle-class voters have their demands met for resources (such as driveways) that go far beyond their legal rights. Marginal voters, such as the Muslim man, may have their legitimate rights denied due to an inability to move the Parshad to help him. The distribution of widow pensions, as just one example, is highly uneven, dependent upon the good will of the Parshad, or put differently, the capacity of the person in need to engender emotions that animate, mobilize, or compel the Parshad to act. Such factors shape citizen entitlements in ways that are related to (in the sense they may augment), but are not fully captured by moral economies. The differential capacity to affect is therefore an important, and heretofore relatively under-examined aspect of people's uneven access to resources and services.

Voters' differential capacity to affect is related to the differential susceptibility to be affected of Parshads. I have identified two aspects of women's affective biographies that make them particularly susceptible in ways that motivate them to respond to voters' requests and demands. First, the sense of self as being primarily a social worker makes many women Parshads particularly susceptible to feeling pity, compassion, and a genuine desire to help others. For Padma and Kashi who identify strongly as social workers, the prompt to help is 'natural', something they feel satisfied by and animated to do. By highlighting how women are particularly susceptible in this way, I am not referring to a natural and essential feminine quality. Rather the institutional context and lived experiences of women within gendered societies (Goetz 2007) lead to particular ways of being, of emotional repertoires and affective biographies (Chapter Four) that shape the ways they are affected in encounters.

The second element of women's affective biographies is related to these same gendered conditions. Women are more likely to have less experience and be less competent during their initial years as Parshads. The experience of feeling lost, incompetent, anxious, makes them highly susceptible in situations in which their capability can be questioned, and perhaps over-responsive when they are uncertain about what is right. At the same time, having achieved a degree of competence brings its own affective highs, so that being able to enact and demonstrate an ability to do things can be an animating force in itself. Affective biographies therefore matter when examining the susceptibility of municipal councillors and other development actors to be affected in encounters with citizens. This finding also points to the importance of interventions (such as capacity building) that help women to quickly become competent in their role so that such affective patterns are not established in the first place, or are more easily dispelled (Jakimow 2017b).

Not all women Parshads are affected in the same way. Gender, class, and caste all shape their susceptibility to be affected in encounters with citizens. Parshads' personal self-making projects, sense of self and affective biographies influence the ways they are recruited into affective slots (Wetherell 2012), that is, their susceptibility. Likewise, not all citizens are able to engender affects in their relations with Parshads that will help them to mobilize resources. Some Parshads are seemingly immune to stories of people's troubles or cannot be intimidated by class assertion. Not all citizens are able to show emotions that will impress the Parshad; social decorum prevents a display of anger, pride a display of helplessness. I am not, therefore, suggesting a *formula* to understand the distribution of resources through the affective dimensions of encounters. There is, however, *a patterning* in the capacity to affect and susceptibility to be affected due to (a) signification, (gendered) ideologies, and discourses; and (b) the gendered and classed nature of self-making projects and self-imaginaries. These social elements produce the routines, or affective configurations in which bodies are disposed towards recruitment into certain affective slots: 'in this situation you do superiority, I do abasement and deference, or *vice versa*' (Wetherell 2012: 125). These routines never exhaust the range of affective possibilities in the social encounter, yet they do make some more likely than others. These affective configurations are (re)productive of certain forms of privilege (Wetherell 2012) with consequences for the distribution of material resources and services.

As the capacity to affect and susceptibility to be affected is relational—that is, one's capacity to affect another is in direct relation to that person's susceptibility to be affected—the relationship between municipal councillors and citizens needs to be the focus of efforts to have more equitable or needs-based citizen entitlements. The aim cannot be to increase the capacity of poor citizens to affect, nor to enhance the resilience of the Parshad to claims made by the better-off, rather the modes of relationality between them need to be transformed. There have been development interventions to change these relationships through accountability mechanisms, giving control over decision-making, and so on. In addition, as seen in Chapter Six, these relationships can also be changed through shifting meanings of democracy or the affective practices of elections. I suggest that attention to the affects engendered in the encounter between different actors may indicate additional means to overcome existing unequal power relations, or at least their material consequences.

The differential capacity to affect and susceptibility to be affected is therefore not only relevant to the specific case of citizen entitlements in urban India. Indeed, the way that affects and emotions are mobilized and engendered is an overlooked factor in the distribution of resources more generally. From the local to the national level, the claims that people make for central funds are based not only on rational arguments, but also emotive appeals. The effectiveness of these appeals depends in turn on the people who are in a decision-making capacity, their susceptibility to be affected by these claims as a consequence of personal characteristics, affective biographies, and social positionings. In the development sector, the micro-decisions that relate to which organization gets funding, and which issues take priority, are also in part shaped by the affective intensities engendered in face to face encounters, and through mediated technologies such as media and documents.

The susceptibility of the people making these decisions is therefore also of critical importance. Having people with different affective biographies and possibilities for self in positions of authority is critical, underlining the need for women, people who have lived through poverty, members of non-normative groups who are marginalized, and so on, in such positions on an equitable basis. Such an approach to understanding power, privilege, and its consequences, rejects the claims that certain racialized or gendered bodies are too 'emotional', and instead sees all bodies as equally but differently emotional. The differential susceptibility to be affected is another point of diversity that needs to be included in hiring and electoral strategies. At the same time, as greater susceptibility can reinforce existing social hierarchies tied to gender in particular, it should perhaps also be a characteristic that is challenged, rather than accommodated as a point of diversity. Concomitant to increasing the resilience of marginal actors to be affected would be efforts to increase the susceptibility of people in positions of privilege. Inculcating an openness to the people who are the targets or recipients of welfare and development—in other words those who are vulnerable—can potentially be a means to achieve more responsive development practice and a more just world. I now turn to the potential of vulnerability in development, and what we can learn from a comparison of local development actors.

9

Conclusion

Vulnerability

As I reached the conclusion of my research, much had changed for the local development agents with whom I had conducted the research. In Medan, the Indonesian government had replaced the PNPM programme with Dana Desa (village funds): a programme that also devolved resources to the local level, but only in rural areas. There was much uncertainty about this change in 2016, with a hope more than expectation among volunteers that the city-level government and NGOs would take over the role of supporting the BKM. By 2017, few BKMs were operational in Medan. A couple sustained activities through the interest earned on rotating loans or had small projects with NGOs, but most were inactive. The loss of activity and their status in the community hit some volunteers hard. They had undertaken a journey of self-realization, and they now needed to find other avenues through which to enact and reaffirm this sense of self. As seen in Chapter Three, for some BKM coordinators like Pak Anto, their time being a local development agent was only a memory. The photos, certificates, uniforms, and other paraphernalia were reminders of a time, and self, past.

My final trip to Dehradun likewise coincided with the end of a period of being a local development agent for many of my friends. Of the ten women municipal councillors that I had followed between 2015 and 2018, only two were re-elected. Aditi a highly competent and popular Parshad won with a party ticket in a seat reserved for women; Deepa was elected in a seat for SC women on behalf of her husband, and was expected to again retreat to her home after the oath-swearing ceremony. Meera and Sushma lost with a party ticket, Devani as an independent, while Padma, Bimla, Kashi, and Rachna decided not to contest after being denied a ticket from their respective parties. Indrani sadly passed away in 2017. Having known them only as Parshads it was a shock to see them without this status. Two days after the election results were announced, we called upon Meera and Kapil. The latter was fixing a bicycle in the small cycle repair shop next to their home: poorly paid and precarious work. Meera, keen to see a friend in these sad times, invited us

Susceptibility in Development: Micropolitics of Local Development in India and Indonesia. Tanya Jakimow,
Oxford University Press (2020). © Tanya Jakimow.
DOI: 10.1093/oso/9780198854739.001.0001

upstairs into her eerily quiet home. She was so bored she said, even as she was still recovering from the intense period of campaigning. They came third in the election: 'we only got 300 votes, 300 after all our hard work for five years'! Her hurt was palpable and inescapable. For Meera, Kapil, and other former Parshads, there was shock, devastation, and a process of rebuilding the self that rarely gets acknowledged in our accounts of personhood.

Personhood is always in process; we become rather than simply be (Biehl and Locke 2017). The end of my friends' becoming as local development agents was due to changes in their circumstances. As I have demonstrated throughout this book, however, their formal status was only one resource for their self-making project. They were dependent on others for the affective reaffirmation of self. As such, the capacity to be affected is integral to the human condition, while we are also susceptible to being affected 'in ways that are radically involuntary' (Butler 2015: 7). That is, while a formal position may provide opportunities to be affected in ways that reaffirm a sense of self, such affective responses are neither determined nor controllable.

This capacity/susceptibility to be affected is relational. In order to be impressed upon, there must be a human or non-human other with the capacity/susceptibility to affect. Susceptibility to be affected and capacity to affect are not attributes of bodies, but rather the forms of relations between them. Bodies are to various degrees susceptible or impervious to the forces of the other in ways that are experienced in the present, but also located within broader webs of signification and histories of contact (Ahmed 2004). In this way, the affective dimensions of life can reaffirm or intensify power relations, hierarchies, privilege, and marginalization (Wetherell 2012). At the same time, there is always an excess of affect that escapes the social, and hence the potential to disrupt and reconfigure power relations (Anderson 2014). It is the contention of this book that attention to the differential capacity to affect and susceptibility to be affected can shed light on power configurations within development terrains, as well as the potential for reconfiguration.

In this book I have focused on two terrains of local urban development: community development in Medan, Indonesia, and municipal governance in Dehradun, India. Both these terrains involve projects and activities to improve the well-being of populations, the delivery of services, and the distribution of resources. Yet only the community development programme fits a conventional understanding of 'intentional' development. The activities of elected representatives and party cadre are the purview of studies of politics, or democracy, of interest to development studies, but not a study of development in a strict sense. I argue that we need to challenge this distinction, in which activities are only considered to be 'development' if they are embedded within an aid chain that can be traced to the *real* development actors of Euro-America.[1] The PNPM that traces its genealogy to the programmes developed by the World Bank Jakarta office that fit a global paradigm of community development is more easily recognizable as a 'development intervention' (Guggenheim 2004). Everyday practices of resource distribution and efforts to improve livelihoods by local institutions, especially the state are, however, much more significant for the well-being of poor and marginalized individuals (Corbridge et al. 2005; Chandhoke 2009). Theorizing development, the frames of analysis and critique, has rarely brought these two types of terrain together, creating a false distinction that maintains Euro-America's dominance in development studies. While I agree as to the importance of international development institutions, taking them out of the frame reveals much about power that has heretofore been overlooked.

Attention to local development agents in particular can be illuminating. Much of the literature of 'Aidnography' focuses on development actors from the global North: expat (and to a lesser extent national) development practitioners, international volunteers, and bureaucrats in international organizations (Chambers 1997; Mosse 2011; Fechter 2012a). In contrast, studies that bring together and compare development agents from the global South as a distinct and separate category are far fewer in number (Horner 2019, see Ballie-Smith et al. 2018; Laurie and Ballie-Smith 2018 for exceptions). This unevenness is despite the vast bulk of everyday development work being undertaken by people who come from or live alongside the populations who need, or are the target of, such activities. Of these, I identify those who implement formal projects, have decision-making authority or distribute resources as local development agents. Their close socio-economic location, relational dependence on the targets and beneficiaries of aid for their social status and sense of self, make their work and experiences distinctly different from development agents from the global North. Local development agents share commonalities across different contexts, making them a distinct object of study within Development Studies (Chapter Two).

Their heightened susceptibility is one such shared characteristic. It was through a trans-local ethnography of two different types of local development

---

[1] By Euro-America I refer to countries of institutions directed by power-holders in Western Europe, USA, Canada, Australia and New Zealand. The distinction is intended to highlight the ongoing dominance of actors in these countries in development, and/or their self-appointed role in 'developing others', rather than a pattern of wealth or other indicators. I purposefully avoid global North as the value of this classification is its ability to transcend geographical borders.

agents that this under-recognized aspect of power became visible, with implications beyond local development terrains. I argue that susceptibility operates across all relations in development, such as those between donor agency and state government, international NGO and national partner, or expat workers and community leaders. Indeed, it is a core contention of this book that the relative lack of attention to local development agents has resulted in a failure to account for how the differential capacity/susceptibility to affect and be affected orders power relations in development more broadly. While I have focused on the local level to explain the affective properties of power configurations in urban development, in this conclusion I turn to how these theoretical insights can illuminate development writ large. Further, by considering vulnerability as an ethical practice, I return to the question of how we can deploy this understanding of power to arrive at a more responsive development and just world.

The Self

In Part I I focused on the significance of becoming a local development agent in the self-making projects of volunteers and Parshads. The literature has only recently started to take the motivations of local development agents seriously, moving beyond the well-worn tropes of calculating individuals seeking material benefit and social influence (Lund and Saito-Jensen 2013) to reveal how the desire to do good and become a better person is a central animating force (Scherz 2014; Watanabe 2017).[2] For many of the local development agents in this study, development was a site where they could achieve long held ambitions to become a better person or achieve a sense of self that was nascent, yet unrealized due to social and/or material conditions. Others were thrust into these positions, or else had new self-imaginaries opened up. For example, Meera developed a new sense of who she was and could become when she became Parshad to fulfil her husband's ambitions; Ibu Rosa was 'just a housewife' until she heard about the PNPM after which something was sparked within her, motivating her to join the BKM.

I contribute to understanding both the nature of these ambitions and the extent to which they are successfully realized by drawing attention to the

---

[2] Anger, at social injustices or otherwise, did not emerge as an animating force, as one might expect with local development agents (with thanks to the series editor for drawing my attention to this possibility). That anger is not an emotion that motivates social action is perhaps indicative of the kinds of self-making projects these development actors are engaged in.

importance of the capacity and opportunity to be affected. In order to become, one must have the opportunity for affective experiences that reaffirm this nascent or emergent self. Class and gender are just two factors shaping the unevenness of these opportunities. In both Medan and Dehradun, I witnessed an expansion in these opportunities. In Medan, low-class *warga* had the opportunity to experience being useful, caring for others, contributing to society with *ikhlas* (sincerity). In Dehradun, gender quotas provide an opportunity for more women to experience public life by contesting elections in reserved seats, and for some, becoming Parshads. The capacity to be affected is a part of the human condition. Yet discourses and ideologies shape how individuals are affected, and the way bodily responses are qualified and expressed as emotions. The capacity to be affected is hence differentiated and embedded within the systems of signification in which we become subjects. A feminine and gender appropriate style of 'social worker' shapes the way women political actors felt in their interactions with others, the kinds of feelings that they experienced and were willing to acknowledge and express. While affect thereby arguably intensifies discourse and ideology, strong affective experiences can also offer moments of rupture and creativity, for example when women openly expressed anger, sparking political ambitions (Chapter Four).

Providing the opportunities for affective experiences and offering new frames for interpreting feeling is empowering inasmuch as it enables an expansion in the possibilities for self (Jakimow 2018b). This positive outcome is rarely acknowledged as a benefit of development, yet alone written into projects to enhance its potential. A vast body of literature examines the success or otherwise of the PNPM, yet none that I know of consider the empowering possibilities for its volunteers. PRAGATI[3] and I have attempted to incorporate an understanding of empowerment as an expansion in possibilities for self in our capacity-building programme for women Parshads (see Jakimow 2017b). Possibilities include affective experiences, such as speaking into a microphone: a small but potentially significant act. Well designed interventions that seek involvement from local actors can contribute to transforming the 'political economy of personhood' (Jakimow 2015) in two ways. First, expanding the possibilities for self helps to overcome an under-recognized form of marginalization: limited avenues of self-realization. Second, as self and society are mutually constitutive, changes to the possibilities of the former have the potential to lead to social transformation (Comaroff and Comaroff 1992).

---

[3] The NGO I work with in Dehradun, see Chapter Two.

At the same time, there are risks in empowering local development actors through an expanded sense of who they are, and are becoming. Volunteers in Medan and women political actors in Dehradun become affectively attached to new self-imaginaries, leading them to make further investments in the self's realization and sustainment. As we draw upon the resources within the topography of self in these processes of becoming, these affective investments are compatible with socio-historical ethical models or regimes of truth (Foucault 1994). When such a self is precarious and the affective rewards for compliance are high, local development actors can be particularly loyal to dominant development discourses. In answering why dominant development discourses stick and are perpetuated despite not serving the interests of local people or their lived experiences (Kapoor 2017), the ways local level development actors internalize and make these objectives their own requires greater attention. At the same time, there is always an imagination that lies outside the ethical frames of the time, sparked by affect, emotion, and embodied experience (Moore 2011). Activating that imagination so that local development agents can contribute to the reconfiguring of socio-historical regimes of truth requires changes to the affective conditions in which they become. Experimentation as much as rule following should engender positive feelings; local development actors need the space to act on their 'instincts' and emotional responses.

A second risk arises from the huge stakes involved in self-making projects through local development: no less than the sense of who one is, and is becoming. To seek new ways of being in relation to others entails a risk to the self that one is (Zigon and Throop 2014). By inviting people to become local development agents, we are asking them to risk their former self, as well as invest in an idea of self that is uncertain and precarious. This risk is particularly high for people who are from the communities in which they work. There is less risk to an expat, as the bubble of Aidland (Apthorpe 2011) provides a liminal space to experiment with new ideas of self with fewer risks to durable self-narratives or relations with meaningful others. The risks are higher for national elites, yet their socio-economic distance from the target populations affords them greater protection than local agents. In other words, the great stakes involved in becoming a local development agent make them highly susceptible to being impressed upon in ways that threaten their sense of self, particularly when development fails to live up to expectations (Fechter 2016). A core contention of this book is that the burdens of this susceptibility are unevenly spread in development, with local development agents bearing a disproportionate load.

Collective Conditions

Part II examined the collective conditions that engender the capacities and susceptibilities to affect and be affected. These conditions are part of the topography for self, containing affective resources upon which people draw in their self making projects as well as productive of affects that impress upon one involuntarily. Part II also focused attention on the susceptibility *to* affect, recognizing that the force of a body in relation may engender affects that are detrimental to that individual. In Chapters Five and Six, we saw how local development agents engendered suspicion, cynicism, and instrumentalism in others, negatively impacting their work as well as their self-making projects. Furthermore, affective conditions also emboldened citizens, that is, enhanced their capacity to be affected in ways that animated them to cast accusations or make demands. These same conditions gave a force to their words and actions, made them plausible and effective, indicative of an enhanced capacity to affect. Collective forms of affect are therefore significant, yet largely over-looked elements of development terrains.

I drew upon two different ways of understanding collective affect in order to account for what I saw as distinct conditions that were at times mutually disruptive (Chapter Five) and at others, mutually reinforcing (Chapter Six). A central debate in affect theory is the role of human actors in the production of affective conditions and the extent to which affect is outside of, or intimately bound to, signification and human action (Anderson 2014; Thrift 2008). Wetherell's (2012) concept of 'affective prac-tice' navigates a path between these two possibilities, arguing that iterative, unconscious, and habitual practices produce anew the affective arrange-ments in which we dwell. These configurations produce affective slots that land on and recruit individuals, positioning them in modes of being in relation: inferiority in relation to superiority, deference to dominance. In Chapter Five I demonstrated how the affective practices of a ceremony to mark the completion of a BKM project enabled the reaffirmation of volun-teers as people 'doing good', while making them less attentive and respon-sive to the recipients of programme benefits. In Chapter Six, affective practices of supplication by women candidates in local elections were pro-ductive of affective configurations that slotted Parshads and voters into arrangements of deference and superiority respectively, seemingly conflict-ing with their formal social status. In both cases, affective practices are a constituent of power relations within local development.

The second understanding of collective affect borrows from Anderson's (2014) notion of affective atmosphere. I introduced the term 'moral atmosphere' in Chapter Five to describe the affective excesses of moral logics; that is, the way that logics generate a sense of potentialities that are an inescapable presence, engendering feelings related to possibilities rather than concrete actions. In contrast to the iterative practices that produce affective configurations, moral atmospheres emanate from ideas, suggestions, and discourses. The moral atmosphere of *bagi-bagi* infected the scenes of community development in Chapter Five, made volunteers sticky with suspicion, susceptible to engendering scorn and derision in others, while intensifying the force of complaints and accusations due to their plausibility. In Chapter Six, a moral atmosphere of clientelism hung over Parshads, reduced their humanity in the eyes of voters who were emboldened to treat them as servants. As a lingering presence, the moral atmosphere influences the susceptibility to be affected of local development actors, as well as the capacity of others—voters, citizens, beneficiaries—to affect them.

Collective forms of affect are therefore critical to the power configurations of development terrains, reproducing or potentially disrupting prevailing hierarchies. The disruptive potential is seemingly greatest in the BKM ceremony, as the moral atmosphere of *bagi-bagi* poses a direct challenge to the affective practice of 'doing good'. That there was no disruption points to a critical question: which actors, under which conditions have the capacity to shape the collective conditions in which we dwell. Volunteers were able to divert their attention away from the metaphorical eye-rolls of the women 'beneficiaries', whose cynicism or perhaps just annoyance was manifestly evident to me and my research assistants, yet seemingly had no capacity to affect BKM members. In Dehradun, the moral atmosphere was mutually reinforcing of the affective practices of campaigning, creating a durable affective configuration that slotted women Parshads into positions of deference. This affective configuration seemingly indicates a reversal of the power relations between voters and elected representatives, thereby indicative of the transformative potential of collective affect (in this case, the moral atmosphere of clientelistic democracy). At the same time, the importance of gender for the extent of these reversals and their durability over time has only partially and provisionally been answered by my account of women Parshads.

Understanding human contributions to collective conditions either through iterative affective practice or the circulation of emotionally charged ideas, can point to new ways to reconfigure power relations in development. For example, attention to the production anew of slots of superiority in the

BKM ceremony may indicate the need for new practices, such as handing over control of the ceremony to the 'beneficiaries', or failing to wait for a late government official. Collective conditions also point to the unintended consequences of campaigns against afflictions such as corruption: emboldening an attentive citizenry but creating difficulties for development agents who may be acting with integrity. In Dehradun, affective practices of supplication during elections may be an under-recognized constraint for women politicians wishing to advance beyond the local level, requiring new modalities of campaigning that engender respect rather than a sense of entitlement among voters. While many will feel that a citizenry emboldened to make demands on elected representatives is positive, the disregard of the humanity of politicians within clientelistic democracy may embolden those who already claim more than their fair share. It is therefore imperative to examine how collective conditions engender *differential* capacities and susceptibilities to affect and be affected, as well as understand the differential power of individuals and groups to *shape* these collective conditions.

Encounters

While the conditions that engender differential capacities and susceptibilities to affect and be affected are collective, operating on various scales from the local to the global, they are realized in encounters between bodies: the focus of Part III. Chapter Seven focused on material consequences, as differently positioned voters were able to mobilize Parshads to meet their demands. This capacity to affect is relational to the Parshad's susceptibility to be affected, with the immediacy of the encounter within longer histories of contact between 'like bodies' influencing the efficacy of the claim. Two key points came out of this chapter. First, affective biographies and ascriptive identities shape the capacity to affect and susceptibility to be affected. Second, and as a consequence, susceptibility to be affected by (and responsive to) constituents is not necessarily always positive, rather the unevenness of susceptibility may reinforce existing forms of privilege.

I argue that we therefore need to pay attention to when, and in relation to whom, local development agents are more or less susceptible (resilient) to being affected. There is no simple formula. In Dehradun, caste, class, and gender were all factors in shaping differential susceptibility, establishing patterns of affective arrangements without determining actual responses. In relation to some Parshads, a poor individual was able to mobilize them to act swiftly, while in relation to others they were 'put in their place', their demands had little force. Some Parshads were highly responsive to people 'living in posh areas', while others were animated to help all people regardless of who they were in order to enact their competence. In each case, the relative capacities and susceptibilities are tied to the affective investments in self: who they think they are, their anxieties in relation to who they can become. The cultural avenues of self-realization (Ciotti 2009) of elected representatives (and other brokers) are therefore affectively tied to citizen entitlements: who can get what. I suggest that this differential susceptibility (or differential responsiveness) points to yet one more reason to ensure that politics and the bureaucracy are representative of people with different types of life experiences.

Part III also pointed to the need for an analytical category that captures our resilience to being affected. Phenomenological anthropology has rightly drawn attention to humans' openness to the world, their inherent susceptibility to be impressed upon in ways that shape their becoming (Jackson 1998; Biehl and Locke 2017). At the same time, we should not overlook the tendency of humans to be protective of the self and our capacity to be resistant to threats to the durable sense of who we are. Berlant (2011) describes the quotidian acts of self-preservation that help us to retain a sense of ongoingness in the world, even when those affective attachments to self are damaging. In other words, the world impresses upon us in ways that are radically involuntary (Butler 2015), at the same time acting to avoid or reduce the potency of these impressions is a part of the human condition. Enquiring as to when we can successfully recover from the impressions that threaten our sense of self (using the term of Chapter Seven, recover from an affective injury) sheds light on our differential responsiveness to others as a critical element of power configurations.

In Chapter Seven, we examined the consequences of volunteers' resilience to being impressed upon by some bodies (their differential susceptibility to be affected) for development practice. Most BKM members were relatively resilient to the affects engendered in their encounters with 'beneficiaries'. They deflected attention away from the hurt caused, produced counter-narratives or reaffirmed their sense of superiority over the complainant. These responses are in part due to the huge stakes involved in development activities as explored in Part I, which makes recovery from affective injuries important for local development agents' sense of ongoingness in the world. Practices close one off from the hurt; one's openness and responsiveness to the world (Throop 2018) is temporarily suspended in an act of self-preservation. Local development agents are susceptible to being affected as a fundamental condition, yet are not always vulnerable, that is with an openness to be affected in ways that lead to a transformation in self, relationships, or practices. In this way, resilience to be affected can act as a 'limit to reflexivity' (Schwittay 2014). Reflective practice that is responsive to the populations who are the target of interventions is seen as critical to development. What we have learnt is that differential susceptibility attunes development practitioners to being attentive to (and learning from) some actors more than others in ways that often map on to conventional top-down development hierarchies.

At the same time, there is always the potential for people who are otherwise marginalized or seemingly powerless to affect local development agents. This under-recognized power does not require changes to the capacities of the 'powerless', but rather to the relationships within the development terrain. As there can be conflicting affective pulls (a woman makes a claim for assistance at the same time as an NGO imposes criteria that would make her ineligible), the relationship to be changed is not only the direct one between local development agent and citizen/resident. Rather attention is required as to the varying degrees of susceptibility within development infrastructures, with transformation across all relationships so that susceptibility to be affected by certain individuals (the poor for example) is complemented by resilience to be affected by others (such as NGO managers). I end this discussion with a caution against advocating a blanket openness to be affected among local development agents. As noted in Part I, there is a great deal at stake for these actors while the claims of members of the public are not always justified or worthy of a response. My argument is simply that differential susceptibility to be affected is a condition shaping power configurations in development terrains, and thereby worthy of analysis. Vulnerability as a practice of being open in order to overcome detrimental power inequalities is a means to use these insights to improve development practice.

Vulnerability

Development studies is a field of study based on using understandings of power, process, and institutions to deliver a better, more equitable world (Fischer 2019). Post-structuralist understandings of power advanced the field of development studies by revealing the ways underdevelopment was created through discourse, justifying technical interventions that were at times worse than the problems they were designed to solve. The sector learnt, to an extent, leading to practices that reversed knowledge hierarchies (Chambers 1997), that led to inclusive processes of knowledge production (McFarlane 2006; Jakimow 2008) reflexive development and development pluralism (Nederveen Pieterse 2010). Development studies scholars are slowly turning towards affect theory to further advance the field (Sultana 2011; Wright 2012). Affect is productive as a concept, as it aids an understanding not only of the apparatuses that sustain unequal power relations (the intensity and force of discourses for example), but also of the potentialities for disruption and transformation (Legg 2011). This book has been a small contribution to extracting lessons from affect theory to produce better understandings of development processes, and thereby improved practices.

Taking the capacity/susceptibility to affect and be affected as an analytical starting point to understand power (Anderson 2014; Massumi 2015) invites new readings of what development should look like. As noted in the introduction, 'development' includes both the immanent processes of change, as well as the intentional practices to ensure such change is positive. In both cases, development should improve the well-being of deprived populations and involve the redistribution of resources so that everyone's needs are met within the earth's limits. It is my contention that the relatively greater capacity of elite groups to affect (drive the debate, set the agenda, establish 'common sense'), and the resilience of decision makers to being affected by marginal groups (a lack of responsiveness to their conditions and a failure to be moved by the consequences of unfair resource distribution) are factors in many of the failures of intentional Development and continuing inequality. It stands to reason that enhancing the capacity of some groups to affect, while making others more susceptible to being affected, could lead to more responsive and just development.

I argue that vulnerability as an ethical practice can be a starting point to transform relational capacities and susceptibilities (Gilson 2014). As Butler notes, susceptibility is 'a condition of our responsiveness to others, even a condition of our responsibility for them' (Butler 2005: 88, emphasis removed). As I have demonstrated throughout this book, however, humans are differentially susceptible, and in many cases resilient to being affected in ways that challenge their fundamental beliefs. In the introduction I posited a difference between susceptibility as a condition of human life and vulnerability as an ethical practice, to acknowledge that being open to being affected may require a purposeful orientation. While this intentionality may be seen as incompatible with the unbidden nature of affect and the way it impresses upon us involuntarily (Thrift 2008; Butler 2015), as other scholars note (Wetherell 2012; Anderson 2014), affect is not devoid of human agency. Without overlooking the way that affect is always in excess of arrangements for life and living, never fully captured by power apparatuses (Legg 2011), it is also the case that the affective dimensions of life can be, and are used to achieve certain objectives (Anderson 2014). I argue that likewise, development agents—those with power or authority over resource distribution and/or decision-making, and/ or who assist others beyond their familial relations—can be attentive to the affective configurations that shape their actions and be intentionally attuned to (open to being affected by) bodies with otherwise diminished capacity to affect.

Vulnerability as an ethical practice for development could be incorporated into each of the three levels examined in this book. In acknowledgement of the importance of selfhood within development terrains, a practice of vulnerability would involve being attentive to the needs for affective reaffirmation of more marginal actors—specifically those of local development agents. Affective feedback from development elites (government officials, NGO workers for example) can have a force that closes off alternative imaginings; what is considered 'right and wrong' therefore needs to be opened up not just discursively, but affectively. Development practitioners and activists can also work proactively to create collective conditions that enhance the capacity of certain actors to affect, and if necessary, reduce the susceptibility of others. Affective practices are largely unconscious. Being mindful of these and the way they sustain unhelpful forms of privilege, can be a starting point for practices productive of new affective arrangements. Vulnerability in this case involves a recognition of one's privileged position in shaping collective forms of affect and intentionally creating space for others to contribute. Finally, vulnerability in encounters requires a practice of reflexivity in the present: taking stock of one's bodily modifications in relation to others, and being attentive to how the 'Other' is affected by one's own force. At each level, vulnerability entails a commitment to new forms of relationality and to transforming the conditions engendering differential capacities and susceptibilities to affect and be affected.

Vulnerability is not a practice that needs to, or should be practised by all. As this book demonstrates, susceptibility is not necessarily an unequivocal good. With whom one is vulnerable is critical. Here I question whether it is fair to expect local development agents to be open to having their sense of self threatened, when development efforts are often successful in part due to the affective investments they make in their self-making projects through these activities. Such affective injuries are arguably most severe for local development agents who live alongside the people, whose relational selves are most closely intertwined with these people, and who must deal most directly with the lived consequences of failed development projects. The central message of this book is thus twofold. First, I argue that we need to consider how suscepti-bility is distributed among aid and development chains. That is, within the network of actors from international donor agencies, national government elites, corporate entities, local government officials, NGOs, and local develop-ment agents, who is made to bear the burden of susceptibility? Second is the need to reflect on how these networks enable, encourage, or make exception-ally risky the kind of vulnerability that I argue is conducive to responsive development and a more just world.

Glossary

Note on Language

I use common spellings for words in Hindi that commonly appear in roman script, but transliterate for pronunciation in the glossary. I do not use diacritical marks for other Hindi words to show long vowels, rather I repeat the letter (for example 'aa') except at the end of a sentence. I do not differentiate between retroflex and dental consonants. Words in Hindi are represented by (H) in the glossary, and words in Bahasa Indonesia by (I). Proper names and acronyms are not identified as either Hindi or Indonesian.

andolan (H)	social movement for a particular cause
andolan kari (H)	fighter in a people's movement
bagi-bagi (I)	*bagi*: share; *bagi-bagi*: to distribute
basti (H)	informal/irregular housing settlement/slum
becak (I)	motorcycle rickshaw, form of cheap public transport
bermanfaatkan (I)	to be of benefit, from *manfaat* (benefit)
BJP	Bharatiya Janata Party (India's People Party)
BKM	Badan Keswadayaan Masyarakat (Board for Community Self-reliance)
dana bergulir (I)	rotating funds, a form of savings and lending
diatas (I)	above: a relational term often used to describe higher social or economic status
dibawah (I)	below: a relational term often used to describe lower social or economic status
ecek-ecek (I)	not serious; doing something only for appearances
hati (I)	emotion seat of the individual, heart or liver (literal)
Ibu (I)	mother/ma'am: used as a polite form of address for women
iklhas (I)	sincerity
jilbab (I)	headscarf worn by Muslim women covering hair and neck
jiwa (I)	soul, or one's nature
kader (I)	cadre, volunteers who help with implementation of government programmes at the local level
Kantor Lurah	government office at the level of the kelurahan
karya karta (H)	party worker
kecamatan (I)	sub-district

kelurahan (I)	level of urban governance (ward level)
kepling (I)	*kepala lingkungan* (head of the lingkungan)
lakh (H)	a unit of measurement, 100,000
lingkungan (I)	environment, level of urban governance (neighbourhood)
Lok Sabha	'House of the People': India's lower house, national parliament
masyarakat (I)	community/people
naukaar (H)	servant (masculine form)
naukraanii (H)	servant (feminine form)
OBC	Other Backward Class: government designation for low caste
orang belum mampu (I)	poor people/people not yet capable
orang biasa (I)	ordinary people/person
pahaar (H)	mountain
pahaari (H)	person who traces familial connections to the mountains
Pak (I)	sir: used as a polite form of address for men
panchayat (H)	level of rural governance (village level)
Parshad/Paarshad (H)	ward member; municipal councillor
peduli (I)	care
pemberdayaan (I)	empowerment
pembinaan (I)	guidance
Pemuda Pancasila	paramilitary organization; *pemuda* means youth, while Pancasila refers to the five principles of the Indonesian state
pejabat (I)	government official
penerima manfaat (I)	recipients of benefits, 'beneficiaries'
PNPM	Program Nasional Pemberdayaan Masyarakat (National Program for Community Empowerment)
Posyandu (I)	*pos pelayanan terpadu*: integrated service post for delivery of local health, particularly child and maternal health
PRAGATI	Panchayati Rule and Gender Awareness Training Institute
pranaam (H)	greeting, with two hands in prayer (signalling obeisance)
preman (I)	gangster/thug
rakyat kecil (I)	little people; ordinary people as opposed to rich or powerful
relawan (I)	volunteer
retinir (I)	usurer; money lender
saree/saarii (H)	an item of women's clothing consisting of a length of fabric wrapped around the body
SC	Scheduled Caste: government designation for Dalit (people outside the Hindu caste system, historically oppressed)

seva (H)	service
sevak samajik (saamaajik) (H)	social worker
sosialisasi (I)	socialization
tenaga (I)	energy, labour power
wajood/vajood (Urdu)	being; sense of self
warga (I)	resident of area; citizen
wirid pongajian (I)	women's group for prayer and reading the Qu'ran

References

Acosta, Alberto (2017) 'Living Well: ideas for reinventing the future', *Third World Quarterly*, 38(12): 2600–16.

Agrawal, Arun (2005) *Environmentality: Technologies of Government and the Making of Subjects*. Durham, NC: Duke University Press.

Ahluwalia, Isher Judge (2019) 'Urban Governance in India', *Journal of Urban Affairs*, 41(1): 83–102.

Ahmed, Sara (2004) *The Cultural Politics of Emotion*. Edinburgh: Edinburgh University Press.

Ahmed, Sara (2010) *The Promise of Happiness*. Durham, NC: Duke University Press

Ahuja, Amit and Pradeep Chibber (2012) 'Why the poor vote in India: "If I don't vote, I am dead to the state"', *Studies in Comparative International Development*, 47: 389–410.

Allahyari, Rebecca Anne (1996) ' "Ambassadors of God" and "The Sinking Classes": visions of charity and moral selving', *The International Journal of Sociology and Social Policy*, 16(1–2): 35–69.

Alm, Bjorn (2010) 'Creating Followers, Gaining Patrons: Leadership Struggles in a Tamil Nadu Village', in P. Price and A. E. Ruud (eds) *Power and Influence in India: Bosses, Lords and Captains*, London: Routledge, pp. 1–19.

Anderson, Ben (2009) 'Affective Atmospheres', *Emotion, Space and Society*, 2: 77–81.

Anderson, Ben (2014) *Encountering Affect: Capacities, Apparatuses, Conditions*, Farnham: Ashgate.

Apthorpe, R. (2011) 'Coda: With Alice in Aidland: A seriously satirical allegory', in D. Mosse (ed.) *Adventures in Aidland: The Anthropology of Professionals in International Development*. London: Berghahn Books, pp. 199–220.

Arvidson, Malin (2008) 'Contradictions and confusions in development work: exploring the realities of Bangladeshi NGOs', *Journal of South Asian Development*, 3(1): 109–34.

Aspinall, Edward and Ward Berenschot (2019) *Democracy for Sale: Elections, Clientelism, and the State in Indonesia*, Ithaca, NY: Cornell University Press.

Aspinall, Edward, Sebastian Dettman, and Eve Warburton (2011) 'When Religion Trumps Ethnicity: a regional election case study from Indonesia', *South East Asia Research*, 19(1): 27–58.

Auyero, Javier (2012) *Patients of the State: the politics of waiting in Argentina*, Durham, NC: Duke University Press.

Ballie Smith, Matt, Nina Laurie, and Mark Griffiths (2018) 'South–South volunteering and development', *The Geographical Journal*, 184(2): 158–68.

Banerjee, Mukulika (2014) *Why India Votes*. London: Routledge.

Bauman, Zygmunt and Rein Raud (2015) *Practices of Selfhood*. Cambridge: Polity.

Beatty, Andrew (2010) 'How did it feel for you? Emotion, narrative and the limits of ethnography', *American Anthropologist*, 112(3): 430–43.

Beatty, Andrew (2014) 'Anthropology and Emotion', *Journal of the Royal Anthropological Institute*, 20: 545–63.

Bebbington, A. (2004) 'NGOs and Uneven Development: Geographies of Development Intervention', *Progress is Human Geography*, 28(6), pp. 725–45.

Beck, Erin (2017) *How Development Projects Persist: Everyday Negotiations with Guatemalan NGOs*. Durham, NC: Duke University Press.

Beckerlegge, Gwilym (2015) 'Seva: The focus of a fragmented but gradually coalescing field of study', *Religions of South Asia*, 9(2): 208–39.

Bedi, Tarini (2016) *The Dashing Ladies of Shiv Sena: Political Matronage in Urbanizing India*, Albany, NY: SUNY Press.

Berenschot, Ward (2010) 'Everyday Mediation: The politics of public service delivery in Gujarat, India', *Development and Change*, 41(5): 883–905.

Berenschot, Ward (2014) 'Political Fixers in India's Patronage Democracy', in A. Piliavsky (ed.) *Patronage as Politics in South Asia*, Delhi: Cambridge University Press, pp. 196–216.

Berenschot, Ward and Gerry van Klinken (2018) 'Informality and citizenship: the everyday state in Indonesia.' *Journal of Citizenship Studies*, 22 (2).

Berenschot, Ward, Retna Hanani, and Prio Sambodho (2018) 'Brokers and citizenship: access to health care in Indonesia', *Journal of Citizenship Studies*, 22(2): 129–44.

Berlant, Lauren (2011) *Cruel Optimism*. Durham, NC: Duke University Press.

Bernstein, Henry (2005) 'Development Studies and the Marxists', in U. Kothari (ed.) *A Radical History of Development Studies: Individuals, Institutions and Ideologies*. London: Zed Books, pp. 111–37.

Biehl, João and Peter Locke (2017) 'Introduction: Ethnographic Sensorium' in J. Biehl and P. Locke (eds), *Unfinished: The Anthropology of Becoming*. Durham, NC: Duke University Press, pp. 1–40.

Björkman, Lisa (2014) 'You can't buy a vote': Meanings of money in a Mumbai election', *American Ethnologist*, 41(4): 617–34.

Boellstorff, Tom (2005a) 'Between Religion and Desire: Being Muslim and *Gay* in Indonesia', *American Anthropologist*, 107(4): 575–85.

Boellstorff, Tom (2005b) *The Gay Archipelago: Sexuality and Nation in Indonesia*. Princeton, NJ: Princeton University Press.

Boellstorff, Tom and Johan Lindquist (2004) 'Bodies of Emotion: Rethinking Culture and Emotion through Southeast Asia', *Ethnos*, 69(4): 437–44.

Boesten, J., Mdee, A., Cleaver, F. (2011) 'Service delivery on the cheap? Community-based workers in development interventions', *Development in Practice*, 2 (1): 41–58.

Bornstein, Erica (2012) *Disquieting Gifts: Humanitarianism in New Delhi*. Stanford, CA: Stanford University Press.

Bourdieu, Pierre (1990) *The Logic of Practice*, Stanford, CA: Stanford University Press.

Brickell, Katherine and Sylvia Chant (2010) ' "The Unbearable Heaviness of Being": reflection on female altruism in Cambodia, Philippines, The Gambia and Costa Rica', *Progress in Development Studies*, 10(2): 145–59.

Brown, Hannah and Ruth J. Prince (2015) 'Introduction: Volunteer Labor—Pasts and Futures of Work, Development and Citizenship in East Africa', *African Studies Review*, 58(2): 29–42.

Budiman, A., A. Roan, and V. Callon (2013) 'Rationalizing Ideologies, Social Identities and Corruption among Civil Servants in Indonesia During the Suharto Era', *Journal of Business Ethics*, 116: 139–49.

Bulloch, Hannah (2017) *In Pursuit of Progress: Narratives of Development on a Philippine Island*. Honolulu, HI: University of Hawaii Press.

Butler, Judith (1997) *The Psychic Life of Power: Theories in Subjection*. Stanford, CA: Stanford University Press.

Butler, Judith (2004) *Precarious Life: The Powers of Mourning and Violence*, London: Verso.

Butler, Judith (2005) *Giving an Account of Oneself.* New York: Fordham University Press.

Butler, Judith (2015) *Senses of the Subject* New York: Fordham University Press.

Butler, Judith, Zeynep Gambetti, and Leticia Sabsay (2016) 'Introduction', in J. Butler, Z. Gambetti, and L. Sabsay (eds) *Vulnerability in Resistance*, Durham, NC: Duke University Press, pp. 1–11.

Carroll, T. (2009) ' "Social Development" as Neoliberal Trojan Horse: the World Bank and the Kecamatan Development Program in Indonesia', *Development and Change*, 40(3): 447–66.

Carswell, Grace and Geert de Neve (2014) 'Why Indians Vote: Reflection on Rights, Citizenship, and Democracy from a Tamil Nadu Village', *Antipode*, 46(4): 1032–53.

Chambers, Robert (1997) 'Editorial: Responsible Well-Being—A personal agenda for development', *World Development*, 25(11): 1743–54.

Chandhoke, Neera (2009) 'Putting Civil Society in its Place', *Economic and Political Weekly*, XLIV(7): 12–16.

Chandra, K. (2004) 'Elections as Auctions', *Seminar*, 539. http://www.india-seminar.com/2004/539/539%20kanchan%20chandra.htm (accessed 29 May 2017).

Chettri, Shradha (2017) 'Illegal Colonies in east Delhi clamour for basic civic amneties before April 23 polls', *Hindustan Times* https://www.hindustantimes.com/delhi-news/wanted-basic-civic-amenities-in-illegal-colonies/story-Zst21Vh97kKxPaW8nrQIaP.html (accessed 5 October 2018).

Chung, Anastasia (2015) 'Colonial Continuities and Impossible Attempts: critical engagements in development', *Progress in Development Studies*, 15(2): 186–96.

Ciotti, Manuela (2009) 'The *Conditions* of politics: low-caste women's agency in contemporary North Indian society', *Feminist Review*, 91: 113–34.

Ciotti, Manuela (2012) 'Resurrecting *Seva* (social service): Dalit and Low-caste Women Party Activists as Producers and Consumers of Political Culture and Practice in Urban North India', *The Journal of Asian Studies*, 71(1): 149–70.

Ciotti, Manuela (2017) 'Away from the Iconic and the Normative: the unlikely subjects of gender and politics', in M. Ciotti (ed.) *Unsettling the Archetypes: femininities and masculinities in Indian politics.* New Delhi: Women Unlimited, pp. 1–24.

Comaroff, John and Jean Comaroff (1992) *Ethnography and the Historical Imagination.* Boulder, CO: Westview Press.

Corbridge, Stuart, Glyn Williams, Manoj Srivastava, and Rene Veron (2005) *Seeing the State: Governance and Governmentality in India.* Cambridge: Cambridge University Press.

Crehan, Kate (2016) *Gramsci's Common Sense: Inequality and its narratives*, Durham, NC: Duke University Press.

Crewe, Emma and Elizabeth Harrison (1998) *Whose Development? An Ethnography of Aid*, London: Zed Books.

Deeb, Lara (2006) *An Enchanted Modern: Gender and Public Piety in Shi'I Lebanon*, Princeton, NJ: Princeton University Press.

Desjarlais, Robert and C. Jason Throop (2011) 'Phenomenological Approaches in Anthropology', *Annual Review of Anthropology*, 40: 87–102.

Doucet, Andrea and Natasha Mauthner (2008) 'What can be known and how? Narrated subjects and the Listening Guide', *Qualitative Research* 8(3): 399–409.

Duranti, Alessandro (2010) 'Husserl, intersubjectivity and anthropology', *Anthropological Theory*, 10(1–2): 16–35.

Ebrahim, A. (2003) *NGOs and Organizational Change: Discourse, Reporting and Learning*, Cambridge: Cambridge University Press.

Effendy, Rochmad (2015) 'The moral values as the foundation for sustainable community development: a review of the Indonesia government-sponsored National Program for Community Empowerment Urban Self Reliance Project (PNPM MP)', *Journal of Economics and Sustainable Development* 6(7): 1–22.

England, Kim V. L. (1994) Getting Personal: Reflexivity, Positionality and Feminist Research', *Professional Geographer*, 46(10: 80–9.

Escobar, Arturo (1995) *Encountering Development: The making and unmaking of the Third World*. Princeton, NJ: Princeton University Press.

Fanon, Franz (1967) *Black Skin White Masks*, New York: Grove Press Inc.

Fechter A. M. (2016) 'Aid work as moral labour', *Critique of Anthropology*, 36(3): 228–43.

Fechter, Anne-Meike (2012a) 'Introduction: The personal and the professional: aid workers' relationships and values in the development process' *Third World Quarterly*, 33(8): 1387–404.

Fechter, Anne-Meike (2012b) 'Living Well' while 'Doing Good'? (Missing) debates on altruism and professionalism in aid work, *Third World Quarterly*, 33(8): 1475–91.

Feldman, Ilana (2007) 'The Quaker way: Ethical labor and humanitarian relief', *American Ethnologist*, 34(4): 689–705.

Ferguson, James (1990) *The Anti-Politics Machine: Development, Depoliticization and Bureaucratic Power in Lesotho*. Cambridge: Cambridge University Press

Fischer, Andrew (2019) 'Bringing Development Back into Development Studies', *Development and Change*, 50(2): 426–44.

Fischer, W. (1997) 'Doing Good? The politics and anti-politics of NGO practices', *Annual Review of Anthropology*, 26, pp. 439–64.

Foucault, M. (1979) *Discipline and Punish: The Birth of the Prison*. New York: Pantheon Books.

Foucault, Michael (1986) *The Care of Self: The History of Sexuality Volume 3*, translated by Robert Hurley. New York: Random House.

Foucault, M. (1991) 'Governmentality', in G. Burchell, C. Gordon, and P. Miller (eds) *The Foucault Effect: Studies in Governmentality*. Chicago: The University of Chicago Press, pp. 87–104.

Foucault, Michael (1994) 'The Ethics of the Concern of the Self as a Practice of Freedom', in P. Rabinow (ed.) *Ethics: Subjectivity and Truth*. New York: The New Press, pp. 281–302.

Fox, Nick J. (2015) 'Emotions, affects and the production of social life', *The British Journal of Sociology*, 66(2): 301–18.

Gaonkar, Dilip Parameshwar (2007) 'On cultures of democracy', *Public Culture*, 19(1): 1–22.

Gardner, Katy and David Lewis (2015) *Anthropology and Development: Challenges for the twenty-first century*. London: Pluto Press.

Geertz, Clifford (1984) 'From the native's point of view': on the nature of anthropological understanding', in R. Shweder and R. LeVine (eds) *Culture Theory: Essays on Mind, Self and Emotion*. Cambridge: Cambridge University Press, pp. 123–36.

Gerke, Solvay (1992) 'Indonesian national development ideology and the role of women', *Indonesia Circle: School of Oriental and African Studies Newsletter*, 59 & 60: 45–56.

Ghosh, Archana and Stéphanie Tawa Lama-Rewel (2005) *Democratization in Progress: Women and local politics in urban India*. New Delhi: Tulika Books.

Gibbings, Sheri (2013) 'Unseen Powers and Democratic Detectives: Street Vendors in an Indonesian City', *City & Society*, 25(2): 235–59.

Gibbings, Sheri Lynn (2017) '*Sosialisasi*, street vendors and citizenship in Yogyakarta', in W. Berenschot, H. S. Nordholt, and L. Bakker (eds) *Citizenship and Democratization in Southeast Asia*. Leiden: Brill, pp. 96–122.

Gilson, Erinn C. (2014) *The Ethics of Vulnerability: A Feminist Analysis of Social Life and Practice*. New York: Routledge.

Giri, Ananta Kumar and Phillip Quarles van Ufford (2003) 'Reconstituting development as a shared responsibility: ethics, aesthetics and a creative shaping of human possibilities', in P. Quarles van Ufford and A. K. Giri (eds), *A Moral Critique of Development: in search of global responsibilities*, London: Routledge, pp. 253–78.

Goetz, Anne Marie (2007) 'Political Cleaners: Women as the New Anti-corruption force?' *Development and Change*, 38(1): 87–105.

Guggenheim, Scott (2004) *Crisis and Contradictions: Understanding the Origins of a Community Development Program in Indonesia*. Jakarta: World Bank.

Guha, Ramachandra (1989) *The Unquiet Woods: Ecological Change and Peasant Resistance in the Himalayas*. New Delhi: Oxford University Press.

Guinness, Patrick (2009) *Kampung, Islam and State in Urban Java*. Singapore: NUS Press.

Gupta, Akhil (1995) 'Blurred Boundaries: The Discourse of Corruption, the Culture of Politics and the Imagined State', *American Ethnologist*, 22(2): 375–402.

Gupta, Akhil (2012) *Red Tape: Bureaucracy, Structural Violence and Poverty in India*. Durham, NC: Duke University Press.

Hall, Stuart (2000) 'Who needs "identity"?' in du P. Gay, J. Evans, and P. Redman (eds) *Identity: a reader*, IDE: Sage, pp. 15–30.

Harrison, Elizabeth (2006) 'Unpacking the Anti-corruption Agenda: Dilemmas for Anthropologists', *Oxford Development Studies*, 34(1): 15–29.

Harrison, Elizabeth (2013) 'Beyond the looking glass? "Aidland" reconsidered', *Critique of Anthropology*, 33(3): 263–79.

Hart, Gillian (2010) 'D/developments after the Meltdown', *Antipode*, 41(S1): 117–41.

Hauser, Walter and Wendy Singer (1986) 'The Democratic Rite: Celebration and Participation in the Indian Elections', *Asian Survey*, 26(9): 941–58.

Heaton-Shrestha, Celayne (2006) '"They Can't Mix Like We Can": Bracketing Differences and the Professionalization of NGOs in Nepal', in D. Lewis and D. Mosse (eds) *Development Brokers and Translators: An Ethnography of Aid and Agencies*. Bloomfield, CT: Kumarian Press, pp. 195–217.

Held, Virginia (2006) *The Ethics of Care: Personal, Political, and Global*. Oxford: Oxford University Press.

Hemmings, Clare (2005) 'Invoking Affect: Cultural Theory and the Ontological Turn', *Cultural Studies*, 19(5): 548–67.

Herzfeld, Michael (2015) 'Anthropology and the inchoate intimacies of power', *American Ethnologist*, 42(1): 18–32.

Hickey-Moody, A. (2013) 'Affect as Method: Feelings, Aesthetics and Affective Pedagogy', in R. Coleman and J. Ringrose (eds) *Deleuze and Research Methodologies*. Edinburgh: Edinburgh University Press, pp. 79–95.

High, Holly (2014) *Fields of Desire: Poverty and Policy in Laos*. Singapore: NUS Press.

Highmore, Ben (2010) 'Bitter after Taste: Affect, food, and social aesthetics' in G. J. Seigworth and M. Gregg (eds) *The Affect Theory Reader*. Durham, NC: Duke University Press, pp. 118–37.

Hilhorst, Dorothea (2001) 'Village Experts and Development Discourse: "Progress" in a Philippine Igorot Village', *Human Organization*, 60(4): 401–13.

Hilhorst, Dorothea (2003) *The Real World of NGOs: Discourses, diversity and development.* London: Zed Books Ltd.

Hilhorst, Dorothea (2018) Arenas, in T. Allen, A. MacDonald, and H. Radice (eds) *Humanitarianism: A dictionary of Concepts.* London: Routledge, pp. 30–51.

Hilhorst, Dorothea, Leos Weijers, and Margit van Wessel (2012) 'Aid Relations and Aid Legitimacy: mutual imaging of aid workers and recipients in Nepal', *Third World Quarterly*, 33(8): 1439–57.

Hobart, M. (1993) 'Introduction: the growth of ignorance?' in M. Hobart (ed.) *An Anthropological Critique of Development: The Growth of Ignorance.* London: Routledge, pp. 1–24.

Hochschild, Arlie (1983) *The Managed Heart.* Berkeley and Los Angeles, CA: University of California Press.

Hoffman, Lisa (2013) 'Decentralization as a Mode of governing the Urban in China: Reforms in welfare provisioning and the rise of volunteerism', *Pacific Affairs*, 86(4): 835–55.

Hoffman, Lisa (2014) 'The Urban, Politics and Subject Formation', *International Journal of Urban and Regional Research*, 38(5): 1576–88.

Horner, Rory (2019) 'Towards a new paradigm of global development? Beyond the limits of international development', *Progress in Human Geography*, online first, 1–22.

Huang, Julia Qermezi (2017) 'The Ambiguous Figures of Social Enterprise: Gendered flexibility and relational work among the iAgents of Bangladesh', *American Ethnologist*, 44(4): 603–16.

Jackson, Michael (1998) *Minima Ethnographica: Intersubjectivity and the Anthropological Project.* Chicago: Chicago University Press.

Jackson, Michael (2014) 'Ajàlá's head: Reflections on Anthropology and Philosophy in a West African Setting', in V. Das, M. Jackson, A. Kleinman, and B. Singh (eds) *The Ground Between: Anthropologists engage philosophy.* Durham, NC: Duke University Press, pp. 27–49.

Jakimow, Tanya (2008) 'Answering the Critics: The Potentials and Limitations of the Knowledge Agenda as a Practical Response to Post-Development Critiques', *Progress in Development Studies*, 8(4): 311–23.

Jakimow, Tanya (2010) 'Negotiating the Boundaries of Voluntarism: Values in the Indian NGO Sector', *VOLUNTAS*, 21(4): 546–68.

Jakimow, Tanya (2012) *Peddlers of Information: Indian Non-government Organizations in the Information Age.* Bloomfield, CT: Kumarian Press.

Jakimow, Tanya (2013) 'Spoiling the Situation': reflections on the development and research field', *Development in Practice*, 23(1): 21–32.

Jakimow, Tanya (2015) *Decentring Development: Understanding change in agrarian societies.* Houndmills, Basingstoke: Palgrave-Macmillan.

Jakimow, Tanya (2017a) 'Becoming a Developer: Processes of Personhood in Urban Community-Driven Development, Indonesia', *Anthropological Forum*, 27(3): 256–76.

Jakimow, Tanya (2017b) 'Empowering Women Municipal Councillors in Dehradun', *Economic and Political Weekly*, LII(23): 120–6.

Jakimow, Tanya (2018a) 'Voluntarism and Citizenship in Indonesia: Practices of care as a model for state-citizen relations', *Citizenship Studies*, 22(2): 145–59.

Jakimow, Tanya (2018b) 'Beyond 'State Ibuism': Empowerment effects in state-led development in Indonesia', *Development and Change*, 49(5): 1143–65.

Jakimow, Tanya (2018c) 'A moral atmosphere of development as a share: consequences for urban development in Indonesia', *World Development*, 108: 47–56.

Jakimow, Tanya (2018d) 'Negotiated Impossibilities and the Responsibilization of failure in an Urban Community-Driven Development Program', *Journal of Developing Societies*, 34(1): 35–55.

Jakimow, Tanya and Aida Harahap (2016) '*Gaji Sejuta*': Moral experiences and the possibilities for self in a community-driven development program in Indonesia', *Critique of Anthropology*, 36(3): 264–79.

Jakimow, T. and Yumasdaleni (2016) 'Affective Registers in Qualitative Team Research: interpreting the self in encounters with the state', *Qualitative Research Journal*, 16(2): 169–80.

Jakimow, Tanya, Kurniawati Hastuti Dewi, and Asima Yanty Siahaan (2019) 'Unpacking public care in Indonesia: women's perspectives on care in politics and policy', *Asian Studies Review*, 43(2): 276–94.

John, Mary E (2007) 'Women in Power? Gender, Caste and the politics of urban governance', *Economic and Political Weekly*, 42(39): 3986–93.

Kapoor, Ilan (2017) 'Cold Critique, faint passion, bleak future: Post-Development's surrender to global capitalism', *Third World Quarterly*, 38(12): 2664–83.

Kar, Sohini (2013) 'Recovering debts: Microfinance loan officers and the work of "proxy-creditors" in India', *American Ethnologist*, 40(3): 480–93.

Koskimaki, Leah (2017) 'Youth Futures and Masculine Development Ethos in the Regional Story of Uttarakhand', *Journal of South Asian Development*, 12(2): 136–54.

Kothari, Uma (2005) 'Authority and Expertise: The Professionalisation of International Development and the Ordering of Dissent', *Antipode*, 37(3): 425–46.

Kumar, Anup (2011) *The Making of a Small State: Populist social mobilisation and the Hindi press in the Uttarakhand movement*. New Delhi: Orient Blackswan.

Kunreuther, Laura (2018) 'Sounds of democracy: performance, protest and political subjectivity', *Cultural Anthropology*, 33(1): 1–31.

Laidlaw, James (2014) *The Subject of Virtue: an anthropology of ethics and freedom*. Cambridge: Cambridge University Press.

Lama-Rewal, Stephanie Tawa (2009) 'Studying Elections in India: Scientific and Political Debates', *South Asia Multidisciplinary Academic Journal*, 3.

Lamb, Sarah (2000) *White Saris and Sweet Mangoes: Aging, Gender, and Body in North India*. Berkeley, CA: University of California Press.

Laurie, Nina and Matt Ballie-Smith (2018) 'Unsettling geographies of volunteering and development', *Transactions of the Institute of British Geographers*, 43(1): 95–109.

Lawson, Victoria (2007) 'Geographies of Care and Responsibility', *Annals of the Association of American Geographers*, 97(1): 1–11.

Legg, Stephen (2011) 'Assemblage/apparatus: using Deleuze and Foucault', *Area*, 43(2): 128–33.

Lewis, David (2019) '"Big D" and "little d": two types of twenty-first century development?', *Third World Quarterly*, 40(11): 1957–75.

Lewis, Simon (2015) 'Learning from Communities: the local dynamics of formal and informal volunteering in Korogocho, Kenya', *IDS Bulletin*, 46(5): 69–82.

Li, Tania Murray (2006) 'Neo-liberal strategies of government through community: the social development program of the World Bank in Indonesia', International Law and Justice Working Papers, 2006/2.

Li, Tania Murray (2007) *The Will to Improve: Governmentality, Development and the Practice of Politics*. Durham, NC: Duke University Press.

Long, Norman (2001) *Development Sociology: Actor Perspectives*. London: Routledge.

Lund, Jens Friis and Moeko Saito-Jensen (2013) 'Revisiting the Issue of Elite Capture of Participatory Initiatives', *World Development*, 46: 104–12.

Lutz, Catherine (1986) 'Emotion, Thought and Estrangement: Emotion as a cultural category', *Cultural Anthropology*, 1(3): 287–309.

McFarlane, Colin (2006) 'Knowledge, Learning and Development: A post-rationalist approach', *Progress in Development Studies*, 6(4): 287–305.

McFarlane, Colin and Renu Desai (2015) 'Sites of entitlement: claim, negotiation and struggle in Mumbai', *Environment and Urbanization*, 27(2): 1–14.

Mahler, Matthew (2006) 'Politics as Vocation: Notes toward a sensualist understanding of political engagement', *Qualitative Sociology*, 29: 281–300.

Malkki, Liisa (2015) *The Need to Help: the domestic arts of international humanitarianism*. Durham, NC: Duke University Press.

Manor, James (2016) *The Writings of James Manor: Politics and State-Society Relations in India*. Hyderabad: Orient BlackSwan.

Mansuri, G., and V. Rao (2004) 'Community-based and -driven development: a critical review', *The World Bank Research Observer*, 19(1): 1–39.

Marcus, A. and S. Asmorowati (2006) 'Urban Poverty and the Rural Development Bias: some notes from Indonesia', *Journal of Developing Societies*, 22(2): 145–68.

Markell, Patchen (2000) 'Making Affect Safe for Democracy? On "Constitutional Patriotism"', *Political Theory*, 28(1): 38–63.

Massumi, Brian (2015) *Politics of Affect*. Cambridge: Polity Press.

Michelutti, Lucia (2007) 'The Vernacularization of Democracy: political participation and popular politics in North India', *Journal of the Royal Anthropological Institute*, 13: 639–56.

Michelutti, Lucia (2010) 'Wrestling with (Body) Politics: Understanding "*Goonda*" Political Styles in North India', in P. Price and A. E. Ruud (eds) *Power and Influence in India: Bosses, Lords and Captains*. London: Routledge, pp. 44–69.

Mittal, Gaurav (2014) 'Delusory Transformations: Transportation projects under JNNURM in Dehradun' *Economic and Political Weekly*, XLIX(48): 62–8.

Moore, Henrietta (2007) *The Subject of Anthropology: Gender, Symbolism and Psychoanalysis*. Cambridge: Polity.

Moore, Henrietta (2011) *Still Life: Hopes, Desires and Satisfactions*. Cambridge: Polity Press.

Mosse, David (2005) *Cultivating Development: An Ethnography of AID Policy and Practice*, New Delhi: Vistaar Publications.

Mosse, David (ed.) (2011) *Adventures in Aidland: the anthropology of professionals in international development*, Oxford: Berghahn.

Mosse, D. and D. Lewis (2006) 'Theoretical Approaches to Brokerage and Translation in Development', in D. Lewis and D. Mosse (eds) *Development Brokers and Translators: An Ethnography of Aid and Agencies*. Bloomfield, CT: Kumarian Press, pp. 1–26.

Muehlebach, Andrea (2012) *The Moral Neoliberal: Welfare and citizenship in Italy*. Chicago: Chicago University Press.

Munshi, Shoma (1998) 'Wife/mother/daughter-in-law: multiple avatars of homemaker in 1990s Indian advertising', *Media, Culture and Society*, 20: 573–91.

Munsoor, M. (2015) 'The soul (heart) and its attributes: An Islamic perspective with reference to self in Western psychology', *Afkar*, 16: 93–118.

Nederveen Pieterse, Jan (2010) *Development Theory*, Second Edition, Los Angeles: Sage.

Nilan, Pam (2009) 'Contemporary Masculinities and Young Men in Indonesia', *Indonesia and the Malay World*, 37(109): 327–44.

Olivier De Sardan, J. P. (1999) 'A Moral Economy of Corruption', *The Journal of Modern African Studies*, 37(1): 22–52.

Ong, Jonathan Corpus and Pamela Combinido (2018) 'Local aid workers in the digital humanitarian project: between "second class citizens" and "entrepreneurial survivors"', *Critical Asian Studies*, 50(1): 86–102.

Oppenheimer, Joshua (2012) *The Act of Killing*. Denmark: Final Cut for Real Production Company.

Ortner, Sherry (1996) *Making Gender: The Politics and Erotics of Culture*. Boston, MA: Beacon Press.

Ortner, Sherry (2006) *Anthropology and Social Theory: Culture, Power and the Acting Subject*. Durham, NC: Duke University Press.

Paley, Julie (2002) 'Toward an Anthropology of Democracy', *Annual Review of Anthropology*, 31: 469–96.

Paley, Julia (2008) 'Introduction' in J. Paley (ed.) *Democracy: Anthropological Approaches*. Santa Fe, CA: School for Advanced Research Press.

Pandian, Anand (2009) *Crooked Stalks: Cultivating Virtue in South India*. Durham, NC: Duke University Press.

Parry, Jonathan (1986) 'The Gift, the Indian Gift and the 'Indian Gift', *Man*, 21(3): 453–73.

Pattenden, Jonathan (2011) 'Social Protection and Class relations: Evidence from Scheduled Caste Women's Associations in Rural South India', *Development and Change*, 42(2): 469–98.

Pedwell, Carolyn (2012) 'Affective (self-)transformations: Empathy, neoliberalism and international development', *Feminist Theory*, 13(2): 163–79.

Pedwell, Carolyn and Anne Whitehead (2012) 'Affecting feminism: Questions of feeling in feminist theory', *Feminist Theory*, 13(2): 115–29.

Perman, Tony (2010) 'Dancing in Opposition: Muchongoyo, Emotion and the Politics of Performance in Southeastern Zimbabwe', *Ethnomusicology*, 54(3): 425–51.

Philip, G., C. Rogers, and S. Weller (2012) 'Understanding care and thinking with care', in C. Rogers and S. Weller (eds) *Critical Approaches to Care: Understanding Caring Relations, Identities and Cultures*. London: Routledge, pp. 2–21.

Pigg, Stacey Leigh (1992) 'Inventing social categories through place: social representations and development in Nepal', *Comparative Studies in Society and History*, 34(3): 491–513.

Piliavsky, A. (2014) 'Introduction', in A. Piliavsky (ed.) *Patronage as Politics in South Asia*. New York, Cambridge University Press.

Piliavsky, Anastasia and Tomaas Sbriccoli (2016) 'The ethics of efficacy in North India's *goonda raj* (rule of toughs)', *Journal of the Royal Anthropological Institute*, 22: 373–91.

Prahara, Hestu (2016) 'Rethinking Populist-Developmentalism in Indonesia', in *ISRF Best Essays 2015*, Jakarta: ISRF, pp. 169–77.

Price, Pamela and Arild Englesen Ruud (2010) *Power and Influence in India: Bosses, Lords and Captains*. London: Routledge.

Raghuram, Parvati, Clare Madge, and Pat Noxolo (2009) 'Rethinking Responsibility and care for a postcolonial world', *Geoforum*, 40: 5–13.

Rai, Shirin M. (2012) 'The Politics of Access: Narratives of Women MPs in the Indian Parliament', *Political Studies*, 60: 195–212.

Redfield, Peter (2012) 'The Unbearable Lightness of Ex-pats: Double binds of humanitarian mobility', *Cultural Anthropology*, 27(2): 358–82.

Richard, Analiese and Daromir Rudnyckyj (2009) 'Economies of Affect', *Journal of the Royal Anthropological Institute*, 15: 57–77.

Robertson-Snape, F. (1999) 'Corruption, Collusion and Nepotism in Indonesia', *Third World Quarterly*, 20(3): 589–602.

Robinson, Kathryn (2008) *Gender, Islam and Democracy in Indonesia*. Hoboken, NJ: Taylor and Francis.

Robinson, Kathryn (2014) 'Citizenship, identity and difference in Indonesia', *Review of Indonesian and Malaysian Affairs*, 48(1): 5–34.

Rose, Nikolas (2000) 'Community, Citizenship, and the Third Way', *American Behavioral Scientist*, 43(9): 1395–411.

Ross, Aileen D. (1961) *The Hindu Family in its Urban Setting*. Toronto: University of Toronto Press.

Roth, Silke (2015) *The Paradoxes of Aid Work: Passionate Professionals*. London: Routledge.

Roy, Srila (2017) 'Enacting/Disrupting the Will to Empower: Feminist Governance of "Child Marriage" in Eastern India', *Signs: Journal of Women in Culture and Society*, 42(4): 867–91.

Rudnyckyj, Daromir (2011) 'Circulating Tears and Managing Hearts: Governing through affect in an Indonesian Steel Factory', *Anthropological Theory*, 11(1): 63–87.

Rudnyckyj, Daromir (2014) 'Regimes of Self-Improvement: Globalization and the will to work', *Social Text 120*, 32(3): 109–27.

Russell, S. and Vidler, E. (2000) 'The rise and fall of government—community partnerships for urban development: grassroots testimony from Colombo', *Environment and Urbanization*, 12(1): 73–86.

Sardesi, Shreyas and Vibha Attri (2019) 'Post-poll Survey: the 2019 verdict is a manifestation of the deepening religious divide in India', *The Hindu*, 30 May 2019.

Scherz, China (2014) *Having People, Having Heart: Charity, Sustainable Development, and Problems of Dependence in Central Uganda*. Chicago: Chicago University Press.

Schwittay, Anke (2014) *New Media and International Development: Representation and affect in microfinance*. London: Routledge.

Scott, James (1987) *Weapons of the Weak: Everyday forms of peasant resistance*. New Haven, CT: Yale University Press.

Seigworth, Gregory J. and Melissa Gregg (eds) 2010. *The Affect Theory Reader*. Durham, NC: Duke University Press.

Sevenhuijsen, Selma (2000) 'Caring in the third way: the relation between obligation, responsibility and care in *Third Way* discourse', *Critical Social Policy*, 20(1): 5–37.

Shah, Alpha (2009) 'Morality, Corruption and the State: Insights from Jharkhand, Eastern India', *The Journal of Development Studies*, 45(3): 295–313.

Shekhar Swain, Satyarupa (2012) 'The Unequal Access to municipal services and the role of local elected representatives', *N-AERUS*, XIII.

Shutt, Cathy (2012) 'A Moral Economy? Social interpretations of money in Aidland', *Third World Quarterly*, 33(8): 1527–43.

Simon, Gregory M. (2009) 'The Soul Freed of Cares? Islamic Prayer, subjectivity, and the contradictions of moral selfhood in Minangkabau, Indonesia', *American Ethnologist*, 36(2): 258–75.

Singer, Wendy (2007) *'A Constituency Suitable for Ladies': and other social histories of Indian elections*. New Delhi: Oxford University Press.

Slaby, Jan and Rainer Mühlhoff (2019) 'Affect', in J. Slaby and C. von Scheve (eds) *Affective Societies: Key Concepts*. New York: Routledge.

Smith, Daniel Jordan (2003) 'Patronage, Per Diems and the "Workshop Mentality": The practices of family planning programs in Southeastern Nigeria', *World Development*, 31(4): 703–15.

Sultana, Farhana (2011) 'Suffering *for* water, suffering *from* water: emotional geographies of resource access, control and conflict', *Geoforum*, 42: 163–72.

Suryakusuma, Julia (2011) *State Ibuism: The social construction of womanhood in New Order Indonesia*. Depok: Komunitas Bambu.

Tarigan, Ari K. M., D. Ary Samsura, Sut Sagala, and Anthoni Pencawan (2017) 'Medan City: Development and Governance under the decentralisation era', *Cities*, 71: 135–46.

Thrift, Nigel (2008) *Non-Representational Theory: Space, politics, affect*. London: Routledge.

Throop, C. Jason (2012) 'Moral Sentiments', in D. Fassin (ed.) *A Companion to Moral Anthropology*. Malden, MA and Oxford: John Wiley and Sons Inc.

Throop, Jason (2018) 'Being open to the world', *HAU*, 8(1/2): 197–210.

Throop, Jason and Alessandro Duranti (2014) 'Attention, ritual glitches, and attentional pull: the president and the queen', *Phenomenological Cognitive Science*, 14: 1055–82.

Tidey, Sylvia (2013) 'Corruption and Adherence to Rules in the Construction Sector: Reading the "Bidding Books" ', *American Anthropologist*, 115(2): 188–202.

Tidey, Sylvia (2016) 'Between the ethical and the right thing: How (not) to be corrupt in Indonesian bureaucracy in an age of good governance', *American Ethnologist*, 43(4): 663–76.

Tronto, Joan C. (1995) 'Care as a Basis for Radical Political Judgements', *Hypatia*, 10(2): 141–9.

Trundle, Catherine (2012) 'The transformation of compassion and the ethics of interaction within charity practices', in S. Venkatesan and T. Yarrow (eds) *Differentiating Development: Beyond an Anthropology of Critique*. Oxford: Berghahn, pp. 210–26.

Tsaputra, Antoni (2019) 'Disability Inclusive Budgeting in Indonesia: A pathway to *difabel* citizenship', unpublished PhD Thesis, UNSW Sydney.

van der Veer, Peter (2016) *The Value of Comparison*. Durham, NC: Duke University Press.

van Dijk, Tara (2011) 'Networks of Urbanization in Two Indian Cities', *Environment and Urbanization, ASIA*, 2(2): 303–19.

Wandita, Galuh (2014), 'Preman Nation: Watching the Act of Killing in Indonesia', *Critical Asian Studies*, 46(1): 167–70.

Watanabe, Chika (2017) 'Development as pedagogy: on becoming good models in Japan and Myanmar', *American Ethnologist*, 44(4): 591–602.

Weinstein, Liza, Neha Sami, and Gavin Shaktin (2014) 'Contested Developments: Enduring legacies and emergent political actors in contemporary urban India', in G. Shaktin (ed.) *Contesting the Indian City: Global Visions and the Politics of the Local*. Malden, MA: Wiley Blackwell, pp. 39–64.

Wetherell, Margaret (2012) *Affect and Emotion: A new social science understanding*. London: SAGE publications.

Wetherell, Margaret (2013) 'Feeling Rules, Atmospheres and Affective Practice: Some reflection on the analysis of emotional episodes', in C. Maxwell and P. Aggleton (eds) *Privilege, Agency and Affect: Understanding the production and effects*. Basingstoke: Palgrave Macmillan, pp. 221–39.

Wetherell, Margaret (2015) 'Trends in the Turn to Affect: a social psychological critique', *Body and Society*, 21(2): 139–66.

White, Daniel (2017) 'Affect: an Introduction', *Cultural Anthropology*, 32(2): 175–80.

de Wit, Joop (2017) *Urban Poverty, Local Governance and Everyday Politics in Mumbai*. London: Routledge.

Witsoe, Jeffrey (2011) 'Corruption as Power: Caste and the political imagination of the postcolonial state', *American Ethnologist*, 38(1): 73–85.

World Bank (2013) 'Indonesia: Evaluation of the Urban Community Driven Development Program: Program Nasional Pemberdayaan Masyarakat Mandiri Perkotaan (PNPM-Urban), Policy Note', http://documents.worldbank.org/curated/en/2013/01/19140048/indonesia-evaluation-urban-community-driven-development-program-program-nasional-pemberdayaan-masyarakat-mandiri-perkotaan-pnpm-urban (accessed 19 March 2015).

Wright, Sarah (2012) 'Emotional Geographies of Development', *Third World Quarterly*, 33(6): 1113–27.

Zigon, Jarrett (2009) 'Morality and Personal Experience: The Moral Conceptions of a Muscovite Man', *Ethos*, 37(1): 78–101.

Zigon, J. and C. J. Throop (2014) 'Moral Experience: Introduction', *Ethos*, 42(1): 1–15.

Index

For the benefit of digital users, indexed terms that span two pages (e.g., 52–53) may, on occasion, appear on only one of those pages.